# GOLD WARS

GOLD WARS

# GOLD WARS
## THE BATTLE
## FOR THE GLOBAL ECONOMY

BY

KELLY MITCHELL

CLARITY PRESS, INC.

© 2013 Kelly Mitchell
ISBN:       978-0-9860362-6-2
EBOOK: 978-0-9860362-7-9

In-house editor: Diana G. Collier
Cover:  R. Jordan P. Santos

Library of Congress Cataloging-in-Publication Data


Mitchell, Kelly.
  Gold wars : the battle for the global economy / by Kelly Mitchell.
    pages cm
  Includes bibliographical references and index.
  ISBN 978-0-9860362-6-2 (alk. paper) -- ISBN 978-0-9860362-7-9 (ebook)
  1. Gold. 2. Gold--Purchasing. 3. Precious metals. I. Title.

HG293.M66 2013
332.4'5--dc23


                        2013032174

                     Clarity Press, Inc.
                 Ste. 469, 3277 Roswell Rd. NE
                  Atlanta, GA. 30305 , USA
                  http://www.claritypress.com

# TABLE OF CONTENTS

# TABLE OF FIGURES

zerohedge.com/article/shadow-bank-liabilities-plunge-700-bil-
lion-q2-21-trillion-year-date

24 **Consumer Inflation - Official vs Shadowstats.** shadowstats.com/
home

25 **Annual Inflation Rate (%)** comparativepoliticseconomics.com/his-
toricalinflationrate

26 **Annual Inflation Rate - Japan %.** azmytheconomics.wordpress.
com/2013/06/19/overview-of-the-japanese-economy-part-1/

27 **Gold and US Real Rates.** marketoracle.co.uk/Article26187.html

28 **Gold YoY vs Real Interest Rates (since 1978).** hks.harvard.edu/
fs/jfrankel/Commodindex&r1950-2005.jpg

29 **Gold Kept Rising Despite Analysts' Forecasts.** financialsense.
com/contributors/frank-holmes/how-gold-miners-leverage-price-gold

30 **Performance of the S&P 500 v. Gold and Gold Stocks.** smart-
knowledgeu.com/blog/2013/01/the-one-chart-that-explains-the-
massive-risk-in-investing-in-gold-gold-stocks

31 **Gold Intraday Average and PM fix 1998-2011.** goldsilverworlds.
com/gold-silver-insights/gold-price-manipulation-proven-on-the-
intraday-charts

32 **Gold August Future intra-day chart June 7, 2012.** safehaven.
com/article/26474/a-high-frequency-attack-on-gold

33 **Gold August Future intra-second chart June 7, 2012 at
21:21:20.** safehaven.com/article/26474/a-high-frequency-attack-on-
gold

34 **US Federal Reserve Gold Holdings vs US Public Debt.** tfmetal-
sreport.com/comment/323548

35 **LBMA Gold Forward (GOFO) Rates.** news.goldseek.com/Gold-
Seek/1272866760

36 **Separation of Physical Demand and Paper Demand in Gold.**
zerohedge.com/news/2013-05-16/gold-demand-one-chart-physical-
vs-etf

37 **Canada's Silver Maple Coin Sales (in millions).** agorafinancial.
com/research/html/ost_westpoint_061313/?code=EOSTP805&ver=
1&n=OST_Westpoint_061213

38 **Silver Lease Rates.** kitco.com/lease.chart.silv.html

39 **Two Banks Net Short as Percent of Commercial Net Short &
Silver Price.** news.goldseek.com/GoldSeek/1238360122.php

40 **U.S. Gold Import-Export Deficit Jan-Jul 2012.** financialsense.
com/contributors/steve-angelo/u-s-exporting-record-amounts-of-
gold-overseas

41 **Chinese Gold Imports from Hong Kong.** rocksituationreport.
com/2013/02/10/february-2013-7th-13th/

42 **Gold arbitrage between Shanghai and Comex exchanges
12/3/12.** goldenjackass.com/members/dec2012_v2.htm

43 **Paper Gold and Physical Gold Divergence.** zerohedge.com/
news/2013-02-26/februarys-strange-divergence-precious-metals

# ACKNOWLEDGMENTS

Thanks to all the people who contributed to this book through their awesome knowledge and insight into our modern financial insanity. Jim Willie (the golden jackass), Eric Sprott, John Embry, Dimitri Speck, Turd Ferguson, Nate Martin, James Turk, Chris Powell, Bill Murphy (and all the GATA warriors), Eric King, Egon von Greyerz, Stephen Leeb, Jim Sinclair, Dan Norcini, Michael Pento, Gerald Celente, John Hathaway, Andrew Maguire and Max Keiser.

# FOREWORD

A book like this can benefit from a guiding metaphor – like a handle to grab. The Paul Krugman con is appropriate. Economist Paul Krugman, according to the mainstream media, won the 'Nobel Prize in Economics.' However, there is no such prize. The Sveriges Riksbank Prize in Economic Sciences in Memory of Alfred Nobel was created in 1968 and passed off by the Swedish Central Bank as a true Nobel in an effort to save the dismal reputation of economics. "It's most often awarded to stock market speculators," one of the Nobel heirs claimed. Robert Merton and Myron Sholes won it for their formula valuing derivatives to minimize risk. Nine months later, their firm LTCM nearly imploded global bond markets and required an emergency intervention.

The bank managed to slip the prize in with those created by Alfred Nobel. They did it to get scientific validation and wrest control from democratic processes – a relentless central bank strategy in all countries. Scientists are miffed but the public is none the wiser. That's the way it is with central banks in particular. Most non-insider experts more or less despise them as a renegade force that has seized control, but the public is treated to a steady diet of propaganda and little understands the intense debate. Far worse, they have no idea that the stakes could not be higher.

Modern economic theory is useless. In fact, it is dangerous. The global economy is undergoing a paradigm shift. Mainstream economists see the series of crises (real estate bubble pop, banking crises, sovereign debt problems) as external – problems stemming from various participants and their inability to properly manage their situation in the overall context. Economics, as it is said, is very useful as employment for economists. In the real world, the theories are mismatched and worsen the situation. The problems are not external, nor are they a series of isolated events. The problems are the early warning signs of the failure of the global monetary system. We are witnessing a worldwide paradigm shift. The current way of doing things is crumbling. The process is not reversible, nor can it be stabilized at a lower level. The imbalances are too large. It can be slowed somewhat, and has been. It can also be broken apart to let separate pieces fail without dragging the entire system down as rapidly.

This is meeting with little success, however. The globalized system is quite integrated. It is failing as a whole, but few people see this.

Here's the prime question: is it somehow feasible to create enough money simply by printing it, so that we can pay out the globe's debt with no serious consequences? Mathematically, the answer is no. Credit and debt are inherently unbalanced systems on which to base a currency, though this is indeed the foundation for fiat (paper money) currencies where money is introduced into the system through debt – which must be repaid with interest.. Debt (the money supply) must be perpetually expanded in order for existing debt to be repaid, leading to money's loss of value. At some point, the rate of increase required overwhelms the real, productive economy's ability to cope. The currency fails. Hyman Minsky proposed the 'financial instability hypothesis' to explain this. Prior to now, unbacked and debt-backed currencies have failed one at a time. But now, for the first time, the world is without any sound currency and is facing multiple currency failures simultaneously. It is, as they say, uncharted territory.

Certain nations do perceive it and are taking steps to create a new paradigm. The 'BRICS', led mainly by China, are making significant efforts in this direction. The efforts are well known to those who research modern economic realities closely and honestly, but they are unreported in the mainstream media. The details of these efforts, insofar as they are known, are discussed in the final section. The new paradigm will almost certainly include a gold 'anchor.' This is the most fundamental aspect, among many, of this shift – the current, non-gold system is being silently replaced by a sounder currency system. It appears to be far less centralized and more open, but will shut out the ruling Western monetary powers. It is, effectively, war by another means.

*Gold Wars* is not for everyone. It targets the swelling mass of awakening readers who want to know what is really happening in the world's economy and financial power centers. It is not for the mainstream watcher of Fox or CNN – it is for the alert citizen who requires a deep and broad understanding of this system. It is for the citizen who will invest real time and energy in a very important endeavor – the attempt to secure and protect their families and future. It is not light reading. It is not intended as salacious entertainment. Most readers should have or be seeking a radical reorientation of perspective, or at least a serious questioning of the mainstream narrative. An entirely different global picture is presented here – and it's not a comfortable one.

This book differs from most economics books in a number of ways, but especially in the balance of information. Most books are prescriptive – they tell the reader the author's single notion of what is best for the economy and for their own protection, and use a few cursory chapters to describe certain significant problems. Prescriptions are not critically examined, but are presented as the 'best' possible idea. This book takes the tack of trusting the reader to make their determination among competing views, rather than talking down. An extensive detailed description serves to broadly educate the reader as to the nuances and problems facing the world. That's about 80% of the book. The probable outcomes are then addressed – 10%. Finally, we see a variety of different prescriptions and ideas for economic reform. It is my firm belief that a strongly educated reader will be in a far better position to protect wealth and the family future. This reader will not be swayed by feeble arguments of friends, relatives, and nightly news, but will have a host of counter-arguments to feel secure in the knowledge that they are acting intelligently.

# INTRODUCTION

*The world will soon wake up to the reality*
*that everyone is broke and can collect nothing from the*
*bankrupt, who are owed unlimited amounts by the insolvent, who*
*are attempting to make late payments on a bank holiday in the*
*wrong country, with an unacceptable currency,*
*against defaulted collateral,*
*of which nobody is sure who holds title*
*– anonymous*

At opening bell of April 30, 2012, an anonymous player sold short $1.24 billion worth of gold. At three quarters of a million ounces, the sale slammed through over 1000 bids, up to 8400 ounces apiece in a fraction of a second. Even the *Wall Street Journal* ran an article on manipulation – the dump exceeded an entire average day's trading. The perpetrator broke the law and took rapid losses of $75 million as the gold price reasserted itself in a few hours.

**Figure 1**
**$24 Billion in gold sold short in seconds**

04 00  05 00  06 00  07 00  08 00  09 00  10 00  11 00  12 00  13 00  14 00  15 00  16 00  17 00  19 00  20 00  21 00

The *WSJ* failed to note that these contracts were not longs liquidating, but naked shorts – a party selling gold they did not have. These are done without posting margin. The activity is blatantly illegal.

Nonetheless, sells of this type (though not this size) are fairly common. Many occur in a thinly traded period of the day – 3am – making it doubly suspect a profit point of view. Without multiple buy orders to hold up the price, the seller gets less and less money with each bid filled. No trader would do this for profit – if they were seeking a profit, they would have parceled it out over a period to avoid dropping the price.

The Fat Finger has been offered as an explanation. A trader could have keyed in an extra zero after the number of contracts. While this is possible, it's highly unlikely that a sophisticated trader or trading system would have no safeguards against hundred million dollar losses because of a single accidental keystroke. The accident theory is implausible. The move more or less screams manipulation. Somebody controlling a lot of money wanted to slam the price of gold and could afford to take a sizeable loss. But why do it?

One potential seller works at the Bank for International Settlements (BIS). Mikael Charozé's bio at the BIS listed "interventions [and]... proprietary positions on all currencies including gold," until the Zerohedge website posted it. A few days later, those parts of his job description had been removed from the BIS site.[1] It cannot be proved, of course, because everything lies under layers of what seems to be intentional confusion. And central banks have a wall of silence policy against any criticism, especially from the people they claim to serve. It's all part of the gold wars.

The logic is simple enough from the bird's eye view. A swiftly rising gold price reveals the mismanagement of the currency, like the expiring canary in the mine. Therefore it is suppressed surreptitiously. Because paper currencies rely totally on faith, central bankers take it as part of their duty to manage that faith and maintain confidence in the currency. If gold shot up to $10,000, world banks and investors would become very, very concerned about their dollar holdings. Most other items are openly managed – food and oil prices (through subsidies and reserves), inflation, inflation perception, interest rates, money supply and financial risk. Those who question the manipulation of gold should be asking the polar opposite question: why wouldn't it be manipulated? It's the *key* metric of faith-based currencies. Managing the gold price is a central banker's job.

The gold wars are the cornerstone of a much larger overall context – currency, trade and actual wars. As part of the gold wars presentation, it's important to establish that the financial system is secretive, corrupt and highly beneficial to a few. In short, it's rigged. To prove this contention, it's necessary to establish motive, means, and escape. The motive here is to preserve a failing system, the means is control of regulators, and escape from public detection is through control of public perception – the cover-up. People never know what really happened. The MF Global fiasco and other financial crimes that we will explore are an easy way to prove corruption and elite benefit. The Petrodollar/ global reserve currency system and its stunning hegemony over world politics is the principal motive. The primary means is by control of the currency. The secondary means include repeal of the Glass-Steagall Act, emplacement of corporate execs into regulatory bodies, the entrenchment of too big to fail notions and policies, and countless other methods. The escape vehicles include the loss of independent media, consolidation of media into a few companies, ignoring the public, foot-dragging investigations, obfuscation, ridicule of opposition, and secrecy by claiming national security interests. These are among the topics to be covered.

Figure 2 below may be the scariest chart in the entire book.[2] Around 1965, the debt to GDP ratio crossed 1:1. Before then, a dollar of debt created at least a dollar of GDP increase. That's sustainable. Since then, the long-

Figure 2

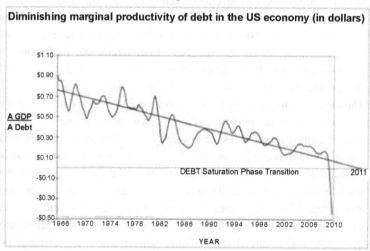

term chart is vicious and steadily downward. In 2010, it crossed the zero bound – more debt created no GDP increase. It's actually been forced to occur sooner because of the enormous extent of monetary creation since 2008. The sharp jag below zero is clear and striking. Debt saturation is in full swing. Incomes have not kept pace – they can no longer service the debt. It's tough to say what happens now, but probably (and strangely) new debt will contract GDP.[3] As the zero bound is more clearly left behind, economic dislocations become more and more violent. Volatility goes haywire. The debt creation becomes a black hole. As this book shows, we're already there.

The central economic problem in the world today is debt saturation. This is a direct offshoot of the current monetary system – fractional reserve banking. The public has almost no understanding of how money is created and that's extremely unfortunate. "It is well enough that people of the nation do not understand our banking and money system," Henry Ford said. "For if they did, I believe there would be a revolution before tomorrow morning." Money, in today's world, is created from debt. All money is created when a bank loans it into existence. It is extinguished when the loan is paid off, but sufficient money to also pay the interest (bank profit) is not created. Consequently, there is always much more debt than money to pay it – scarcity is built in to the system. Numerous problems result, some obvious, some not. We will explore this strange system in much greater detail, but one salient fact is most disturbing. It requires perpetual growth at an increasing rate to sustain the system without implosion because of the inbuilt shortages of money. It *inevitably* leads to a debt crisis, as Ludwig von Mises postulated six decades ago. He called it a systemic crack-up – a global reset. Leaders have greatly increased sovereign debt in response, but the solution to debt is not more debt. It is default. What cannot go on forever not only must but will end.

In the past, money was directly issued and backed by precious metals. Or it was coinage. This required no debt and no perpetual growth. It was stable. Gold systems are not perfect – no system is. However, they have proved far more durable and self-sustaining than debt based money. True gold standard economies do not need to be centrally planned – they have built in self-corrections to prevent modern excesses. Central bankers express great disdain for such systems publicly because they prevent excesses. Gold is the mortal enemy of modern money.

Without the gold anchor, the world economy has become seriously unbalanced. Greek one-year debt hit a high of 140% interest in 2011. Under Generally Accepted Accounting Principles, the 2011 US deficit exceeds $5 trillion – far more than the government-accounted $1.5 trillion. The entire US obligations would be $60 to $200 trillion, depending on who did the estimating. The total of accounted for derivatives is $600 trillion by BIS measures and undisclosed bets might easily double that total to over a quadrillion – twenty times the world's economy. Central bank balance sheets are bleeding red from buying worthless paper to prop up failing banks. Financial giants are leveraged at many times their reserve assets, making them insolvent in even a slight downdraft. The Federal Reserve has issued $23 trillion in zero interest loans since 2008. Something is seriously wrong. The global economic system is dying and the illness is being hidden from view.

Trust is one of the great missing elements of today's system. That lack is a primary reason that precious metals will continue to steepen in demand –

they alone require no trust. There are many components of trust necessary for a strongly functioning economic system. Virtually all of these components are now AWOL. A citizenry must believe that its leadership has their best interests at heart, even if the actions taken are less than perfect. If the leaders are seen not as flawed, but as corrupt, deeply self-interested, or worse, tyrannical, then many decades of trust will evaporate in a few years. We are close to that point.

Likewise, the citizens must believe the banks are functional utilities serving a basic societal need rather than profit-driven entities focused on investment and returns. Today, most people think that banks are wildly speculative enterprises, risking the nation's very health. The truth is less important than the perception. Some make the case that in actuality leadership and finance have been utterly self-interested for a very long time and have simply managed to disguise that fact from the public through skillful and extensive PR. Because the increasing systemic strains are making it impossible to paper over, the truth is emerging. The evidence of long-scale deception is an interesting topic we will address.

One very strange lacuna in our civilization is the lack of monetary knowledge. In a well-educated system which prides itself on fundamental capitalist values, a knowledge of money would seem to be *de rigeur*. America lives and breathes money: it "makes the world go 'round." Yet mysteriously, almost no one understands this most basic and essential fact of our lives. What is money? Where does it come from? The old saw that money does not grow on trees is no longer true – money is paper. *Gold* has been de-monitized. It is less than paper in the case of electronic money – it is just a number in a computer.

Why the ignorance? It seems fair to blame the educational system. According to John Taylor Gatto, the missing substance is deliberate. Gatto, named Teacher of the Year, the highest honor in education, condemned the system in his acceptance speech. He roundly criticized it for deliberate mal-education of the entire population. The Department of Education was more or less designed by large private endowments. Big capital, Gatto claimed, wants a society of citizens poorly informed about many things, especially money creation and its link to their exploitation and manipulation. Citizens are kept more compliant due to their ignorance and far less willing to question the system of big capital presently in place, or who benefits. This is breeding a society of workers, not entrepreneurs capable of innovative and nimble planning, whether on a micro scale suited to meager resources, or larger. We have a system of unbridled paper money creation, a citizenry totally ignorant of its mechanics, and a deliberate veiling of the powers that actually control it. If money is power, then the government-given authority to create it affords the exponential manifestation of that power. Keeping citizens uninformed safeguards the power holders from revolution – or at least, revolution directed at them. Cattle are easy to control.

The deeper implications of these facts are frightening when fully understood, and history bears this out many times over. Governments with too much centralized power – whether from misguided public trust or harsh repression – inevitably abuse the privilege of unbacked currencies. We'll get into some instances in the hyperinflation section. The warfare/welfare state is as old as repressive government. Rome achieved citizen compliance through a system of public dole and extravaganzas, featuring slaughter of undesirables; historians called it 'bread and circuses.' Politicians buy loyalty or enforce obedience. Both are extraordinarily expensive, beyond a sound currency's ability to support. Paper (or digital) currencies permit terrible abuses, including unrestrained war, and tyranny because there is no check on spending (or rather, printing.) The current system is out of all control. Black Swan events are causing bouts of alternating debt deflation and the policy response of firehose monetary inflation. The real economy is being destroyed by the far larger speculative economy. Short term solutions are only making the long-term problems worse.

There is now a tremendous amount of confusion, complexity, and uncertainty in the financial system. It might even be described as chaos. New terms are emerging – debt holocaust, Europocalypse, and financial Armageddon. Phrases such as "uncharted territory," "never before seen conditions," seem to be popping up all over the net and even in the mainstream. *No one* fully comprehends the depth and breadth of the issues – it's too vast. Therefore no one can create a real solution to save the existing mechanisms. Indeed, no solution may be possible. The reset button has been hit before – four times in the twentieth century.[4] But this time the problems are much larger and aggravated by real resource constraints. The planet is tapped out. Growth is at its maximum. The wall is right in front of us and we are flying towards it at full speed. The system may somehow muddle through, but fools ignore these problems at their peril. In such situations, vast wealth has a historical tendency to disappear. That's because this paper-based wealth is largely illusory.

Some wealth denominators, like derivatives, are far more insubstantial than others, like the value of precious metals. Derivatives require trust in the system and the organizations holding the other end of the contracts. The system must hold fast the value of the currency, the other party must honor the letter and intent of a complex contract, a regulatory agency might be needed to enforce it, that agency must not be compromised, and the other institution must have both the solvency and liquidity to back it up. That's actually a lot of links requiring trust. It's been taken for granted – up to now. We will examine recent events that have shaken the system upside down. Hordes of honest investors and deep pockets are jumping out of major markets. They cite manipulation, lack of confidence, and even fear of outright theft.

Precious metals (PMs), held in one's own possession, require very little trust. Gold is corruption insurance. It has no counterparty obligation. There is no other entity required to uphold the value of PMs – society as a whole is the guarantor of value (though a concern remains re their market manipulation). Metals have retained value for thousands of years – their manipulation is only short-term, and largely unsustainable. Unlike paper, gold never goes to zero. Other than that, the only risk is theft of actual physical holdings – a relatively low risk, especially if holdings are kept secret and are well-secured. In times of massive distrust, fear, and economic corruption, gold and silver become highly valued for many reasons. Systems which seek power and control hate gold. The gold wars are not new. In ancient China, people were put to death for refusing the paper currency and demanding gold. Likewise in 18th Century France. Examples are plentiful and we will cover some very instructive ones.

Nowadays, serious problems, even crises, are popping up more frequently. Fear and suspicion reign. Class war is raising its head. According to Warren Buffet, class war is already ongoing and his class, the wealthy, is winning. That's because only the wealthy understand the need to pay attention to economics. This failure by the middle class is already destroying it. People who are otherwise well educated have lost their life savings in a puff of rehypothecated smoke. Today's financial markets are little more than casinos. The long cold trade war between the uneasy great power allies – China and the US – is heating up. It is becoming a currency war. Bank runs are already happening silently (because uncovered by the mainstream media) in southern Europe. The Greek government has failed. Portugal, Spain, and even Italy are teetering on the cliff of default. The derivatives based on their sovereign bonds number in the hundreds of trillions of dollars – they're like quicksand under the global banking system. Sovereign debt is going parabolic -- rising at an ever-increasing rate. Realistic unemployment numbers are approaching Great Depression levels. Tent cities are appearing nationwide. Municipalities are going bankrupt. Bizarre crime is escalating.

States are beginning to rise against the Federal government. Federal laws like Obamacare and NDAA are being rejected by state governments as unconstitutional. Some even declare a right and intent to arrest federal agents enforcing unconstitutional laws. Ron Paul made a serious run at the presidency by bucking the establishment. He fathered a groundswell of public outcry to audit the Federal Reserve, even shut it down. Occupy Wall Street became a global movement against the bankers. Particularly targeted is Goldman Sachs, which has or has had former executives as head of the European Central Bank, the Federal Reserve, the Bank of Canada, the NY Fed, the US Treasury, and in line for the Bank of England, as well as serving as unelected prime ministers of Greece and Italy, and as creators of the Euro currency. GSax has a less flattering moniker – the great vampire squid with its tentacles sucking blood from the world economy. The policy of too big to fail has created moral hazard on a scale that threatens the world's financial system. The drums of war beat louder every day against the oil-rich Middle East and especially Iran to forestall or divert attention from financial collapse. Bizarre political issues arise, such as birthers questioning Obama's natural born citizenship status and claiming he is thereby an unconstitutional president. Meanwhile, the executive branch conducts wars without Congressional approval, burdening the nation with out of control debt. The world grows increasingly skeptical of US good intentions and perhaps more worrying for its leadership, of its capacity to enforce its will, leading to increasingly open hostility towards the United States. No one trusts anyone anymore. Amidst these situations, the idea of the world economy erupting in flames appears not only more and more possible. To those paying attention, it's already happening.

## Endnotes

1    Tyler Durden, "Today's $1.24 Billion Targeted Gold Slam", Zerohedge.com, April 30, 2012 and "BIS FX/Gold 'Intervention' Profiles – Before And After", Zerohedge.com, April 16, 2012.

2    $1 for $1 Rubicon crossed in 1968. http://thewe.cc/weplanet/circus/2008/circus_october_2_2008.html

3    Since 2010, the chart has turned positive again; part of this is statistical manipulation, discussed later. Another caveat: if GDP contracts even slightly, the chart flips negative.

4    This sequence is covered in the Petrodollar section.

# 1

# MONEY
# FORM AND FUNCTION

*Gold is money, everything else is credit*
—**J.P. Morgan**

Against this awesome chaos, there is a single, timeless counterweight. Valued around $10 trillion in total, the world's supply of gold would fit into a cube 64 feet on a side and weigh 150,000 tons – 5 billion troy ounces. It represents the opposite of chaos, the opposite of clever, the opposite of corrupt. Gold is too simple to be used to connive, too monolithic to confuse, too straightforward to deceive. It just sits there and holds value. That is its beauty and its promise. If history is any judge, gold will be the last man standing in a holocaust economy.

The relationship is shown from a different perspective by Exter's inverted pyramid. John Exter was a Federal Reserve Board governor during the 1950s. He also helped found the central bank of Ceylon. His pyramid is a powerful teaching and visualization tool. It shows (see Figure 3 adjacent) the relative size and risk of various asset classes. When he made it, third world debt was at the top – now derivatives have taken that position of infamy. They are the largest, riskiest and most destabilizing asset on the planet. One very interesting note is that size of the asset also corresponds to risk of the asset. This is a law-like characteristic, at least in a non-manipulated market. A huge size means that fewer and fewer buyers exist for the amount that is for sale. And since price is set by the latest sale, rather than an average, the entire pool is pegged to a few sales. So a huge pool of derivatives is valued on very few transactions. When the large market players swing away from them, the market collapses. This is why the Federal Reserve has such a bloated balance sheet. It has bought enormous sums of derivatives to bolster the mega-banks.

The second lesson is the vaporization of wealth. When times are good, money moves up the inverted pyramid. The big money borrows to invest, putting it in higher-risk assets to generate more profit. Gold, currency, and now T-bonds just sit there – in such a context, they don't generate a sufficiently appreciable return. But when the downturn comes, just sitting there seems pretty desirable, much better than vanishing into smoke. Asset

**Figure 3**

**Exter's Pyramid**

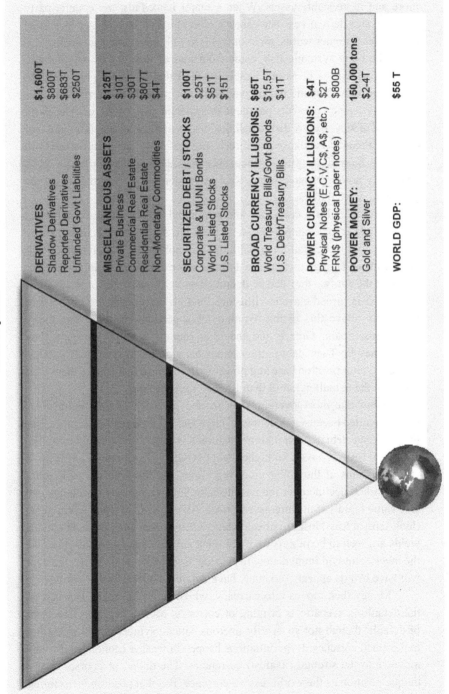

| | | |
|---|---|---|
| **DERIVATIVES** | | $1,600T |
| Shadow Derivatives | | $800T |
| Reported Derivatives | | $683T |
| Unfunded Govt Liabilities | | $250T |
| | | |
| **MISCELLANEOUS ASSETS** | | $125T |
| Private Business | | $10T |
| Commercial Real Estate | | $30T |
| Residential Real Estate | | $807T |
| Non-Monetary Commodities | | $4T |
| | | |
| **SECURITIZED DEBT / STOCKS** | | $100T |
| Corporate & MUNI Bonds | | $25T |
| World Listed Stocks | | $51T |
| U.S. Listed Stocks | | $15T |
| | | |
| **BROAD CURRENCY ILLUSIONS:** | | **$65T** |
| World Treasury Bills/Govt Bonds | | $15.5T |
| U.S. Debt/Treasury Bills | | $11T |
| | | |
| **POWER CURRENCY ILLUSIONS:** | | **$4T** |
| Physical Notes (E,C,V,C$, A$, etc.) | | $2T |
| FRN$ (physical paper notes) | | $800B |
| | | |
| **POWER MONEY:** | | 150,000 tons |
| Gold and Silver | | $2-4T |
| | | |
| **WORLD GDP:** | | $55 T |

values will disappear from the top of the pyramid as money runs down to more and more stable assets. When a major bank fails, the counter-party risk activates derivatives. The cascade effect begins. This causes leveraged companies (in other words, most of them) to fail; their stocks go south.

The other systemic risk, aside from loss of market value, is default. The preponderance of assets, concentrated at the top, are highly prone to a counter-party default: the derivative is not paid on some pretext, or a regulatory agency prevents payment as systemic risk, or the counter-party lacks the money. Below that, small businesses are failing regularly and real estate is already in collapse and foreclosure crisis. It's also intertwined with mortgage backed securities which disappeared from the market in 2008 since they no longer have value. Real estate derivatives – at the top of the pyramid – were the first to go.

Next to fail are corporate and municipal bonds – Detroit defaulted in June, 2013, for example. These entities are not legally backstopped by anything else. If they fail, their liabilities will not be met and their stock will be worthless. Though their assets do have some collateral backing – the net worth of the entity – they can be defaulted on in a bankruptcy or insolvency.

Next is 'broad currency illusions,' mainly sovereign debt. Euro-debt is slightly above this in the pyramid for a peculiar reason – the dodgy sovereigns, Spain, Greece and the like, cannot print the currency they owe money in. Their debt is thus somewhat akin to the debt of US states. However, their taxation base and power is stronger, so that pushes them a bit lower on the default pyramid than Illinois, for example.

At any rate, most sovereign debt lies above US debt in the pyramid. This seems inverted because US debt is so large and the problem is insoluble. But the aggregate debt of other nations combined is larger, and some nations, like Japan and Britain, have a far higher debt to GDP ratio. Moreover, the reserve currency status of the dollar gives it a stronger safe-haven status, in spite of its gradual decline over the past decade. Sovereign debt instruments can lose value rapidly if the interest rate rises. All previously issued instruments (long-term at least) lose significant value when current rates exceed theirs. If yields are seen to be in a rising trend, then nobody wants to invest because the investment will immediately lose value. Eventually, most sovereign debt will have lost its appeal. Too many have defaulted in one way or another.

Money then moves into currency, which spikes in value. But part of the defaulting scenario is printing of currency. Monetizing debt is a form of default, though not so overtly onerous, since payment is still made but in devalued currency. Hyperinflations happen in weaker economies. Money moves into the strongest (safest) currencies. The dollar, of course, is in a unique position as the world reserve currency. But that position is declining and such long-term trends are virtually impossible to reverse. Confidence takes decades to gain and a few years to lose. The dollar index (USDX) has slipped from 120 to 80 since 2001. Monetary value declines can take a long time. However, psychological declines can be lightning fast. The seemingly strong German Weimar currency went from deflation to hyperinflation within a year. Attempting to specifically predict this phase and its effects on the general populace is a fool's game. The dollar may last for another hundred years and it may be gone in ten. But one thing is sure – it will continue to lose real value. A dollar will buy less and less. The long-term trend has been taking place for a hundred years. The dollar will get bounces, some major ones, but they won't last. And when big money realizes more and more that the US government has to massively inflate the currency supply to feed the maw of failing banks, states, and the bloated warfare/welfare state, it will move to solid money – precious metals, which cannot be inflated over a duration or artificially created. The paper illusions created on top of them – derivatives – will be destroyed in the conflagration. Only the physical metals will retain value. And, if Exter's map is right, these will increase in price astronomically.

One of the best illustrations of the power of gold is the chart comparing it to US Treasury debt. They have been highly correlated since 2000. This is a very strong trend; as long as debt increases, the price of gold will track that increase (see Figure 4, below) Short-term fluctuations disappear over a long-term view. Of course, the trend continuation does depend on the debt remaining viable. At the zero bound mentioned earlier, or in the event of US default, the situation will become unpredictable. Probably a short crash (buy

**Figure 4**

**US DEBT & DEBT LIMIT vs GOLD**

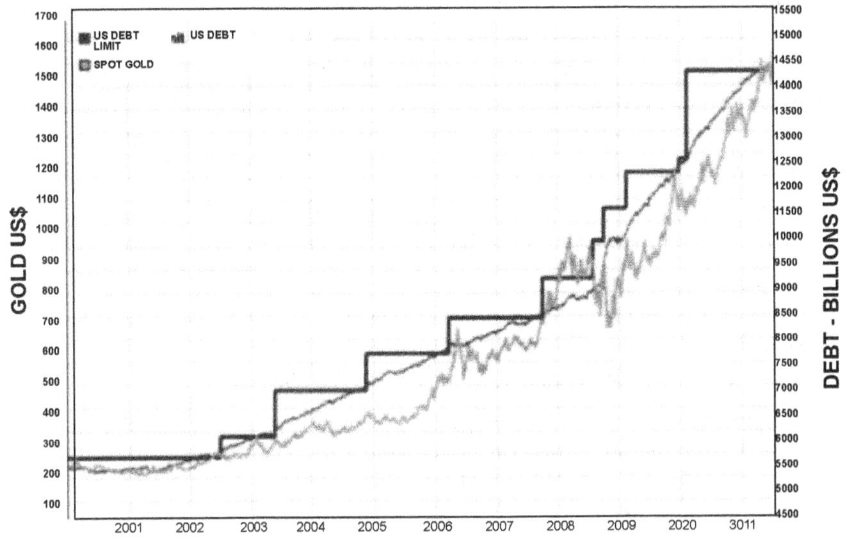

world gold charts © www.sharelynx.com

with both hands), then a super-spike in the gold price would result, at least in US dollar terms. So far, the Treasury market has been linear with a jump and a steepening in 2008. A serious dislocation makes the results unknowable.

A significant part of the gold wars is the psychological battle to make PMs look like a speculative bet and a bad one, rather than the traditional form of money. So far, the middle class has bought this idea. PM participation is incredibly small on the part of the general public. Less than 1% of the populace owns any investment gold or silver. Total investment hovers around .8% of holdings versus 20% and higher a few decades ago. When this reverses, based on the fear trade, the rise will be epic. It will make the greed-based dot-com and real estate bubbles look tiny. But PMs are not now and will not then be in a bubble. Real money, being limited in supply by nature, cannot be in a bubble.

To understand this, we must make clear what a bubble is. The definition is simple – a situation where demand overwhelms supply and the price rises exponentially and, most importantly, unsustainably. Once supply greatly exceeds the recently burgeoning demand, the bubble deflates.

A bubble results from the availability of too much credit. The enlarging of the supply of money results from the excess creation of credit by the dark magic of fractional reserve banking. This book will cover that topic in detail, but for now, a bubble happens when demand first exceeds supply. Everybody wants dotcom stocks, real estate, or tulip bulbs. People borrow, margin, or straight-out invest in the bubble instrument in herds. Prices explode because five times the amount of money is chasing the same number of instruments. Speculation takes hold – people are buying for no other reason than that they see the numbers rising. Derivatives mushroom – investment bankers devise different ways of investing in the arena. This soaks up more capital, but inflames investors' passions and attracts more interest. The ostensible rise in supply created by the intervention of derivatives generates a 'heat' with it and draws in more demand. As long as these are balanced or demand is stronger, the bubble can keep inflating. But at some point, the supply exceeds demand – there's just too much product for the money. All the creative instruments explode out of control. Big money panics, or skillfully exits, and that's the pinprick. Once bubble prices drop too much, everybody runs for the exits, trying to get out with as much money as they can retain. The slow-moving sheep are sheared and the bubble can never be reinflated. Prices drop to zero or to realistic levels. Often, they overshoot reasonable valuations to the downside.

The speed of bubble formation depends on the tangibility and labor required to produce the underlying asset. Tulips are easy to grow – so the Dutch tulip mania (documented thoroughly in *Extraordinary Popular Delusions and the Madness of Crowds* by Charles Mackay) flowered extremely quickly by the terms of the day. According to records, people paid more for a tulip bulb than for a house! It wilted far faster. The dotcom bubble took two years or so. Stocks are easy to create, so the supply took little time to overwhelm the demand. The real estate bubble lasted for about six years; real estate takes time to build. But this was foreshortened by the overlay of mortgage backed securities and the use of variable rate loans to people with no assets or income. These paper instruments created overwhelming supply on top of the basic instrument: real buildings. Those paper instruments overwhelmed the demand and the bubble deflated. The securities failed with lightning speed – nobody wanted the valueless paper. Central banks bought it to save the too big to fails. The real estate market declined more slowly, since buildings do have actual value where paper does not. But real estate should have fallen much further. The slow decline resulted in large part from artificial measures to uphold home values – again to protect the banks from insolvency.

A bubble is marked by a rapid rise then rupture of price. The rupture must be market driven, not instigated by regulatory agencies. We will analyze the notorious Hunt brothers' silver play, along with the concurrent gold 'bubble,' and present evidence that regulatory attacks destroyed a speculative run-up. Gold may have been overvalued, but Figure 5 shows that it fell far less in percentage terms than the NASDAQ. It was not a popping bubble, it was a forced revaluation to end speculative strength.

Sound money cannot be in a bubble for two reasons. One, the supply is definitively limited. Gold cannot be created; it can only be mined and refined. However much can be found is how much there is. Equities can be created without any limit. This is an important bubble criteria – the capacity for unrestrained supply creation to overwhelm demand.

**Figure 5**
**Gold is not in a Bubble**

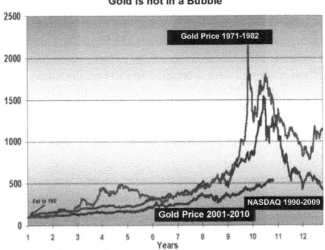

25

Second, money is the yardstick to measure all other instruments and whether they are overly inflated or not. If gold becomes not money – highly unlikely in the world's political arena – then a commodity bubble is possible. Of course, gold derivatives can still easily blow up with speculative excess, then pop. That's because the speculative excess can proliferate without restraint – it is only made of paper. These mechanisms are a key topic in this book. When the paper gold bubble pops, then the paper price of gold and the physical price will likely separate. Paper should drop and physical soar. Central banks realize that gold is money and the trend for them to buy it is increasing. It only seems like "not-money" to the general public, as Western central bankers want. It's an old game.

People that respect gold in such a way are disparagingly called goldbugs, as if they felt that the metal had some sort of sacred properties. But it's not that – gold is just a metal. However, it has specific characteristics that make it uniquely suitable for the role it has. Gold is money, and many insist it is the ultimate form. Aristotle defined money by five criteria (more have been added), and gold fulfills them all. It is fungible, divisible, portable, a store of value, universally recognized, limited in quantity, convenient and durable.

Fungible means that all units of equal weight are equivalent in value. One dollar is the same value as another. Any PM (precious metal) one ounce coin is the same value as another of the same metal (except numismatics which have collectible value). PMs, like dollars, can be infinitely divided or recombined to make money of any desired value. Paper and electronic currencies are quite superior to gold in portability – a small rectangular card can hold virtually any amount. It can be wired around the globe in minutes. Still, gold and silver are more portable than most commodities and physical assets. They fit in the pocket and an enormous value can be moved with a van. Unlike paper currency, PMs are a store of value because they have a relatively stable value for millennia – they have never gone to zero. This is because everyone knows they are money (like the dollar), they cannot be infinitely created (unlike the dollar), and the work to create them is a proxy value by itself since it is always required to increase the supply (unlike the dollar). Like the dollar, PMs are quite convenient. Minted into well-known forms, they carry instant recognition with understood value. Finally, they last. Coins do wear down, but it takes a long time and lots of use. Except for its poor portability, gold is a superior form of money to paper and electronic currencies.

Money and currency are not the same. Money is a store of value, currency is a medium of exchange . No national currency possesses a stable value. All have declined over the past 40 years or more. Historically, every single unbacked currency has steadily declined. If a person had $35 to invest in 1972 and he stored it in US dollars, now it would be worth $35. If he had invested it in Treasuries, he would have $375 or so. If he had bought an ounce of gold, it would now be sellable for multiples of that.

Money's origins are debatable. The reigning theory is that money was an emergent phenomenon of the open market. People need a standard measure of trade. As such it was made of some commodity – silver or exotic seashells, for example. The Romans paid their soldiers in salt, which is where the word salary comes from. Which brings up the contrary theory of money – it's a creation of the state, originally meant to pay soldiers. The military is always an empire's greatest expense. This system allows the same advantage to be derived from money – a standard measure of trade – but confers a number of hidden advantages available only to rulers. The government can tax its own currency and it gets seigniorage – basically free money – from creating the supply. (More on this later).

Money, as such, stems from an issuing body and survives only so long as that body survives. When Rome fell, so did its coin – which had been radically debased prior to the fall. Likewise with other nations. Today, issuing bodies are central banks; some, like the European Central Bank, are clearly supranational. They are not synonymous with what we call 'government.' Nevertheless, the power to control a currency is effectively a form of governance. As this book shows, it is *the most powerful* form of governance. When that power operates secretly and is exempt from democratic controls or legislative oversight, it is, by definition, highly concentrated in those few hands which are in a position to decide how it is to be deployed. This is a terribly dangerous situation – it leaves the door wide open to the most unscrupulous and power-hungry, potentially permitting a small group of sociopaths to exert de facto control over the globe. That may not be the current situation, but since sociopaths seem more likely to enter politics and/or fixate on money than other people,[1] such a situation may be emerging.

Historically, as money became more sophisticated, representative money emerged – money backed by a commodity, usually gold. The paper was exchangeable for the physical. Nowadays, all state currencies are fiat – latin for 'let it be done' – decreed by government to serve as the medium of denomination for all debts, public and private. Currency, with its connotation of 'current,' is 'now' money. It is immediate and of the present time. More stable currencies are backed by gold.

There is a long-standing debate about two conflicting uses of money. As the old rhyme goes: Money is a matter of functions four, a medium, a measure, a standard, and a store. In other words: a medium of exchange, a measure of value (for settling contracts), a standard of deferred payment (a defunct usage), and a store of value. The first and last are in conflict – exchange media are meant to circulate, store of value media are meant to be held. Hence, some economists separate these into two terms: currency as medium of exchange and money as store of value.

As such, gold is more money than currency. It's not easy to use gold as a circulating medium – even small quantities of it are too valuable. From one perspective, it would appear to be an increasing store of value, but it's quite difficult to demonstrate this over periods of time. Up until the mid-20th Century, the benchmark of value was gold (and silver). In a series of steps, beginning in the 1930s, global public perception of monetary value was shifted from gold to the US dollar. The dollar became 'as good as gold,' and universally sought after.

Silver is the little brother of gold in that sense. In 51 countries, the word used for silver is the same as that for money. The French word 'argent' means money and silver. There have been hundreds of silver and silver-backed currencies in history. It has had a number of names associated with it, including 'The Devil's metal.' Silver probably has the best ability to function as both money and currency, insofar as it has a number of serviceable traits that distinguish it from gold, sufficient to warrant its own chapter in this book. But one fact is stunning: above-ground silver is more plentiful than above-ground gold. That's because industry is ravenous for silver and uses it up. This gives it some very enticing investment criteria.

In times of extreme monetary creation, such as currently, it behooves the central bank to control the rise of gold price to prevent it spiking out of control. Short sales, gold leasing, unallocated exchange-traded funds (ETFs) are some of the mechanisms – we'll cover all of these shenanigans. More intense methods are also used, like letting it rapidly rise, then issuing repeated margin calls to slam it back down. This increases volatility and scares away short term investors.

Central to all this is the world reserve currency status of Federal Reserve notes. Exactly what a Federal Reserve Note (FRN) is will be covered later. It's not what most believe. The creation of money and a much deeper picture of all the above issues will also be covered. This introductory section is only intended to set the stage, to give an initial idea of the relative complexity involved – and financial engineering has made that complexity infinitely worse. And that's one reason gold is a threat: it's so simple. It functions as a counter-lever against this entire illusory fiat currency system.

Accordingly, the powers that be dislike it, and even take steps to prohibit public ownership of gold. In 1933, gold ownership for US citizens became illegal, and the penalties for owning gold could lead to a fine of $10,000 and up to 10 years in prison.[2] The real problem was that public ownership of gold could portend the deflation of the money supply. When people wanted to redeem their gold certificates in 1933, as agreed by law, the Federal Reserve declared it a national emergency on March 2. On March

4, FDR was inaugurated and called a session of Congress within a few days. Shortly thereafter, Proclamation 2039 was issued. "Whereas there have been heavy and unwarranted withdrawals of gold and currency from our banking institutions for the purpose of hoarding...", it began. The word "unwarranted" is interesting. Gold certificates represented a lawful contract between the Federal Reserve and the citizens. FDR declared *force majeure* – permitting abrogation of contract in the national interest. He used the broad War Powers Act and Trading with the Enemy Act to issue a decree making it illegal to own gold. Use of that specific Act was only warranted against enemies of the state. Of course, instead it was applied to the American people. Therefore, Executive Order 6102, declaring the hoarding of gold illegal, implicitly and absurdly names the American people as the enemy of America.

Five hundred tons of gold soon flowed into the Treasury. Gold was redeemed at $20.67 an ounce ($371 in 2010 dollars) under the order. Eight months later, the Gold Reserve Act changed the price of gold to $35 an ounce ($587 in 2010 dollars). The government used the stolen profits to create the Exchange Stabilization Fund whose mandate was to maintain the exchange rate of the dollar. The Gold Reserve Act also made contracts with a gold clause unenforceable, and a subsequent resolution made such dual contracts illegal. The existence of gold clauses reflected an effort to defend business arrangements against the devaluation of the dollar. To no avail: instead, gold was demonetized, removed from circulation, and struck from contractual recourses in a year.

The pretext was nonsensical – hoarding gold was 'slowing the economy.' If hoarding gold was a problem, then turning the Treasury into the ultimate hoarder seems an odd solution. In actuality, it took away people's sound money (barring politico-legal intervention), forcing them to spend their dollars. Part of the intent was to force people to spend. Alan Greenspan offered another perspective, long before he became head of the Federal Reserve.

> The abandonment of the gold standard made it possible for the welfare statists to use the banking system as a means to an unlimited expansion of credit...The financial policy of the welfare state requires that there be no way for the owners of wealth to protect themselves. This is the shabby secret of the welfare statists' tirades against gold. Deficit spending is simply a scheme for the confiscation of wealth. Gold stands in the way of this insidious process. It stands as a protector of property rights. If one grasps this, one has no difficulty in understanding the statists' antagonism toward the gold standard.[3]

He was asked decades later if he wanted to deny the position taken in that essay. In a refreshing bit of honesty, the Maestro replied, "I wouldn't change a word."[4]

Eighteen years after FDR's outlawing of gold, Congressman Howard Buffet (father of Warren) linked gold redeemable money to human freedom. As exhibit A, he noted that Hitler, Mussolini, and Lenin all outlawed ownership of gold at the first possible chance. This enabled them to depreciate all the people's money at the leader's desire. The citizen could not travel with a freely exchangeable currency. All paper currencies, Buffet noted, end in "collapse and economic chaos." Public access to gold gave some leverage to those objecting to government profligacy; they could redeem their notes for gold and "wait for common sense to come to Washington. Politicians of both parties will oppose the restoration of gold, but, unless you are willing to surrender your children and your country to galloping inflation, war and slavery, then this cause demands your support. For if human liberty is to survive in America, we must win the battle to restore honest money."[5]

Nowadays, the problem is more systemically interconnected and being played out on the global stage. The Bundestag – German Parliament – budget committee is pushing for an audit of the country's massive gold reserves and demanding partial repatriation from the Federal Reserve, where it had been deposited after the war, primarily for international trade settlement. There are accusations of cheating on the accounting.[6] Germany holds 4300 tons of gold on its books, second only to the US holding of 8100 tons. The public tentacle of the Bundesbank (their central bank) is Deutschebank, an ally of JPMorgan in the anti-gold arena, each having numerous entanglements with the other. Both are leveraged to the hilt, swimming in bad bonds, derivatives, and toxic assets. They have severe liquidity problems, and would be revealed as insolvent if correct accounting were applied, and face large lawsuits with a dwindling reputation. There is presently a citizen movement[7] that aims to repatriate German gold from New York, London, and Paris vaults. Resistance from mega-banks is high, but explanations for their resistance are few and weak.

Hugo Chavez repatriated Venezuela's gold reserves in 2011, sparking a wave of similar action. India's high court issued an injunction on its central bank to bring back gold from London vaults – after RBI (Royal Bank of India) officials had claimed that India held all her gold. No one from the RBI showed up to defend the case in court. The move signals the wave of distrust of London and New York central bankers. India purchased 200 tons of gold in 2007 from the IMF (International Monetary Fund), but agreed to hold only the gold certificates – a *claim* on the metal actually held in London. Now, they're looking to get the gold and wonder if it's actually there. The IMF lists its gold holdings at 2800 tons, but most is in promissory notes from countries. It holds almost no physical metal.

A deeper, but very uneasy explanation, from *Real World Economics Review*, binds all of this together. The message presented is ominous. Elite accumulation of wealth is highly correlated with physically imprisoning large sectors of the populace, at least since 1940. The US now has 25% of the planet's prison population and incarcerates more of its citizens than any nation in history. There is an 'asymptote of power' that has been reached at the present time. (see Figure 6, below). The top earners are at an historic all-time maximum concentration of wealth. Globally, the top 1% owns 39% of the world's wealth and the lower half owns a scant 1%. In order to consolidate their holdings against the possibility of a majority uprising, and/or to increase their reach even further, a social crackdown is needed. The convict population is already 5% of the US workforce – the highest percent in the world, perhaps in all history. New prison facilities are still under construction, though many lie vacant. A breaking point is coming.

**Figure 6**
**Rising Prison Population**

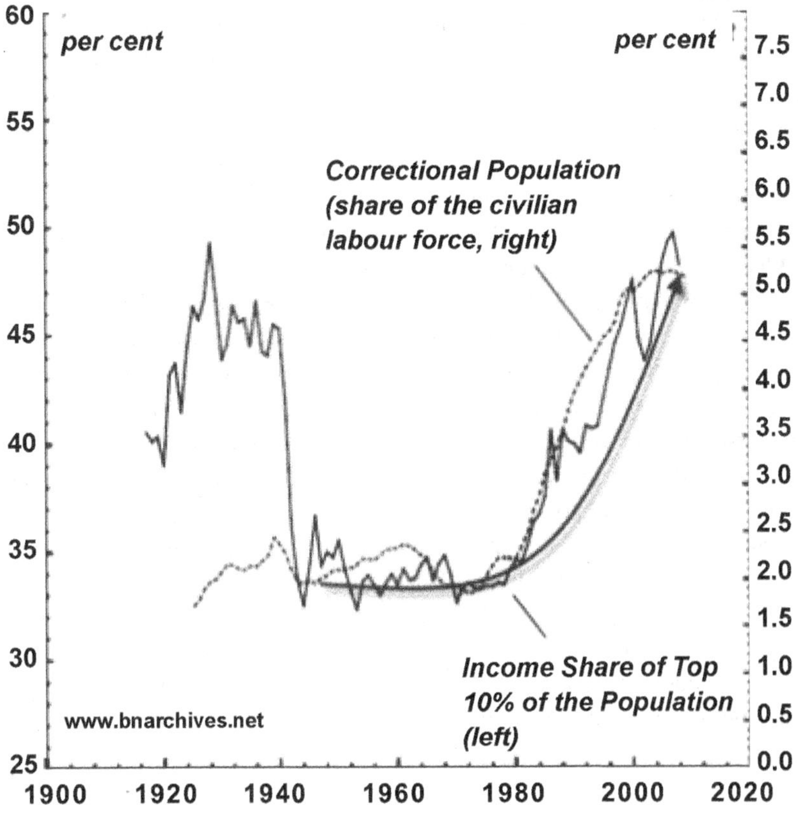

Speculative causes are wide-ranging – left, right, center, fringe, Libertarian, Keynesians, Friedmanites, political theorists, and conspiracists – all have an explanation. The causes cited to explain the present malaise cover a wide range of possibilities, including the issuance of excess credit, excess indebtedness, hyper-regulation, deregulation, asymmetrical enforcement, and use of regulation as a weapon against smaller entities. It's blamed on government, corporatocracy, banksters, a debt-based growth system, peak oil, secret societies, financial system distrust, credit freezes, derivatives, housing and speculative bubbles, central banking, real estate collapse, ballooning trade imbalances, entitlements, greed, wealth disparity, and apathetic citizenry.

The primary fear is that a global economic reset is coming. The global capitalist system is seen to be under threat. There is a common agreement within most theories on a few fundamentals, the *Real World Economics* article finds. First, the state of the economy is the real threat and cause. Politics is secondary. Second, a divergence between real and nominal economics greatly worsens the problems. The real economy – production – is falling. The rising and falling of the nominal economy – the speculative arenas – in an unpredictable manner makes this much worse. Capital cannot find a safe home. Third, we are reaping what we have sown – too much debt, trust in government, leniency to capital creation, etc. The piper has to be paid.

According to *Real World Economics*, these assumptions may be flawed. While Capital may be a tool to produce and consume real goods, primarily it is the locus of social control (which works through the overt function of commerce because everyone needs and wants things). In this case, the economic and political would merge in analysis – they become the same. What is real and what is nominal are not separate.

From this point of view, the current fear is different. It is a systemic fear – one of a total loss of power. Capitalists are driven to accumulate capital, but this is inseparable from the accumulation of power. Capital is power. (see Figure 7 adjacent). This is the key consideration of all societies, and an understanding of this has been lost. But the accumulation has a boundary – the asymptote. At that point, resistance becomes extreme. Instability rules. The need for further power in order to ensure existing power requires greater social violence. It is the point just before failure, when controllers become most afraid. The structure is threatened with destruction by its own success.

As shown, the income of the top 10% is at all-time highs. The previous high saw the commencement of the Great Depression with a slow decline, then a sudden collapse in 1940. The current highs – near 50% of national income – exceed those of the 1920s. The asymptote of capitalist power approaches.[8]

**Figure 7**
**Income Share of hte Top 10% of the U.S. Population**

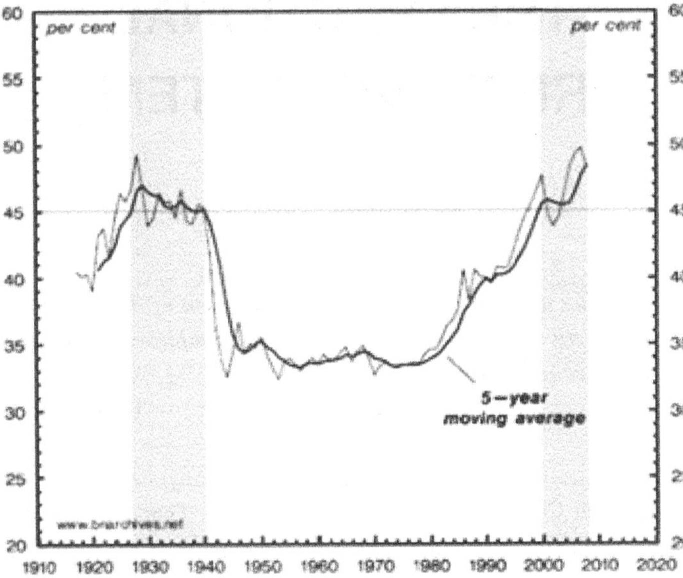

## Endnotes

1 David Freeman, "Are Politicians Psychopaths?", Huffington Post. August 27, 2012.
2 Executive Order 6102, President Franklin Delano Roosevelt, April 5, 1933.
3 Greenspan, Alan. *Gold and Economic Freedom,* 1966.
4 Donald Luskin. 2002 Interview with Ron Paul. Smartmoney.com.
5 Hon. Howard Buffet. Human Freedom Rests on Gold Redeemable Money. May 6, 1948.
6 Welt online, Bundestag-prueft-Bewertung-deutscher-Goldreserven.html, 5/14/2012.
7 gold-action.de
8 Shimshon Bichler and Jonathan Nitzan ,"The asymptotes of power", *Real World Economics Review* 60.June 6, 2012.

# 2

# THE FRACTIONAL RESERVE SYSTEM

*The modern theory of the perpetuation of debt has drenched the earth with blood, and crushed its inhabitants under burdens ever accumulating*

—Thomas Jefferson

In 1776, the Continental Congress declared anyone who would not accept the paper Continental an enemy of the state. That's the essence of a fiat currency – the government mandates its acceptance. Though less overt in the case of modern fiat currencies, their viability is forced nonetheless. But worse, the currencies are not issued by the government, but by privately-held banks. The private enterprise of the central bank is government enforced – the very antithesis of a free market.

There's a lot of context at play in the gold wars. Some of the important components to be understood are fractional reserve banking, shadow banking, and the central banking system. While physical gold is extremely simple in its operation – it just sits there – it can be made into coins for exchange or bars for storing wealth or used to back money and so forth – the banking, financial and investment systems, by contrast, are complex to the point of incomprehensibility. Individuals can only grasp sectors in any depth.

Though gold-holding gave rise to modern banking, the two have radically diverged. Physical gold and modern banking are now mortal enemies, strange as that may sound. Gold has an inherent value due to its scarcity and cost of creation. Banking instruments have no inherent value – they are created from nothing in unlimited supply. The bewildering array of modern instruments serves as a hidden form of money beyond what most people understand as money, i.e. cash. They are the spawn of the fractional reserve system which, at heart, is a system of credit and debt.

The first known use of credit appeared among the Babylonians around 1300 BCE in the form of mortgage security and deposits. Babylon extended it with bills of exchange, enabling trade to faraway nations. Rome refined it much further to assist trade in its complex empire. The notion of credit survived the fall of Rome because traders preferred to rely on it rather than face the dangers of porting solid coin around. The Middle Ages and finally the Renaissance saw a well-developed system arise. During this later period, Great Britain emerged as a world financial power, using credit to devastating effect to create the first "soft" hegemonic empire based on other than military domination. Its great secret was the discovery, by the goldsmiths, of the fractional reserve system.

Goldsmiths held money for the wealthy in vaulted storage. They issued gold certificates, paper claims on the gold, in exchange for the metal. These were used in trade far more than was specie, itself. Physical metal was too bulky and risky to transport. The goldsmiths soon realized that no more than 10% of the metal on hand was ever claimed by the current owners, and began to loan out more paper certificates than they had gold against the claim. They stabilized this at a ratio of 10 paper ounces loaned per ounce of physical. By storing 1000 ounces of gold, the goldsmith could loan, at interest, 10,000 ounces of paper gold. These certificates are now called bank notes – Federal Reserve notes, Euros, Yen and the like.

Bankers had found the means to create money out of nothing. Soon enough, the method expanded from issuing banks to depository institutions. The use of checks allowed banks to simply create a deposit in the borrower's name without putting out any real cash. Many checks simply moved funds from one depositor to another within the bank – no funds were withdrawn from the bank. Bankers fail to explain the enormous power and benefit such money creation confers on the bank – the right to take profits on thin air, based on a power no one else has.

The British defeat of Napoleon illustrated that power. Military war is inevitably fought in large measure as financial war, as wars must be financed. England was the great purveyor of credit, able to access money from nothing. Napoleon was convinced his system of sound money could defeat the vaporous credit creation of the British. He felt that people would reject a paper currency in favor of gold backing. His defeat made clear the awesome power of fractional reserve banking, a point not lost on bankers.

The rest is history. The Federal Reserve was created by private bankers in 1913 and managed to institutionalize itself as if it were a component of government. As it put up a staid and boring façade, clouding. the banking system in a fog of opaque terminology, the public mind simply turned off. After the Great Depression and WWII, the system seemed to work very well, especially for the US. No one wanted to wag fingers at a system that seemed to benefit the entire nation.

Then as now, when the government wants money, the Treasury creates bonds and sends them to the Federal Reserve in exchange for Federal Reserve

Notes. (See Figure 8 below.) Those bonds are the largest share of the national

**Figure 8**
**St. Louis Adjusted Monetary Base**

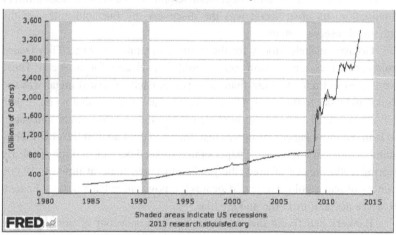

Shaded areas indicate US recessions.
2013 research.stlouisfed.org

debt. There is no particular reason why the government cannot simply create its own currency. In fact, the Constitution specifically disallows the current process of money creation, according to many interpretations.

Most modern systems of banking are based on fractional reserve. When a bank takes money by deposits or borrowing from the Fed (base money), it can loan out 90% of the money. Doing so, it creates the new money to loan out, keeping the original money on its balance sheet. That new currency created by the credit loan is then deposited into the next bank, which can repeat the process. Often the money is deposited right back into the initiating bank. An initial $1000 of base money can turn into $10,000, and through more esoteric means discussed later, up to $40,000. While the 'money multiplier' formula is M=1/R, with R as the reserve requirement – where a requirement 10:1 means supply can be increased by 10 times – banks have many means to stretch the reserve requirements.

An important concept is iterations – the number of times money is cycled through the system. There is an expansion limit defined by the formula: Loans = (Initial Deposit ÷ Reserve Requirement) − Initial Deposit. In real numbers, $9,000 = ($1,000 ÷ 0.1) − $1,000 = $10,000 − $1,000. It's a pyramid scheme. (See Figure 9 adjacent) Banks hold 10% (or less, depending on reserve requirements) of depositor money. When depositors all want their money, due to lack of confidence, there's a bank run. Banks cannot pay in a run

Figure 9

# THE BASIC FRACTIONAL RESERVE BANKING CYCLE

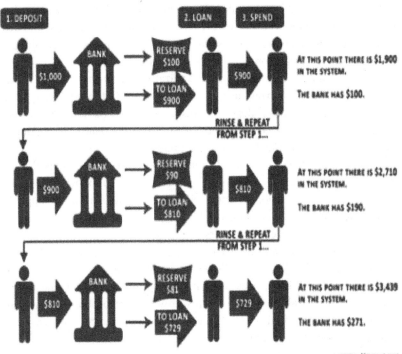

AT THIS POINT THERE IS $1,900 IN THE SYSTEM.

THE BANK HAS $100.

AT THIS POINT THERE IS $2,710 IN THE SYSTEM.

THE BANK HAS $190.

AT THIS POINT THERE IS $3,439 IN THE SYSTEM.

THE BANK HAS $271.

HTTP://CYNIC.ME

because they have lent out more than they held, leaving them soon running out of money. They cannot call in loans to pay off the besieging depositors, because they have no right to change the time requirements on loans.

For the system as whole, interest is the real killer. While the money for the debt is created at the time of the loan – the interest is not. While the principal is extinguished when paid, the interest remains outstanding; there is always a formal shortage of currency. The money supply must be constantly expanded to take care of this. Over a 15 year (or longer term) loan at 5%, the interest even exceeds the principal, yet both must be paid back. Since most loans are of this long-term variety, the amount owed is about twice the amount that exists. The collective outstanding debt can never be repaid. It is impossible and the system is constructed that way. Compound interest eventually eats up all the real wealth of society. It creates an engorging banking system that sucks more money back in than it loans out. That's why people are angry and that's why interest is illegal in certain religions – like Islam. Interest was once forbidden in Christianity and still is between fellow Jews. In fact, total global debt now stands at $170 trillion, but global GDP is only $90 trillion.

This creates the fundamental bind of the modern system. Because of the nature of the fractional reserve system, there is always more money owed than exists. (See Figure 10, adjacent.) The principal is created by the banks, but the interest owed is not created. The system demands perpetual growth in order to maintain the worldwide debt service. Figure 10 adjacent shows debt creation turning parabolic. The system of money creation itself is a major part of the reason for $1 trillion plus federal deficits.

Central banks (CBs), in the standard narrative, exist to manage the system – to monitor the risk of bank runs, to be the lender of last resort, and to set up mechanisms to administer depositors insurance. But CBs have increasingly parlayed the monetary control function to individual banks, attempting to control public borrowing through interest rates.

Most, but not all, central banks mandate a reserve requirement, forcing banks to maintain a ratio of money held in reserve to money loaned out. This limits the overall money supply, allows the CB to control the supply by raising/lowering rates, and (supposedly) keeps the banks solvent and liquid – having the money to meet depositors' demands.

Most systems set a ratio of 10:1, a rate of leverage that seems to work for a while until it hits the wall, which is why it exists. At some point, there is too much debt for existing money supply to service and money creation turns parabolic. That creates downstream problems which are largely the subject of this book. Once they reach that point, however, most banks have sought and found the means to increase leverage dramatically through the shadow banking system. Non-depository institutions (investment banks like Goldman Sachs) have no reserve requirements. G-Sax leverages at several hundred to one. The entire Euro-bank system is 25-1, much worse than the overleveraged US system. MFGlobal was 100 to 1 when it blew up.

The upside of huge leverage is spectacular profits. When a bank has increased its leverage to 100 to 1, a 2% rise in the investment triples the base assets – a 200% profit. The downside is that a 2% drop in the investment pushes the bank deep into the red. Insolvency can happen literally in a few seconds to even fairly large funds of tens of billions, if their risk is bad enough. The problem jumps from institutional to systemic risk in a number of ways. In 2008, it happened through large insurance firms. When AIG widely insured a form of derivative known as collateralized debt obligations (CDOs) against decline for less than .5% of the redeemable value, the downdraft rendered AIG insolvent. Counterparties were left twisting in the wind until the government stepped in to backstop the losses. The Treasury made a number of banks good with a haircut. Only Goldman Sachs was made 100% whole, raising many easily answerable questions as to the source of its clout. The situation is much worse today – a ticking bomb.

**Figure 10**
**Money Creation Cycle**

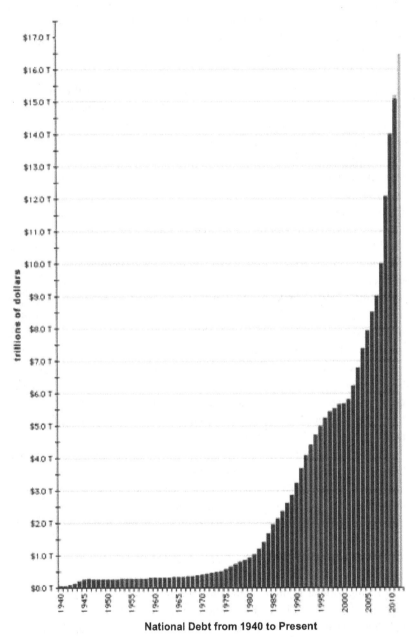

**National Debt from 1940 to Present**

Source: U.S. National Debt Clock
http://www.brillig.com/debt_clock/

To explain it in simple terms:  if Bobby loans Johnny a million dollars and Johnny blows it in Vegas, Bobby owns a million dollar asset plus interest on which he will never collect. Johnny can't get the money to pay back the principal, let alone what Bobby expected to make on the loan. If hundreds of Bobbies loan a handful of Johnnies a million, then the system is at risk through systemic instability.

Minsky's instability hypothesis arose to prominence in 2008, especially during the failure of Lehman Brothers, when the phrase "a Minsky moment" was coined. Hyman Minsky was an economist inspired by the Keynesian school. His basic premise is quite simple: "Capitalist economies exhibit inflations and debt deflations which seem to have the potential to spin out of control. In such processes the economic system's reactions to a movement of the economy amplify the movement – inflation feeds upon inflation and debt-deflation feeds upon debt-deflation."[1] His theory is notable in breaking from classical, Adam Smith doctrine. Smith believed that capitalist systems inherently moved toward stability. Minsky believed that the instability problem is a modern one, created partly by government. Government tries to perpetually goose the markets, to keep the economy growing, at least nominally. This lessens downside business risk, but it increases the inflationary problem. Debt and its modern systemic validation as money are important aspects of the hypothesis. It also takes into account the profit-seeking nature of banks, which Keynes' Quantity Theory of Money ignores.

Minsky is right, of course.  Banks try to make money. As creators and holders of money, this makes their leverage upon the system, the amount of capital they control as a percentage of the national wealth, inherently larger than other institutions. It's a huge problem (covered later), because the whale is now too big for the pool. It's killing everything.

Moreover, innovation is a key approach to generating profits. Since banks are primarily creators of the money supply, that innovation leads to constant change in the character of money. What money is cannot be stably defined in a profit system of banking. This is a very notable concern with shadow banking, where much of what counts as money is not what the man on the street would call money. In fact, with many of the complex derivative structures created by banks, there are some forms of money that are now completely beyond human comprehension.

Trying forever to increase the money supply, banks are, theoretically at least, in constant conflict with regulators, who are forever trying to constrain it. When the banks go overboard, expanding the money supply through extreme innovation to the extent that it threatens systemic stability, the CB is sorely tempted to step in and stabilize the system through intervention. This has the perverse effect of legitimizing the innovation. Ever-more destabilizing innovations become the norm, pushing a stable system into chronic instability.

At that point, the 'income-debt' relationships tend to break down into three distinct kinds: hedge, speculative and Ponzi. Hedge units are the most conservative – they meet payment obligations based on cash flow. Speculative units need to roll over principal debt as it matures in order to maintain financing. A Ponzi unit cannot even finance interest payments on its cash flow. It must borrow more and more just to keep even, watering down its equity.

One of the main sources of stress in fractional reserve banking is the loan duration mismatch. Lenders take in deposit money of zero term duration – it can be immediately withdrawn. They then use it to back long-term loans which will not be paid back, sometimes for decades. When a CD used to back a loan matures, requiring the issuing bank to pay it out, the money loaned out on top of it from which the bank expects to make its money has not yet been paid back. The bank develops massive liquidity problems. In recent years, there have been enormous defaults on the banks' loans. This creates solvency issues on top, because the loans are no longer worth anything. The banks' assets vanish.

Since most capital for these loans comes from savings accounts, the banks cannot pull in the money in the event of a bank run. The mismatch is between zero time and 15 years. The ratio between deposits and loans approaches infinity in theory, but realistically is about 1000 to 1. It takes a few days for a real bank run to crest.

The run is already currently occurring, but in slow-motion. Large investors are letting CDs mature, but not renewing them due to the abysmal returns. Most CDs currently pay less than 1%. As investors continually pull money out of the system, banks have to sell assets to cover this problem and act to get their reserves up. This is a seemingly obvious problem created by allowing a bank to use customer funds as bank reserves – it's not the banks' money, but they use it as if it is. The first assets sold when banks need to increase their reserves are often sovereign bonds. Banks like these instruments because they can hold a lot of money and have a liquid market. They're easy to sell. There is also the lower order of risk – loss of bond values Traditionally, government debt is considered to be safe. However, this isn't all that true – governments can default. If the system experiences massive stress, all banks dump bonds. The bid (buyers for the bonds) disappears and the price tanks. This has been happening with Southern Europe, especially Greece and Spain. In the US, the Federal Reserve has been taking up the slack, but this only converts the risk into an inflationary one, where every paper asset loses value even as it goes up in nominal price.

The systemic effect is hugely amplified, however. The bank first takes a loss on the sold assets (the loans), but because the value of such assets is linked to Treasuries, the unsold assets lose value as well. That's because the interest rate rises, causing newer loans to pay out more than older loans, driving down the value of older loans. Investors obviously want a higher return, so the lower return loans lose demand and value. Banks' asset side of the balance sheet starts to bleed worse and worse, but their liabilities do not go down. So the banks take a double hit. The selling assets go for less and the held assets are priced down. However, mega-banks can disguise their deteriorating situation by legally using fraudulent accounting – permitted by a Bush administration executive order suspending Federal Accounting Standards Board rule 157 for entities deemed critical to national security.

The banks are less solvent than we are being told – probably by a very wide margin. The commercial banks are limited to a 10:1 fractional limit. As their asset base declines, they cannot loan money because their reserve limits are already exceeded. Borrowing short and lending long creates inevitable stresses. There is a limit to how many balls can be juggled.

To bring this back to Minsky – if most institutions are hedges, then the economy tends toward stability. As financialization moves money toward more speculative and Ponzi-type organizations, the economy moves towards instability. Such financial system excesses amplify deviations, rather than suppressing them. Most hedge funds, for example, are no longer hedge funds. They have increased their own leverage to frightening proportions. In a downdraft, their balance sheet suddenly goes negative in unsustainable amounts. All the world's largest banks operate in this manner now. The largest sources of capital, commercial banks, are now Ponzi, or at best, highly speculative schemes. One indication that they are actually Ponzi-financing is the 2008 bailouts. None of the banks were able to make payments on their obligations and had to 'borrow' enormous government sums to stay afloat. It's a classic Ponzi tactic. Even if investment is profitable, leading to increased demand, "moral hazard" – protecting the banks from suffering the consequences of their poor investment decisions by allowing them to fail – merely pushes the system as a whole toward greater speculative frenzy and hence, increased instability.

Theorem 1: any system has stable 'financing regimes' and unstable ones.

Theorem 2: Extended prosperity pushes a system from stable to unstable forms, as investors take the bit in their teeth, and give in to what Greenspan, trying to cool it off, termed "irrational exuberance". Government actions cannot help, and actually worsen the situation. If the system has high speculation and regulators try to contract the money supply to curb it, then speculative units instantly turn into Ponzi units by the decrease in available money. The sudden forced sales of assets cause a deflationary asset price spiral. If government expands the money supply to cover banks' obligations, i.e., the new money goes quickly into parabolic speculation – gambling –

turning the volume on the problem much higher, but pushing the reckoning down the road a few months or years. Buying time, in short.

The hypothesis places the problem squarely at the heart of the system itself, unlike other theories which rely on exogenous shocks. It is internal to fiat economies, like a law of nature. Government and regulatory systems always serve to exacerbate the problem once it arises.

This compelling and seemingly prescient theory misses a crucial point. Fiat currencies are the very stock in trade of instability economics. The gold standard, while not a cure-all for economic ills, definitely has a highly stabilizing effect. It can create deflations, to be sure.[2] These are typically moderate, and self-correcting, due to balance of payment realities when money is restricted by natural law. A deflation causes a nation's goods to be more attractively priced, drawing gold inwards in exchange for goods. An excess of gold (money) causes an increase in price of goods. Neighbors have attractively priced goods, causing gold to flow away. The system is self-balancing. Fiat currencies have no restrictions on monetary creation, annulling the self-correction and leading to amplified imbalances.

When Nixon took us off the gold standard, the fixed relationship of other currencies to the dollar ended, and floating exchange rates came into being. The massive Forex market of currency speculation was born. Tens of billions of dollars, euros, and other currencies flow back and forth, every day seeking a favorable exchange rate advantage to eke out a tiny percentage profit on the transfer of great sums.

Floating exchange rates create horrendous situations for small and developing nations. If they are caught in the eye of the world, then 'hot' money floods in. By this investment in the local banking system, $10 billion becomes $100 billion or more. This upends the economy of a small country. The 1994 Asian financial crisis, triggered in Thailand, is an example. Local inflation rates rose astronomically. Millionaires seemed to be made overnight, mostly by too much leverage, and would go bankrupt. Many citizens were impoverished by an inability to keep up with the inflation rate of goods and services. Development went through the roof. Local resources were purchased by foreign corporations, real estate prices soar for lack of other productive outlet for the increase in capital, the government went up for sale to the neo-liberal economic establishment, corruption and graft became extreme. Eventually, the economy was seen as a bubble and the hot money withdrew, leaving an enormous debt burden and a crushing deflation. The lack of currency leads to ills like a monetary printing binge, currency devaluation and borrowing from the IMF to prevent economic collapse. After, the best companies are picked off for a song by foreign investors. Lesser companies are bought and dismantled for quick sale. With a fixed exchange rate, the ongoing systemic potential for this kind of a problem would not exist.

Similar systemic problems arise due to fractional reserve banking. The legality of the fractional reserve system has been tested, at least once, and lost. In 1967, the First National Bank of Montgomery (MN) tried to foreclose on Jerome Daly. The case went to county court as *First National Bank v Daley*. Daley's defense was curious – the bank could not foreclose because it had not created anything of value in order to purchase the house. The $14,000 it extended to purchase the house was not in silver or gold, i.e. constitutional money, but merely a bookkeeping ledger transfer. The bank's response was that it was following standard practice. The bank could not cite a statute authorizing its right to create money in such a manner. The judge issued a statement after the case:

> There was no material dispute in the facts for the jury to resolve. Plaintiff admitted that it, in combination with the Federal Reserve Bank of Minneapolis, who in the law are to be treated as one and the same bank, did create the entire $14,000 in money or credit upon its books by bookkeeping entry. The money and credit first came into existence when they created it. Mr. Morgan (for the bank) admitted that no United States law or statute existed which gave him the right to do this. A lawful consideration must exist and be tendered to support the note. [There can be] no claim based upon or in any manner depending upon a fraudulent, illegal or immoral transaction or contract to which plaintiff was party. No complaint was made by plaintiff that plaintiff did not receive a fair trial. The path of duty was made clear for the jury. Their verdict could not reasonably have been otherwise.[3]

The bank appealed, paying $2 in Federal Reserve Notes to the court. These notes were refused by the judge who cited article 1, section 10 of the Constitution: "No state shall make anything but gold and silver coin as tender in payment of debts." The bank abandoned its claim at that point. A number of other claims have gone to court, but Daley is the only successful plaintiff against the banks' money creation processes to date.

### Endnotes

1    Hyman P. Minsky, *The Financial Instability Hypothesis*, 1992.
2    Gold has created inflation in the past, but that would be almost impossible now. It would require a massive influx of newly found gold.
3    *Judge Martin V. Mahoney*, December 7, 1968.

# 3

# THE PETRODOLLAR
# STANDARD

*Gold and oil can never flow in the same direction*
*—Another*

In 1971, Richard Nixon infamously closed the gold window. The US was on a gold standard, with a fixed price of $35 per ounce. But the government had expanded the currency base – printing money in order to finance the Vietnam War. Suspecting the lessening value of their dollar holdings, other nations and large traders began to swap dollars for gold. When the trickle became a torrent, Nixon stopped the selling of US gold. Up to this point, other currencies were convertible into US dollars and dollars were convertible into gold. It gave the dollar world reserve status, but also put on pressure to "protect Fort Knox," where US gold was stored.

Figure 11 below shows the resultant sharp upturn after 1971 in the inflation rate. There was far less need for fiscal discipline without the gold

**Figure 11**

## Cumulative Inflation by Decade
## Since 1913

Updated 6/4/2011

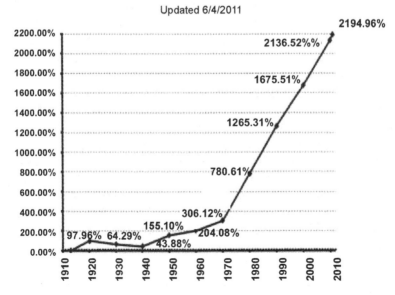

Rottweiler at the government throat. Backing the money with a limited asset (like gold) functions as one of three checks against profligacy. When the issuer overprints, the real treasury is drained; this compels caution, due to the specter of default. The second check is the political one of inflation – the public gets restive – and the far more distant third one is hyperinflation, the kind of economic meltdown experienced by the German Weimer Republic. Having disposed of the first, they ignored the second, and took care of the third in perhaps the most ingenious and powerful pre-emptive economic strike in world history. After 1975, other countries would not desire dollars because they were a good medium of exchange – another reason had been devised to ensure they would have to have them, no matter what.

The system has its roots in the dollar diplomacy policy of President Taft. The US decided to push foreign dollar investment (focusing on Latin America) on terms that would favor America. Military engagement was not stressed, but was a definite option. The stated aim was to maintain "stability" in foreign governments in order to ensure US access to and advantage from foreign markets. It was a soft version of the same thing mastered by the British Empire – monetary hegemony. It was a revolutionary mode of empire.

The monetary hegemon controls access to credit markets, foreign exchange markets, has no balance of payment constraints, and has undisputed ability to force a unit of payment (dollars, for example) for conducting trade. The British monetary hegemon was the world's first, achieved through investment of vast gold reserves – much like the US hegemon began. They were able to set the discount rate (the interest rate charged to commercial banks and other depository institutions) through their central bank and then loan money to other countries in Sterling to facilitate trade. This allowed a consistent method of world payment, which everyone liked. Britain managed to run current account deficits because the currency was so strong and unquestioned. Beginning with 7% of international commerce conducted in sterling, they pushed it to 60% by 1913. World War I initiated a waterfall decline. Patchwork measures were erected, but without a strong anchoring economy, the hegemon failed. Britain eventually lost the world reserve currency due to its inability to convert the pound into gold.

That left the world economy somewhat rudderless until 1944, when the US made its monetary hegemony power grab. But 40 years on, the US had learned the lesson. Leaders recognized that there was no division between foreign policy and monetary policy, or rather, that monetary policy provided the ultimate tool for gaining global dominance. They managed to turn the hegemony, faltering in the 1970s, into global economic domination by linking the dollar to oil.

Probably the most important (though little known) mechanism in the political economy of the world is the petrodollar standard. A full expansion follows, but a brief summary here will allow a handle on the subsequent chain of events, the current state of the mechanism, and the consequences. In 1944, the US dollar became the world reserve currency through the Bretton Woods conference, due to the pre-eminence of its economy, which rather than being destroyed by WWII, had profited from it. When the dollar was formally severed from gold – the so-called Nixon Shock in 1971 – officials scrambled (or had a plan already) to put something else in place. They created a political masterstroke – the petrodollar standard, which ensured that all oil would be sold in dollars, thus requiring all countries to hold dollar reserves.

Petrodollar maintenance was pretty easy until 2000 and remained manageable until recently, though now it seems to be failing. Only a few realize how deep and extensive the consequences for the US will be when it ends. The US policy of maintaining the standard has created very difficult circumstances for the superpower, one that is no longer tenable as US power declines. The end result will be far more tumultuous than any crisis of the past sixty years. For America, it could easily be worse than WWII or the Great Depression. Oil will be far more expensive, and that's the least of the problems. The chain of events leading to the creation of the Standard is instructive.

At the end of WWII, 44 world leaders met at the Bretton Woods hotel in New Hampshire to create a new economic system. The US, being the only nation on the world stage unharmed by the war, was the clear choice to take the role of leader in geo-politics and the world economy. A certain amount of loyalty was bought by the Marshall Plan. The $50 billion in aid that was extended to Europe was sold to the public under the cover of preventing the continent from going Communist under the Soviets.

A number of quasi-governmental organizations were created at this meeting – the IMF, Bank for International Settlements, and the World Trade Organization. More importantly, all currencies were linked to the dollar, and the dollar alone was convertible into gold – at a fixed rate. It was backed by almost 20,000 tons of it in Fort Knox. This system remained stable for twenty years or so. Countries accumulated dollars because they were the easiest token for world trade, as most counterparties carried and traded in them as well. But during the 60s, Johnson's Great Society added a big financial burden to the US economy already stretched by military spending, by seeking to provide both "guns and butter" – Medicare and Medicaid. The military industrial complex alone had required a lot of money creation to wage the Vietnam War.

Clearly, both US political parties were (and still are) guilty in the currency debasement. Social programs from the left, military spending from the right, and bank bailouts from both spiraled the size and cost of government to the point that now it is beyond all sense. When money is freely available, it is easy to buy votes. When big money goes into a few pockets, it is easy to buy political influence. And geopolitical power is ultimately maintained at the point of a gun.

In times of currency debasement, people historically turn to gold and silver. This has been happening for thousands of years and is not likely to change. So, when the 1960s spending put pressure on the dollar and when other nations realized the US currency might be unable to anchor the world economy, mass conversion of dollars to gold began. People always want political and economic stability and with WWII still in clear recall, they were desperate for it. If Uncle Sam couldn't give it, maybe his gold stash could.

When foreign exchange reserves became too great and the US balance of payments deficit (monetary outflow) kept increasing, some countries got edgy and cashed in. After the amount of dollars flooding the world became disproportionate to the amount of gold backing the currency at $35 per ounce, countries exchanged their US dollars for US gold. In 1960, the open market price of gold spiked to $40. The Federal Reserve and Bank of England worked together to defend the price. The 1961 London Gold Pool was a protective measure intended to hold down the price of gold by openly controlling the public market for it. A group of 8 central banks, led by the Federal Reserve, agreed to maintain the dollar convertibility into gold at $35 and to defend it with interventions in the gold market. The US put in half the gold and the other 7 nations the other half. It was a public policy promoting a particular public understanding. If investors thought the gold price would be defended by powerful governments at $35 an ounce, they would realize that there was little point in trying to profit from arbitrage – buying low in one market (US government gold, which only a few had access to) and selling high in another (the London gold market, where the pool operated). Effectively, it was a curb on the demand for gold. But the other nations pulled back-door cheats on the US. By the end of the gold pool, European nations had nonetheless accumulated 12,000 tons of additional gold. US reserves had declined by that amount. In 1967, France pulled out completely and took its gold home. The price could no longer be sustained at the intended level. An attempt to separate the private and government markets for gold was short-lived, as it only created a black market. The Pool collapsed. For a few years, the US continued to try to impose that two-tier pricing system for gold on the world. But it was unworkable, even with full German support. It only limped through a few years until the Nixon Shock. The two-tier system is still parenthetically existent. The Treasury books gold at $42.22/oz. This is an important element in analyzing the secretive activities of the Fed and central banks, to be discussed later.

With the US running simultaneous trade and balance of payments deficits (a rare situation), West Germany pulled out of Bretton Woods and the Deutsche Mark leapt upward. That economy quickly strengthened. Switzerland followed suit and benefitted. The outflow of gold became a torrent, then a flood. It peaked at 400 tons in a single day. In a helter-skelter weekend, the London gold markets closed for a day, London had a bank holiday, and Nixon pre-emptively closed the gold window, surprising the world. Congress backed the move. US dollars were no longer redeemable for gold and still are not.

The government could have simply repriced gold higher to alleviate the pressure for a time. Unfortunately, this would have clearly signaled a policy of increasing spending. It might not have stopped the gold drawdown, but only slowed it for a time. The US credit card would have found a sharp limit afterward. If the dollar had been devalued compared to gold, then every nation would hawkishly watch the ratio of dollars to US gold. Economic prudence would be enforced.

The Zurich gold pool emerged from the ashes, giving wealthy people a place to hold the asset. It continues to this day, with the Swiss franc one of the most valued world currencies. It was 40% gold backed until 1999, the last currency to sever the tie to gold.

Prior to 1971, the US was caught in the Triffin dilemma, pointed out in 1961 by economist Robert Triffin. It holds for any world reserve currency. The nation issuing the currency is stuck with conflicting domestic and international monetary policy goals. It needs to simultaneously maintain a current account trade deficit – putting out more money than taking in – and a current account trade surplus – taking in more than sending out. Obviously, the two are mutually exclusive. The need for the deficit comes from the need to supply excesses of currency to the rest of the world. The need for the surplus is to maintain the strength and confidence in the currency.

On August 15, 1971, the world lost its connection with 'sound money.' Money was no longer connected to a limited supply of a commodity – it became unfixed and has been ever since, floating mainly on an ocean of oil. The dollar was now a fiat currency, mandated for all debts public and private by government decree. In this case, it is not illegal to make or use a competing currency along with the dollar. Local currencies are legal, but the court system will not enforce a contract put outside of dollar terms. If your contract is to be settled in gold or silver, you are on your own collecting. This is the principal method of enforcing use of the dollar.

The actions of Washington were not new. Many nations had gone down the path before. The temptation to inflate the currency to maintain bread, circuses and imperial expansion is as old as government. It has always worked for a time and failed in the end. The length of time it works depends on how forward thinking a government is. Monarchies tend to have a tighter grip on policy because they don't suffer, inter alia, from constant re-election pressures. If a government can think in terms of 10 or 20 year plans, it can hold the system in control for some time. The US government has no such checks. The re-election window is largely a 2 or 4 year cycle. Elected power is widely distributed, so each elected official at federal and state levels wants as much money as they can borrow to spend into the population to essentially buy votes. They want the illusion of prosperity, hence the out of control public debt and monetary inflation.

Owning gold in the US was illegal during this period. In 1975, the law was lifted. This, and monetary expansion, led to the famous gold bull market which saw its price rise from $35 to $850 by 1980.

But before that, a deal was struck in 1973 with Saudi Arabia, from which the so-called Petrodollar emerged. The US agreed to militarily support the unpopular Saudi Royals, making both the country and its government more or less attack proof. No one wanted to go to war with America. US military backup forestalled any possibility of a successful rebellion. In return for bolstering the regime, the royals agreed to sell Saudi oil only in US dollars. They also agreed to reinvest those dollars back into the US banking and Treasury debt complex. Two years later, every OPEC nation accepted only dollars for oil and was reinvesting likewise. The US supplied military support to the other OPEC nations, as well. The skillful power grab by geopolitical architect Henry Kissinger was even nonviolent. After the heated Six-Day War, this was a very enticing promise.

Soon, all oil producers followed suit. Every oil importer needed dollars and every oil exporter received US dollars. All those exporters recycled the dollars right back into the US debt complex. This money was then spent into the general economy (along with a certain amount of new money from the Fed), where it was used to purchase foreign goods, moving those dollars to oil importing countries, to the oil exporters. The cycle of debt has been continually ramped up this way to the present day. In 1973, economics professor, Ibrahim Oweiss, named it the petrodollar standard. While it has never been formalized as a standard it remains an open political secret. Everyone in power knows, but no one talks about it.

According to the enigmatic and verbose analyst, Friend of Another,[1] an even more hidden arrangement was created. The Middle Eastern oil powers like accumulating physical gold in holding for times like now. The West restructured the gold market in order to flatten the price of physical or at least link it to oil, so that if oil prices rose with gold, then OPEC could accumulate equivalent amounts without any real income changes. This restructuring hit a bump with the massive gold price spike – everyone else wanted it in times of gold fever. After slamming the price back down and killing the gold bull (by CFTC rigging and raising interest rates), the West and Middle East went back to business as usual. But the West began operating an increasingly paper gold market – through futures mainly – as a shadow of its equities and bonds markets. The paper market kept the price down for OPEC enabling it to accumulate physical steadily in the open market.

The technique is called seigniorage – the benefit reaped by exploiting difference in money value and cost to produce. It costs the US next to nothing to produce currency – a tenth of a cent per $100 bill. The oil producers, however, took it at full value, surrendering energy resources in exchange. Seigniorage is wildly profitable, especially without a precious metal standard to enforce responsibility.

The US got a second bonus – the agreement meant they were already in place militarily in the largest oil producing countries. When the region gets tense, the system is threatened, and military action is desired, 'getting there firstest with the mostest' is a fait accompli. The military has 600 bases in 130 countries and hundreds of weapons caches already set in place.

It's not hard to see that the system requires perpetual growth. The money supply must constantly expand to service the debt. The use of oil must constantly increase to soak up the money supply and limit inflation. But the two are not organically linked in a supply-demand sense. Imbalances in one do not dampen and correct the other – in fact, quite the reverse can happen. One such scenario, frightful to central bankers, is called deflation.

Deflation is shrinkage, the opposite of growth. A system which incorporates growth is not bad in itself, but a system that *requires* perpetual growth is a catastrophe in the making. It is obviously unbalanced because it cannot handle normal cyclical processes. The mechanics are a bit complicated, but well worth the brainpower invested in understanding them. Deflation, inflation and so forth will be covered in detail in a separate section. They are quite important.

The gold wars are integrally linked to this system of monetary inflation and oil purchases. According to some, gold backing provides a counterweight to monetary excesses. This thesis will be expanded later, but gold clearly provides a brake on monetary creation; even in the absence of an official gold standard, gold still provides a standard. Thus it is an enemy of central banking – it infringes on the ability of central bankers to do as they please. It threatens them with loss of control of the currency when people flee to the safe haven of precious metals. Central bankers will do anything to prevent that – it is the entire basis of their power.

Bretton Woods and the petrodollar standard both created an enormous and consistent demand for US dollars. This offered a tremendous boon for the United States – it is the primary source of all the country's might. The government is allowed to inflate its currency without a rapid decline in its value. No other nation benefits from this privilege. It's always important to ask, in any given situation, *cui bono*: who benefits? The Federal Reserve can print far more money than otherwise possible. This in turn enables the US to fight endless wars. It is also why government, corporate and private debt can go out of control to the extent that it has. For every dollar spent, the US government taxes, borrows from the available supply of dollars, or borrows from the Fed, which creates the money out of nothing. The last borrowing is inflationary, of course. Over the long term, at minimum.

A fascinating feature of this hegemon is its rapid transition from world's largest creditor to world's largest debtor. This was an incredible innovation in monetary geopolitical control systems. Normally, the process of control was exerted through lending money, but the US showed that being the world's debtor gave it even more power. As the saying goes – If I owe the bank a million dollars, it's my problem. If I owe them a hundred million, it's their problem. The Treasury complex is the largest market in the world. Nobody wants it to fail suddenly because all nations have an economic stake in it. But the BRICS are working to slowly undermine it by converting their share of its power into a new system – probably gold based and decentralized. They seem to be allowing the debt-based construct of the West to tear itself apart from its excesses. Meantime, they are gathering strength to fill the void of US dollar power. That power is fading, it seems, and causing enormous volatility in its wake.

The world has been forced to absorb all US debt. As it ceases to do so, the value of the dollar holdings declines and trade to the US declines, as well. Since the US has been the main Chinese customer for so long, China has had a vested interest in supporting the dollar. But that is gradually ending. The Shanghai Cooperation Organization (SCO) is mounting a slow attack on dollar hegemony. It includes Iran (provisionally), China, Russia and other 'rogue' nations. Their trading with each other in non-dollar instruments, including gold,is a threat to the petrodollar system.

Some governments simply borrow US dollars to purchase oil. US banks buy foreign bonds, thus loaning the money, usually through fractional creation of it. This is one of many mechanisms for petrodollar recycling. The IMF also has a facility for helping poor governments with balance of payment problems to purchase oil.

In recent years, oil producers have questioned the strength of the dollar. The increases in monetary creation are seriously out of step with the increases in oil demand, and cannot be justified by that. Global oil consumption increased by 30% since 1988. MZM means money of zero maturity, i.e. liquidity. That money supply has increased 1000% in the same time frame. There are a lot more FRNs being created than the petrodollar standard can accommodate. The world is choking on US dollars. Figure 12 shows a curve with an upturn in money creation compared to a linear increase in oil consumption. Dollars

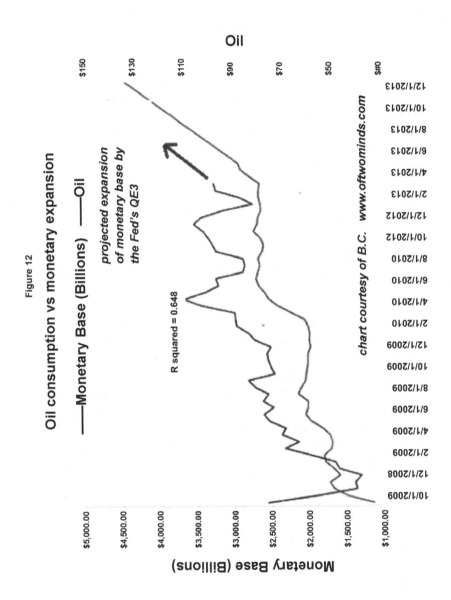

Figure 12

Oil consumption vs monetary expansion

——Monetary Base (Billions)    ——Oil

outpace oil. Moreover, the money supply steepened dramatically since the 2008 crisis while oil consumption has actually declined. The petrodollar system has lost its balance – the oil supply may be hitting its peak, unable to increase daily production. Meanwhile, the money supply is hitting its debt limit, and forced to accelerate its increase. This mismatch will become worse and worse, and lead to extreme consequences as the financial, economic, monetary and production systems of the world struggle to cope. (See Figure 12 adjacent.)

Until now, the US could issue lower interest bonds and run higher deficits than other countries. However, the value of the currency is declining too fast. OPEC investments are losing value. More and more questions are arising about the intrinsic value of a currency that has no brakes on expansion with an out of control government. Most of the countries have people angry about the loss of their national resources and sovereignty to hegemonic empire.

While this is not offered as proof of a US political deception, it is worthy of investigation. Is the demand to maintain the petrodollar standard the primary driver of US geo-political activity? Are the military actions and wars conducted under a false flag of fighting terrorism and concern over rogue nations in actuality an effort to maintain the petrodollar standard? JPMorgan now operates the Iraq central bank, appointed by the occupying forces. Strangely, they use Iraqi oil as collateral for letters of credit.[2]

The system creates enormous wealth disparities and allows a few elites to plunder the national resources for their own benefit. On the OPEC side, the Saudi Royals are the worst offenders, claiming the titanic underground wealth as their own personal property. The price is growing civil unrest. This has been managed for decades, on the US end, by a number of covert actions and propaganda tools. But these have limits, so the next level of management is the age-old answer of ultimate control: war.

'We must guard against the acquisition of unwarranted influence by the military industrial complex,' President Dwight Eisenhower said, just before leaving office. He was ignored. The Carter doctrine claims that the US will, with full right, engage in military activity to protect access to oil. An unbreakable oil supply is officially a matter of the highest national security – a policy definitively in effect today. Jimmy Carter created the Rapid Deployment Task Force to address it, the precursor of Centcom, a military arm responsible for providing stable US control over Middle East oil – not that it needs access to the oil for its domestic needs, but that it must control and protect the petrodollar standard: that oil, globally, must be purchased in dollars. This is not a hidden doctrine. It is not a secret. It is openly acknowledged, but not brought up by leaders or the media, which might anchor it in the public mind. The Bush administration publicly acknowledged after invading Iraq that Hussein had nothing to do with 911 and had no weapons of mass destruction. A number of newspapers carried articles about the fake evidence (yellow cake uranium and other deceptions). The charges against Hussein had been fabricated as an excuse to invade. This is no longer in contention -it's an unpleasant truth that has just been forgotten.

Iraq boasts the third largest oil reserves in the world. On September 24, 2000, with his country having been under US/UK-initiated, UN-imposed sanctions for a decade, Saddam Hussein announced that Iraq would begin accepting Euros for oil.[3] He did not say that sales of oil to the US would be curtailed – in fact there were none at the time, due to US sanctions. Sales of Iraqi oil to the US could easily have been managed as part of a process of normative trade. But the petrodollar system is not about oil, per se. It is about a system of sustaining the worldwide need for a paper currency by linking it to a true global necessity – oil.

In a 2006 press conference, Bush was asked what Hussein had to do with 911. "Nothing,' he replied, "and nobody's ever suggested that Hussein ordered the attack."[4] After the denials, there were some admissions. Former commander of US Centcom Gen. John Abizaid said, "of course the Iraq War is about oil – we can't deny that."[5] Russia, China and France didn't back the invasion, but any moral reasons they might have had were supplemented by other reasons: they had a vested interest. Agreements were already on the table for billions of Euros. With Hussein gone, the agreements were null and void.[6]

After US forces took Baghdad, they first guarded the oil fields and oil ministry. Looters were allowed to ransack the Baghdad Museum which housed ancient treasures from a long-lost world formerly on that land, widely referred to as the cradle of civilization. Within weeks, Iraqi oil was being sold only in US dollars again. A few years later, the oil fields were officially parceled out to Western corporations.

In 2007, similarly sanctioned, Iran requested all oil be paid in non-US currencies. The Iranian oil bourse opened in February, 2008 and began selling oil in gold, Euros and other currencies. The drums of war against Iran beat louder every day. The WMDs and connection to 911 were shown to be false about Hussein. Perhaps we should be skeptical of current claims about Iran. Many analysts do not find the accusations of Iranian nuclear weapons development credible. Iran is much stronger than Iraq, with powerful allies. A war on Iran could pull the trigger on WWIII. Caution is an excellent idea. If the issue was about domestic supply for the US, as the government insists, the oil could have simply been purchased – there was no restriction from the Iranian side. The claim of supply shortages is deceptive – it's about maintaining the petrodollar standard.

Any notion that a Democrat administration represents peace must be questioned by the $900 billion military budget for 2012, far higher than Bush's.

Military expenses are 59% of the discretionary budget. All this spending is not for defending US sovereign territory. The last attack on the US was Pearl Harbor. No nation is going to attack the US directly. The military spending is for offensive purposes. It is to pursue hegemonic control and to protect the Petrodollar. The 'kinetic military action' in Libya, too, was an act of war against a sovereign nation that had never attacked the US. Similar to Iraq and Iran, once under US threat, the Libyan government sought to pursue every avenue towards peace short of abject capitulation, and similarly following rejection of such overtures, Qaddafi pushed for a currency to trade oil – the gold-backed dinar. It never happened.

Saddam Hussein began taking Euros for oil shortly before his demise. Iran first began taking Euros for oil in 2005. Venezuela now accepts foreign payments or the dollar. More and more importers, like North Korea, want to quit using US dollars to purchase oil. Perhaps this portends an ever-growing list of so-called "rogue states"?

According to this analysis, the gigantic US military expenditure (more than all other nations combined) is a necessity. The military is not serving as the world's policeman or defending the US from its enemies. It is guarding the world reserve status of the currency by forcing the payment of oil in US dollars. It is a very big job, done by coercion, intimidation, largesse, and failing that, by war

The US debt machine and standard of living can only be maintained under the petrodollar standard. If any countries manage to back out of it successfully, then others will follow suit. This entrapment generates tremendous resentment toward US hegemony throughout the world. Countries want to get out from under the imperial thumb. Saudi Arabia began talks with China for a protectorate of the Persian Gulf in 2006,[7] for example. If most countries really divest from the reigning oil payment system, there will be no worldwide need for dollars. Only a few will invest in US debt instruments. All that money will come flowing right back to the US. The many creditors may panic and dump all their imperial paper at once.

The government then has two choices: have the Federal Reserve monetize the debt (which it's already doing) or default. No government using its own fiat currency for debt has ever defaulted. They always try to print their way out. Some of the moneys coming in will recycle through the government debt complex, but most will go to buy US assets and resources. When countries no longer need to hold dollars, they will buy up pieces of the US (and anywhere else in the world they can). They will want out of those massive stockpiles of depreciating money.

Freeways will turn into Chinacorp toll roads, foreign banks will appear, private schools will be foreign owned, as will airlines, land, and almost everything else. It's already happening. The People's Bank of China is opening four branches here, with the Fed's blessing. It's a gradual insertion, with more to follow. They will use their dollar holdings and be allowed to multiply them through the US fractional reserve system. A somewhat antagonistic foreign creditor will be able to create US currency in the fractional reserve system.

The enormous influx of dollars will combine with a second inflow – new currency issued by the Fed. With no one buying government debt using existing dollars, the Fed will be forced to print massively, purchasing government debt itself, monetizing it. Enormous inflation will follow. When people want to protect themselves from serious inflation, they turn dollars into assets. But this only exacerbates the pace of inflation. Dollars go down because lots of wealth is transferring away, increasing the velocity of money and decreasing its desirability. The value of assets rises, because so many want to transfer their wealth into them and out of the currency.

Interest rates should rise to extreme levels unless the Fed can hold them down. Companies relying on short-term debt to finance long-term operations will be in deep distress. The price of oil will go sky-high. Oil and commodity dependent businesses will fail. Theatrical political divisions between left and right will become extreme with each side blaming the other. Debt encumbered assets will dramatically lose real value, although nominal prices may rise due to extreme inflation. People with a floating interest rate will be forced to default. The derivatives complex will go haywire, spiraling the world's largest banks into open insolvency. The US currency might even hyperinflate and face extinction.

The US (with British, Canadian and a few other) leaders are therefore highly invested in maintaining the petrodollar standard. A number of other countries – the BRICS, mainly – are looking to escape or subvert it. Some countries are waiting on the sidelines and hedging to see how it plays out – Germany is probably the most important. The battle is on.

The most desirable asset during such dangerous times for the wealthy is gold; for poor people, silver; and for the middle class, a balance. One government/central bank strategy is to keep the allure of gold down. The gold market must be seen as highly volatile. So reminiscent of campaigns against the leadership of the targeted "rogue states," the campaign of slander begins: "It's very easy to invest at the wrong times, it doesn't behave as it should, and if you buy at the wrong time, you'll lose your shirt. It's not worth the risk. It's a 'barbarous relic.'" That's the message. The establishment mouthpieces are sowing propaganda. "Gold just sits there and does nothing," Warren Buffet said.[8] His partner, Charlie Munger, strangely said "Gold is something pre-holocaust Jews sew into their clothes. It's not for civilized people."[9] They try to push the big money – pension and hedge funds – into Treasuries, the safe investment of the last 40 years.

But like it or not, gold is the historical sound alternative to a government mandated currency. Like the US dollar, it is universally recognized as money.

Unlike the dollar, it has been so for 5000 years. Gold is the enemy of fiat currency, and even though the dollar was born as gold-backed currency, it has turned on its parent and seeks to destroy it. But it's impossible to destroy the idea of gold as money. Most people in the world refuse to believe it's not. Only a select population does. Most are in the US. They have a vested interest in believing that because the petrodollar standard has been so beneficial. However, that is the set of people needing to understand it most, because the failure of the petrodollar will have the greatest negative impact on the US, for obvious reasons. Failing to realize the refuge of gold will cause many people's savings to be wiped out.

China, Russia, India, Iran, Brazil, and South Africa, called the BRICS, are systematically delinking oil from the dollar. These countries have instituted trades in their respective currencies for other goods in addition to gold. [Russia and China, in 2012, announced a major deal to trade oil in Yuan – the Chinese currency]. More and more, these nations are accumulating gold and using it as money.

The BRICS trade movement, away from US dollar hegemony, is creating an enormous strain on the Western government financing and the entire Western debt and banking system. There are other strains: out of control sovereign debt, the need to continually increase debt to counter deflation, real estate collapse, derivative issues, and endless and pervasive corruption. All these have contributed to a huge loss of trust, which are fundamental for a fiat economy, which runs on trust in the currency and on counterparty good faith.

The Machiavellian genius of the petrodollar standard – that nations have no choice, they must obtain dollars to get oil – has had a multitude of ramifications. It's why Asia has developed an export-led strategy tied directly to the US. It's also why the US is drowning in cheap foreign goods. Every country needs oil, requires dollars to get it, and must export – whatever – to the US to get those digital tokens. The US gets three massive advantages right out of the gate. Because everybody must have dollars, they are worth more than any other currency and continue to be the de facto world reserve currency. Second, nations that reap a lot of dollars for their oil become a pre-arranged, automatic market for US debt. Third, the US can buy all the oil it wants for nothing, just by turning on the printing press. For forty years, that incredible inflation of dollars has caused enormous price rises, and US wage rises, sending American manufacturing to lower wage countries. It led to the creation of the warfare/welfare state, then became necessary to enable it to continue to function.

That Niagara Falls of dollars churned out by the fractional reserve multiplier may get soaked up overseas, but all things come to an end. The system is breaking down. There are a lot of dollars in some hands, especially in the East and Middle East, and there's a lot of debt around other necks, especially Western financial organizations, governments, and citizens. A big enough debt yokes creditor to debtor, because if debtors are unable to pay, then creditors are unable to collect on their worthless assets.They are both in the same boat. They are both bankrupt – as is evidently the case with southern European banks and their failing sovereign debt assets. Most of that money has left the US. Even as it's recycled through debt mechanisms, the debt grows without the available currency growing. This is the concern over debt deflation. And that's the razor knife right now we are walking on – deflation on one side and inflation on the other. We'll get to deflation later.

While any economic system has an element of artificiality to it, this system is artificial on a much grander scale. Enormous debt imbalances, trade imbalances, and cash flow imbalances all stem from this system. The numbers are in the multi-trillions. Add derivatives and it exceeds the global economy by orders of magnitude. The petrodollar system *is* the world economy, the backbone of the globalized trading system. When the system comes to an end, and it will, the unwinding of it will cause international havoc. Gold stands in the background.

While other currencies will be exchangeable for oil, no currency will become the single choice. No country wants to own the reserve currency, because the rapid increase in demand would drive up their export prices and their industry would collapse. The slow decline of US manufacturing illustrates the problem. Being the holder of the global reserve currency drives up the cost of living, wages and asset prices in the issuing country. For producers, this means they cannot compete using US labor. If a company can pay someone $5 a day, like Apple does, then US-based companies are sunk. That's why US manufacturing has been gutted. It's why the US economy has shifted to become a FIRE (finance, insurance and real estate) economy. Any country with a sharply rising currency value loses its export industry. A nation like China is export dependent just to keep its populace employed and happy. Germany will be in a similar situation if it exits the Euro.

A group of strong currencies is likely to emerge to supplant the dollar over time. Certain countries want to participate and develop a strong world reserve currency without being the sole issuer of that currency. That's why so many of these countries are holding more and more gold. Those with political awareness realize that the story of Middle East tensions is being utilized in a crafty game of chess.

## Endnotes

1    Friend of Another, "The Inside Story on the Gold-for-Oil Deal that could Rock the World's Financial Center", usagold.com, Oct.-Nov. 1997.

2      Jim. Willie, Hat Trick Letter, April, 2006.
3      William Clark, *Petrodollar Warfare,*, May, 2005, p. 28..
4      White House press conference, August, 2006.
5      "Courting Disaster – fight for oil, water and a healthy planet", Oct. 2007. Stanford Univ.
6      Samer Shehata, "Oil after Saddam: All bets are in", Center for Cont. Arab Studies, 2002
7      John Defterios, "Middle East and China forge ties over oil", CNN, November 15, 2012.
8      Berkshire Hathaway Annual Report, 2011.
9      "Berkshire's Charlie Munger Speaks" CNBC interview with Becky Quick, May 12, 2012.

4

# SHADOW BANKING, QE AND ZIRP

*Financiers ... played a central role in creating the crisis*
—S. Johnson, IMF Chief Economist

Lehman brothers was engaged in a full-scale fraud. They rotated debts to London to get them off-books in time for annual shareholder reports. Then they moved them back home afterwards. The financial quarterlies were intentionally falsified with full CEO knowledge and repeated warnings to him. It's not isolated, according to Academy Award documentarian, Charles Ferguson, a muckraker on the finance industry. Rico offenses, bribery, perjury, accounting and equities fraud, insider trading, prostitution, drugs, and drug laundering are primary components of the system.[1]

Twenty-five percent of Wall Street executives believe that fraud is necessary for success in the financial arena.[2] That means that at least 1 in 4 financial service players (and probably the ones doing the biggest volume) are committing fraud. Since sharks don't always like to show their teeth, the number is probably far higher. It helps explain what might be the largest-scale financial fraud ever. The interest rate swap market – the largest nominal market in the world, by an order of magnitude – is based on the LIBOR. Under the cloud of this scandal, both the Chairman and the CEO of banking conglomerate Barclays resigned on July 3-4, 2012. Executive Jerry del Missier, prominently implicated in the operation, was let go with a bonus of £8.75 million. The company was exposed for manipulating the LIBOR – the London Inter-Bank Offered Rate.

The average rate of inter-bank lending sets the mortgage rate. By manipulating it upward artificially, Barclays was able to overcharge interest on millions of home mortgages. By manipulating it downward, it scalped municipalities. This is complicated. Municipalities were locked into interest rate swap deals by the banks: if interest rates went up, then they could swap out of their payments to avoid paying more. If interest rates went down, the cities' swap arrangements lost their value, but municipalities had to keep paying on them anyway. Interest rates indeed went down, artificially manipulated by the central banks for their own reasons. However, Barclays (and all other mega-banks) were told rates would decline beforehand and capitalized on it with secret knowledge. Commercial bankers sit on central banking boards and help to set policy. The banks' payments declined to nothing. So banks are collecting 5% average on muni bonds while paying out .1% average on the swaps. They conned the naive muni managers.

The defense? "Everybody's doing it, or at least or at least the top execs at big banks are." Barclays was just the first one caught. This 'defense' turned out to be true – what one does, most do. And plenty of evidence is there. Multiple governments are conducting inquiries on all the major banks. Emails were traced back to the Bank of England which sanctioned the behavior. London is known for being even softer on white collar crime than the US. Policies are only changing because the public is so angry.

The banks have been charged with collusion by many governments. Presently, they are turning evidence against each other and ceasing communications on legal advice. The sharks are trying to kill each other for regional immunity. Litigants are now in the thousands and include small banks, state and local governments. The problem for the banks is very, very big. European politicians are running successful campaigns as bank enemies.

*The Economist*, known for its bank-friendly policy, reported that the rigging went back to the late 1980s.[3] It's global, too, of course. Cities all over are choking. The swaps were supposed to be risk hedges, they were promoted to municipalities as a safety net, but instead they toxified muni assets everywhere. The Philadelphia school system coughed up $331 million, for example, just to get out of its odious contracts. The problem is massive – 50% of all California local governance bodies are struggling as a result. "These financially unsophisticated local officials were being exploited by the big banks," Nobel Prize economist, Joseph Stiglitz, said. The cities cannot exit from the deals without huge penalties. The financing is made deliberately inscrutable to baffle the naïve. Is this capitalism? Hundreds of municipalities, counties, provinces, and states have been pushed into bankruptcy by these instruments. They are huge, too. For a comparison: the CDS problem involved about $50 trillion. IR swaps involve $350 trillion – seven times the size.

This illustrates where the true power lies. Several trillion dollars were mobilized in weeks to prop up the big banks in 2008. It got media airplay 24/7. The propaganda was off-the-charts – the too big to fails would bring down the economy if they crashed. Obama pledged to eliminate the too-big-to-fail danger. Now, the banks are bigger than ever, with larger and more interconnected derivative positions. The problem is far worse than when he took office.

Now whole cities are going bust and the media is silent. No bailout is forthcoming, even though it was the banks themselves who engineered both sets of problems by the same means. They hung themselves and the government cut the rope with a taxpayer funded knife. They hung the local citizens and the government collaborated, then ignored it.[4]

The Libor is the most important interest rate index in the world. Such things may sound boring, but they engage massive financial markets. A tiny change in the index can cause billions in profits or losses. The Fed funds rate rides on the LIBOR, so manipulating it allows the Fed to maintain its ultra-low interest rates. It also keeps the Interest Rate Swap machinery from breaking down.

It carries a deeper twist, as well. Since 2008, the LIBOR has steadily declined. This, Paul Craig Roberts argues, is deliberate. As rates decline, older assets holding higher rates increase in value. By manipulating the rates downward, the banks can overvalue these older assets to appear more solvent. All asset-based derivatives, the core of bank balance sheets, would be revalued higher. The Fed and the BOE both knew and supported the fixing as part of the game to keep the too big to fails from going under.[5]

In 2007, Paul McCulley and Bill Gross, managers at the enormous bond trader, Pimco, warned that there might be some concerns over "the whole alphabet soup of levered up non-bank investment conduits, vehicles, and structures." They coined the ominous term shadow banking system (SBS) to describe it. "We are witnessing the breakdown of our modern-day banking system.,"[6] Gross announced. This shadow banking system is entrenched and it's powerful – Romney and Obama each received $300 million from the financial lobby. The shadow banking system bought both candidates.

Shadow banking arose largely from the repeal of the Glass-Steagall act. At a trim 37 pages, Glass-Steagall was a masterpiece of simplicity by today's 1000-page legislative standards. Enacted in 1933, it established the FDIC and more importantly, separated commercial and investment banking. This created a number of beneficial effects, which were not realized until its repeal and the dark consequences thereof. The 1999 Gramm-Leach-Bliley Act, repealing Glass-Steagall's critical sections, allows for commercial banks to speculate and have that insured. In other words, if banks screw up, they can pay for it from the public till of the FDIC. That's because of a second ill consequence – banks can use depositors' money to gamble in equities markets – or any markets. That 'any markets' phrase has led to the creation of the vast shadow banking complex and the enormous derivatives problems.

Zerohedge posted a pretty interesting definition. "Shadow banking is the near-infinite fungibility of electronic credit-money equivalents within the infinitely interconnected modern financial system." It's the ability to collateralize any asset into an obligation for any financial derivative with any major party and to string these pieces of debt into a vastly larger tangle.

The critical factor of derivatives is the underlying basis for them. A derivative is a value 'derived' from an underlying asset. According to the IMF, $600 billion in assets is backing up $600 trillion in derivatives. [7] This is leverage of 1000 to 1 – an unavoidable catastrophe. If the value drops by 0.1%, the global derivatives portfolio is broke. If it drops by 1%, the total is $6 trillion in the red. That's why derivatives are the financial black hole of the planet.

Bankers surrendered banks' utility function in a race to cash in on their highly profitable new investment function. So they grew enormously in asset allocation, size and risk. The repeal of the Glass-Steagall Act allowed banks to become extremely interconnected and 'too-big-to-fail.' They were allowed to become systemically critical to the global system, while at the same time taking on fantastic risk. Moral hazard became acute and worsens by the day. There is no provision for loss on these bets – indeed, nor can there be – only for gain. Insofar as individual trading desks reap small percentage fees on numerous, huge transactions – derivative bets, they have a vested interest in making these bets to increase their paycheck. This ties the banks up in a spiderweb of interlocking agreements for trillions of dollars. The CEOs encourage the behavior, or at least allow it, because they know the government will backstop them because they are systemically important. Risk is encouraged, even celebrated, because the taxpayer foots the bill while the banks get the profits. Mussolini called fascism a partnership between corporations and government. The reader can decide if the definition fits here.

The SBS consists of hedge funds, special investment vehicles, investment banks, pension funds and other non-bank financial institutions. It's called shadow because it is unregulated, since it does not perform deposit banking. The system holds about $60 trillion in assets. Because they can leverage so high and cannot use FDIC, these institutions are risky in contractions or downturns. They pose systemic risks because of the many credit based interconnections to the conventional banking system.

In finance, a 'weak sister' is an element that undermines the entire system. The major banks and even governments, have all become weak sisters. They suck in capital at an astounding rate, far higher than the productive economy can produce real capital. The twin vortexes of the sucking are the shadow banking system and the Treasury complex.

Aside from the loss of faith in banks, the point for this book is the loss of trust in the system as a whole. Many view the system as rigged – a casino where the average player cannot win. Casinos are fine, but Main Street should not be forced to gamble – as in fact it is, both in terms of the investment opportunities for its pensions and savings, as well as the possibility of SBS-induced systemic collapse. The global economy should be a place for honest business and trade, not a giant craps table where your home can be taken. Analyst George Washington (pseudonym) compiled a list of big bank fraud that has come out since 2008, but been ongoing for decades.[8]

- Mortgage and foreclosure fraud.
- Multiple collateralizing and sales of mortgages to buyers.
- Robbing veterans through foreclosure law abuses.
- Using mafia rigging tactics in municipal affairs.[9]
- Fraudulent accounting.
- Manipulating and coercing ratings agencies for false ratings.
- Selling short, then crashing bad investments to their own clients.
- Frontrunning markets.
- Scalping managed pension funds for many years.
- Helping Enron and others to manipulate energy markets.[10]
- Drug money laundering.[11,12]

The banks are no longer what they were meant to be: a public service utility. Bank of America reaps below 10% of its assets from traditional banking. Other banks are similar. They have become engines of speculation. Big bank lending has declined by 3.4% since the bailouts. Small banks have taken up the slack.[13] Most bank profits come directly from the bailouts – 77% for JPMorgan.[14] Economist Michael Hudson calls it warfare on society by the banks. By an ongoing process of transferring their bad debts to the public balance sheet and getting bailouts, they have transferred the mass of society's wealth to the top shareholders.[15] Goldman Sachs made $2.3 billion in profits in 2008 and received $10 billion in bailout money. It paid $4.2 billion in bonuses – giving away almost double its profits by using taxpayer bailout money. Most banks have similar situations. Some analysts call it a financial takeover.

In April, 2009 the Financial Accounting Standards Board fed honesty to the sharks. They suspended normal accounting rules – but only for the too big to fail banks. These were allowed to set their assets at whatever value they chose. If the market price was too low to maintain the appearance of solvency, the banks could (and did) claim the sinking assets were still worth the original price. These methods are used to disguise massive quarterly losses as the toxic paper rots. The favored accounting gimmick – a 'trading' portfolio is marked to market. An 'investment' portfolio (supposedly held until maturity) is not marked to market. This hides the balance sheet's true position.

Credit markets are frozen. Britain's banks have a £40 billion undeclared hole on their balances. Royal Bank of Scotland, with £18 billion, is the dirty stepson, as usual. None of the banks will lend into the economy because of this. It's the same everywhere – banks have no capital and show enormous losses on their books. They cannot lend – their reserve requirements are hopeless. If they came out with authentic accounting, almost all the largest banks in the world would be insolvent.

John Cruz was a VP and relationship manager for HSBC. He became a whistleblower in 2012, presenting a thousand pages of documents proving illicit activity by HSBC. Visiting many clients as part of his job to sell them additional banking services, he discovered they were not what they seemed. One 'shipping company' deposited millions of dollars through paypal. They had no evidence of any shipping activity at their place of business. He had hundreds of examples. Many businesses were just a house with a desk and phone – no evidence of business activity. The transactions were hidden – the money came from an unknown source and left for an unknown source. One bank manager learned from Cruz that 75% of the branch's investigated accounts were fraudulent.

The businesses used identity theft to get social security numbers. These were used to set up shell businesses for several hundred billion dollars in money laundering. A single social security number was used for 5000 accounts with $800 million transferred through them. The actual holder of the social security number had no idea this identity theft was going on. "The whole system," Cruz said, "is designed to be a culture of fraud to make it look like it's a legalized system. But it's not. HSBC is a criminal organization." Cruz was fired for "poor job performance" when he refused to halt the investigation.[16] The bank has been under criminal investigation by a Senate committee for several years now regarding the activity.[17] They made a public apology in front of the Senate on July 17, 2012 and admitted to laundering $881 million six months later. No one was prosecuted, no activities were stopped. They are *still* doing it.

Other mega-banks are involved, of course. The Council of Europe made a presentation on July 4, 2012, naming JPMorgan as the conduit for money laundering through the Vatican. £20 million was frozen by Rome authorities during the investigation. The bank then questioned the Vatican on the source of the funds, but apparently received no reply and stopped asking. The transfers were egregious violations of anti-money laundering regulations.[18]

The mortgage fraud deserves special details for its stunning breadth. Mortgages gradually increased from 20% to 60% of US GDP. Excepting derivatives, they are the biggest game in town. The increase was due to deliberate bubbling of the sector. Loans were given to buyers with no income or assets, and requiring no down payments. Appraisals were palm-greased to raise value, or no appraisals happened. Interest rates were manipulated by LIBOR machinations. A fistful of AAA paper was bundled with millions of F- mortgages into toxic securities. They were sold with ratings rigged by payoffs to ratings agencies. The MERS (Mortgage Electronic Registration

System) database was put together to facilitate the con game, focusing on the mountain of bonds linked to the investors – it tried to legitimize the mess. The database was found to be fraudulent in court and thrown out. MERS property titles are legally invalid. Then the robo-signing scandal erupted. Banks were fraudulently foreclosing on millions of homes without any due process. People without mortgages – full ownership of their homes – were evicted by sheriffs. A number of soldiers serving overseas, with legally suspended payments, had their families evicted under false pretenses. The settlement for trillions in mortgage fraud was a paltry $20 billion accompanied by a banker's reward of strict limits on future lawsuits, i.e. relative impunity for carrying on as usual. The TARP program was billed as needed to keep the credit and economy flowing. Instead, the money went to preferred stock and record-setting executive bonuses to the executors and planners of the crisis. None of it went to lending.

William Black was a prominent prosecutor in the DOJ during the S&L crisis in the 90s. His team made over 10,000 referrals for prosecution resulting in 1000 convictions. This time, he says, the scale is vastly larger, but there are zero referrals for criminal investigation.[19] Stats show that about one-third of loans in 2006 were liar loans, hence fraudulent. The Mortgage Bankers Association report shows definite knowledge of the activity by bank executives. Execs fully empowered the activity, helping to put the lie in the loans. The game was 'bankruptcy for profit.' Banks elevated appraisals to get bigger loans and bigger commissions. They grew the book as rapidly as possible, but did not underwrite the loans. They sold them. They made terrible loans at premium yields and held a tiny amount of capital for loan loss reserves. This system booked huge short-term paper profits with obscene return percentages over capital base. Executive pay rose astronomically. But the profits were not real – they were accounting gimmicked because the loans, as was foreknown, would never be paid off. The executives walked away filthy rich and the banks imploded. Then the taxpayer took the hit. The criminals won big-time. The FBI investigated this starting in 2004 and issued repeated warnings about the dangers. The best way to be ignored is to be right, with bad news that implicates the powerful.

This happened with Eileen Foster. As head of internal investigations at Countrywide, she blew a big whistle. Worse than being ignored, she was hounded out of her job and thoroughly discredited. The labor department exonerated her, finally, with their conclusion: Countrywide had "multiple incidents of egregious fraud spread throughout the entire region, including loan document forgery and alteration, manipulation of borrower's assets and income, manipulation of the company's automated underwriting system, the destruction of valid client documents, and evidence that blank templates of bank statements from several different financial institutions were emailed back and forth among loan officers in various branches for use in forging proof of borrower income and assets."[20]

With all the banks doing it, they created an enormous bubble. When the bubble collapsed, the entire economy sank into recession. Black calls it the 'greatest financial crime in history.' The FBI was hamstrung. First, the regulators didn't refer anyone for prosecution. Worse, the investigative force for white-collar crime shrank from over 1000 agents to 120 under Bush. Since it required 100 agents for Enron alone, the task is hopeless. They are pathetically understaffed to investigate a fraud of this magnitude. Why are resources not diverted to this important issue? Is there a willful blockage of any and all criminal investigation into the crisis? If so, what does that say about the future of the financial system, let alone American democracy? Since Inspector General Mukasey refused the FBI request to create a national task force on mortgage fraud, no large-scale investigation has ever occurred. The FHA has 15,000 records, with paper trail, of massive serial fraud by the largest financial institutions in the country and not one criminal indictment or systematic investigation against a major bank has occurred for mortgage fraud.[21]

If an insurance company backstopped serial gamblers when they ran out of money, the gamblers would vastly increase the risk of their bets, looking for higher returns. This is exactly what the government has done for the financial industry. Looking for bigger returns, banks are drawn to higher risk. Thus, the methods to prevent a crisis actually make worse crises inevitable and more frequent.

The five largest US banks hold about $8.5 trillion, equal to 56% of the US economy. The big five banks are consolidating into titanic fortresses. They have gone from 17% of all bank assets to more than half. Small banks went bust, and medium size were absorbed into the giants during the crisis. How did they manage to grow so much with all the stresses from 2008? Bailouts, of course. From a Government Accountability Office report, here's the tally:

| Citigroup | $2.513 trillion |
| Morgan Stanley | $2.041 trillion |
| Bank of America | $1.344 trillion |
| Goldman Sachs | $814 billion |
| JPMorgan Chase | $391 billion |

Add to this list a number of foreign banks, salvaged as 'systemically important.' In total, the Fed put out a freakish $16 trillion – more than the national debt – in a few months.[22] A year later, they put out another $7 trillion.

When the AP contacted 21 banks about the use of the taxpayer funded TARP bailouts, all refused to answer any questions. To add insult, the Fed paid the same banks $600 million to administer the disbursal. All this was done in secret; they fought against disclosure.

From December 2010 to the following June, Morgan Stanley beefed up its derivatives sheet by $8 trillion dollars, mostly in IRSwaps. This was a 30% increase in high-risk instruments inside of 6 months – far beyond insane. It is very dangerous and extremely high-risk positioning. MS has steadily moved these derivatives from its holding company to its insured banking unit, making the enormous derivatives pool theoretically backed by the FDIC in the insured unit. A big reason for the transfer is the credit rating – the holding company features an anemic Baa versus Triple-A for the banking unit. Anyone on the other side of the bet wants real money backing it. Of course, the real money is depositors' money.

It's a bit odd that MS was on the auction block during the 2008 crisis, but could not find a buyer. Now, they are leveraged up to many times their net worth in derivatives. The global economic system lacks sufficient credit lines for the company to create this positional increase, even if all means were focused on the task. With a failing balance sheet, what entity would take the other side of these trades? What entity would fund MS to take these positions, given it would be bad business to do either?

Enter the Plunge Protection Team, formally known as the Exchange Stabilization Fund. The ESF is part of the Treasury, officially. But it publishes no financial statements, even though it has a large funding. Among its operations, in 2008 the fund put $50 billion to shore up money market funds. Most of its activities are secret. Congress has no oversight. According to Rob Kirby, the ESF helped Morgan Stanley with an "undeclared stealth bailout / recapitalization of Morgan Stanley on the public teat in conjunction with arbitrarily controlling the long end of the interest rate curve."[23] MS was the front-man to make Treasury Bonds look good by a complicated scheme involving interest rate swaps – covered later.

On May 5, 2006, President Bush amended the 1934 Securities Act. "With respect to the matters concerning the national security of the United States, the President or the head of an Executive Branch agency may exempt companies from certain critical legal obligations, [including accurate] books, records and accounts [and] a system of internal accounting controls sufficient [for] generally accepted accounting principles." The President can selectively excuse companies from honest accounting for national security reasons. If there is any economic threat to national security, it is the ballooning debt. The ESF, Kirby says, has its fingerprints on the Treasury trade. As a counterparty, they can purchase interest rate swaps on the ten-year bond. The seller of the swaps must buy the bonds in the open market to hedge the position. Enough of these low-cost swaps, and the market is pushed lower by the artificial buying pressure. Only the Treasury or Federal Reserve can be the counterparty. No other entity has the ability and the wish to do this through these massive portfolios.

Large portfolios strive to maintain a delta-neutral position. Delta is the symbol for change. In derivatives it represents the rate of change in value of the position versus change in value of the underlying asset. Example: you own a mortgage with 20% equity. If house prices fall by 20%, your entire equity is wiped out, even though the house value drops only 20%. Commercial traders establish off-setting positions to hedge the risk. When the asset moves in price, a raft of puts or shorts offsets a raft of longs or calls. By using leverage, the positions can be profitable. However, when the positions get too large, delta-neutral is far more difficult to maintain.

The JPMorgan loss in June, 2012 is an example. Iksil (the London Whale) created outsized positions in a moderate-sized market. When the market moved against the position, it was already too big to manage without pushing prices around. The fix made the situation worse because the fix forced prices in the wrong direction. Morgan was stuck. It went public and the sharks came out. They waited for the giant to move and ate up the other side of the trade, deepening Morgan losses. And that's a typical state of play for most of the derivative positions. They have to hold them frozen, but they are so large, that exponential amounts of capital are required just to sustain the delta-neutrality. The situation spiraled out of control and JPMorgan lied about the losses being $2 billion. Piling multiple accusations of deception and economically dangerous practices on top, a Senate hearing found the losses were greater than $10 billion.

Too many banks are betting against each other. They also rely on each other as counter-party to these trades. The idea that derivatives can safely unwind is called 'netting out.' If A owes B $1, B owes C $1, and C owes A $1, then the net is zero. This is a fantasy, however, because derivatives cannot be simplified in this way. One firm will eventually fail as the tower climbs to heaven and eventually falls. Morgan Stanley, Deutschebank or JPMorgan will lose control of their book. As an example, the ratio of Deutschebank's derivative exposure (€55 trillion) to Germany's GDP ($2.7 trillion) is 20 to 1. When a single bank has nominal obligations 20 times its country's GDP, the situation is getting impossibly out of balance.

Volatility is increasing and it is very damaging to delta-neutral trades. The Fed's ability to monetize (paper over) these problems has failed. If a large holder of T-Bonds dumps on the market, the yields go up quickly. This causes outsized losses to the derivatives portfolios. More hits will come. This is a currency war, as well as an East-West bank war.

The shadow institutions borrowed short term money from the money market and other highly liquid sources, then invested in long-term, illiquid assets such as mortgage backed securities and collateralized debt obligations. So, when the piper called, they had to pay back the short term moneys immediately. The only way ahead was to sell off the long-term, now toxic assets. But without buyers, the market collapsed. Because they were leveraged so high, the downturn wiped them out. At a not abnormal 35 to 1 leverage, a 3% loss in the value of assets destroys all equity. But the losses were much higher, leaving the companies deep in the hole with no shovel. So, the government stepped in. The canard that no one could have predicted the problems is a patent lie. Many did predict them. Warren Buffet called derivatives a 'weapons of mass destruction.' In fact, Long Term Capital Management and Enron both caused massive market failures through this type of activity.

The biggest financial transaction company in the world is virtually unknown. DTCC, Depository Trust and Clearing Corporation, oversees the lion's share of derivatives transactions. In 2008, the company settled transactions valued at over $1,800 trillion – over a quadrillion dollars in notional value. The Fed legally sanctioned the DTCC as a trust company in 2010. Now several hundred trillion dollars are backstopped by the Fed and the US taxpayer.[24]

The SBS operates off-balance sheet. The transactions are not regulated. All the major banks engage in SBS activities with these assets. That's why their stated values are not based in reality. They have obligations and assets which do not appear in their financials. The top four conventional US banks had $10.2 Trillion in the SBS. Similar numbers exist in Europe.

These structured asset pool type of assets are just the thin end of the wedge. Credit and other derivatives overwhelm them by 10 to 1. The notional value of the derivative market is impossible to really know, but it's knocking on the door of a quadrillion dollars, and it may already be inside the 16 digit house. That makes the notional derivatives tally 20 times the entire global economy.

Zerohedge is probably the largest alternative financial media out there. The readership and articles are sophisticated and well informed. According to the pseudonymous Tyler Durden (main writer), MF Global demonstrated a common trait of "virtually unlimited leverage via the shadow banking system in which there are no hard assets backing the nearly unlimited layers of debt created above, and which, when finally unwound, will create a cataclysmic collapse of all financial institutions because of the daisy chain of rehypothecation."[25] Rehypothecation, covered in detail later, is a legal, but highly questionable banking practice of using customer money – *your money* – as collateral for speculation.

Highly leveraged institutions do not want to write-down bad collateral. When they do, they have to put the losses onto their balance sheet and make up the cash. But without good, unencumbered assets, they cannot. They can sell gold, but that's a minor asset in relation to the enormous derivatives tower. If they sell pre-existing derivatives products – MBS, CDS, and so forth – they will take a massive loss on them in the current market. This only worsens their leverage situation. They have no good assets to sell. They are trapped with hostile forces closing in.

This is the fascinating part of the gold wars. Jim Willie talks about attacks on Western Banks.[26] Gold is one of the few good assets they own since it's unencumbered. Eastern banks loan them money, then wait. When the market moves against them, they issue margin calls which cannot be met. They're using the Western banks' transformation of maturity problem and their excessive leverage against them. The banks have to post something or declare bankruptcy, so they fork over the gold. Since both sides are suppressing the price of gold (for now), they're getting a lot less return than they would in an open market. The Western banks have to post the gold because the Eastern powers bought it and have the power to enforce the contract. They don't want paper and will expose the scheme if they don't get metal. The Western banks are trapped in a prison of their own making.

A primary new method to raise cash is so bizarre that it's almost indescribable. The banks sell $1 million of derivatives, for example. They then find a reverse to the derivative at a better price. If it activates, they get the counter-party to pay off and pocket the spread between the payout. If it doesn't activate, they pocket the spread between the cost of the derivative. The problem comes when the counterparty does not or cannot pay. And derivative payouts are insurance – they payout in many multiples of the premium. So one counterparty default can wipe out gains from 100 derivatives policies. It's a Ponzi house of cards. The failure of a major bank opens a derivatives black hole – no one gets paid from their bad bets. The entire system gets sucked down.

The debt is so large that no amount of selling good assets can ever get the black back on the balance sheet. The game is to get what they can, hoping the bad assets will reinflate to former values. But once the cycle goes global, as it has done, this is impossible. There are simply no buyers. No one has a spare $500 trillion, not the entire globe combined. Prices are set by only a few assets. The latest sales establish the current price, so no matter how much or little of an asset there is, it is all valued against the last sales of just a few units. That's why the Fed is buying so much bad paper.

Moreover, the Fed is stuffing the banks full of cheap money for its own reasons. The banks take this low interest money and buy higher interest Treasuries with it – risk-free profits, supporting the expansion of the national debt. Growing the debt is inevitable – otherwise the government defaults. The Fed's job is to keep the interest low enough to allow expansion of the debt and to bolster the large banks, keeping the system limping along. The Fed has to manage a lot of major, conflicting economic stresses to keep the wheels from coming off. The banks 'Treasury carry trade' also locks the citizens out of new loans – the money remains inside the banking trough. Of course, the economy stays in recession. All the new money stays parked at the Fed and in Treasuries. Velocity goes to zero.

Aside from the ethical implications of buying your competitors with taxpayer funds, another big problem is the banks' need for profitability. Where do institutions this size go in order to get real returns? They will need to soak up the real economy to feed themselves, and will then, nonetheless, still starve. The Dallas Fed is going against the policy.

> Too big to fail must end now. Normal market rules don't apply to the rich, powerful and well-connected. Concentration amplified the speed and breadth of the subsequent damage to the banking sector and the economy as a whole. Mammoth institutions were built on a foundation of leverage, sometimes misleading regulators and investors through the use of off-balance-sheet financing. Their balance sheets deteriorated—too little capital, too much debt, too much risk. The troubles weren't always apparent. Financial institutions kept marking assets on their books at acquisition cost and sometimes higher values if their proprietary models could support such valuations. These accounting expedients allowed them to claim they were healthy—until they weren't. Write-downs were later revised by several orders of magnitude to acknowledge mounting problems. With size came complexity. Many big banks stretched their operations to include proprietary trading and hedge fund investments. Complexity magnifies the opportunities for obfuscation. The too big to fail term disguises the fact that they did fail."[27]

Does the Fed at least know what it's doing in managing the economy? Here are Bernanke's past predictions: 2006, house prices will continue to rise; 2007, subprime is contained; 2008, -no recession, and Fannie and Fred are in no danger of failing.

In spite of the manipulations and control, the banks are trapped. When runs happen and depositors pull out, they need liquidity. They need to recapitalize. Their only large-scale assets are sovereign bonds. But states' need for banks to buy ever more sovereign bonds is acute. So yields rise, making older bonds lose value. But these are the same bonds banks need to sell to raise money to buy more bonds, which similarly would lose value when sold. It's called a death spiral.

Central banks are out of options. Zero interest rate policy (ZIRP), Quantitative Easing (QE), capital controls, forced investment, covert monetization, direct monetization – all are failing. There is only one other option: default. Sovereign defaults will begin happening more and more as the crisis worsens. Bonds will become even less trustworthy. Precious metals, commodities, real estate and other hard assets will become more attractive. Bill Gross, head of Pimco, the largest bond firm on the planet, is buying hard assets, especially gold.

Bailouts support the financial sector only. They never go to the real economy, even though that is the advertised message. Deception is part of the game. At a 2011 Brussels conference, Euroland President Jean Claude Junker said, "when it becomes serious, you have to lie." The situation is, and has been, serious for years now, on many fronts. If other leaders agree with Junker, then it is safe to say we are being lied to, systematically. Indeed, Greenspan shrugged off the housing bubble in 2005, and Bernanke said subprime problems were contained in 2007. He also said the Fed was not monetizing the debt, among other whoppers. Spanish PM Rajoy claimed Spain would not be requesting a bailout less than two weeks before it requested a bailout. In some sense, that is the entire subject of this book. Business and political leaders are deceiving the public for a host of reasons – to avoid panic, calm markets, maintain trust in the system, keep it limping along for as long as possible, increase power and get re-elected/appointed because no one votes for a bad news bringer. And there is no way out that does not challenge not just the interests, but the social domination of the powerful.

High-profile bankers are no better. Blythe Masters, head of JPMorgan's Commodity's division and from CFO, claimed that the bank did not speculate or manipulate markets. A few weeks later, traders detected a gargantuan position and tracked it to a JPMorgan desk. CEO Jamie Dimon said it was a hedging position, but a hedge position of $100 billion that dominates its market sector is a contradiction. Dimon also called it a tempest in a teapot before admitting soon after that losses were $2 billion, then $3 billion and rising. Many analysts set the number at $18 billion or more.

The mega-bank is concealing massive asset losses, which it has openly admitted in a back-door way. In a Harvard law school presentation, the bank reckoned that a hypothetical $50 billion loss, when transferred to the FDIC, would be valued at a $200 billion loss. In other words, they admitted that their assets are mismarked. The company has a far lower asset base than it shows on balance sheet. The report then goes on to state that the equity base is $184 billion. The $50 billion loss is a hypothetical, so it should not be used, but the $150 billion (to bring the above losses to $200 bn) was treated as a realistic assessment of the current shortfall – meaning JPMorgan has only $34 billion in assets minus liabilities.[28] That's not much against a $2 trillion balance sheet and a $70 trillion derivative exposure.

JPMorgan is being investigated by 11 (or more) government agencies. These range from Singapore to Germany to the US. Meanwhile, their Tier 1 capital (strength under strain) has declined from 10.3 to 9.8%. It's a big drop, increasing leverage and instability significantly.

It may be impossible to really know what's going on at a global level, even given far more information than we have. Large banks in every country, central banks and even governments are notoriously secretive about their financial practices, and if secrecy doesn't pose enough difficulties for getting a grip on the situation, then there's the rampant lying and fraud. Banks have off-balance sheet transactions to hide their real bets. Governments do, too. Federal liabilities are estimated at $60 to $100 trillion by credible estimates, when Medicare and other programs are included. The largely off-balance derivatives complex is between $600 and $1400 trillion. It's the world's largest economic unknown, a mushroom cloud waiting to blow up the global economy. When it goes off in a chain reaction, the world's biggest institutions will become black holes, sucking in more and more money to stay alive.

Derivatives exposure is highly concentrated:

| | |
|---|---|
| JPMorgan Chase | $70.1 Trillion |
| Citibank | $52.1 Trillion |
| Bank of America | $50.1 Trillion |
| Goldman Sachs | $44.2 Trillion |

Similar amounts are spread among the Euro-mega-banks. The derivatives total of a quadrillion dollars is 10 times the value of all stocks and bonds on earth combined. It's 20 times global GDP. It's a big, big number and an even bigger problem.

JPMorgan's $70 trillion in derivatives is backed by its $156 billion in risk capital, a leverage of 516 to 1. Goldman Sachs wins the prize with $44 trillion in derivatives backed by $19 billion in risk capital, an over 2000 to 1 leverage.

Derivatives were at the heart of the 2008 crisis. The agreement with bailouts was to step down derivatives activity. It's increased dramatically. So has the risk. When counterparties became alarmed, Bank of America moved trillions in derivatives from Merrill Lynch, which it owns, to its central deposit institution. Now these are theoretically backstopped by the FDIC.

One derivative form, credit default swaps, courtesy of Markit Group, are not reliably priced. Markit Group could be compared to Moody's, except they actually set valuations, mostly on exotic derivatives. The company's indexes set the industry standard. Prices are sent in from various banks and funds as to what value they assign to the CDS. Then Markit takes the data and makes a best fit scenario. Markit is notoriously secretive, not even revealing its founders. But the biggest banks are part owners and they stand to gain big from Markit evaluations. And big may not be legal. If the valuations are wrong, then good companies can be attacked by bogus valuations. Their equity shrinks because everyone thinks their assets are tanking. Their debt is sold short and their cost of borrowing goes sky-high. Short sellers with inside information front run the process, buying or selling CDSs against debt assets they never purchased. It's casino speculation by house rules. When the debt rises, the CDSs are activated or expire worthless, depending on the initiator's intent.[29]

The Dodd-Frank Act was supposed to regulate derivatives, getting them out into the open, where problems would be easier to anticipate and solve. But it does something pretty frightening, as well – it ostensibly backstops the massive derivatives complex. Dodd-Frank opens a Fed borrowing line to derivatives clearing-houses that are found to be 'systemically important.' This is the essence of moral hazard. No one has had access to this channel of cheap money before except savings banks, which are regulated in their use. The clearing-houses are not regulated. They can do anything they want with the money they borrow at ultra-low rates. If they get into a serious derivatives rats-nest, they borrow money for nothing, and never pay it back. It's all reward and no risk. Again, bet the farm and bet big. Become systemically important by taking the counter-bets to the biggest institutions. If the clearing-houses go bust, those institutions go bust, too. Now, they're systemically important. If their bets win, they win. If their bets lose, the Fed pays off. There is no reason not to bet the farm, because they can't really lose.

Easy money is a policy of low interest rates from the Fed combined with money printing. Banks can borrow quite readily. Initially, easy money leads to a boom in asset prices – wherever the hot money goes. In the 2000s, it was to real estate and its derivatives. After a time, the value is eroded by excess capacity of the assets – the system chokes on the flood. The values plummet – called the popping of the bubble. The government and banks are trying to re-inflate, but a popped bubble, once gone, is gone. During TARP, the Federal Reserve issued $26 trillion in zero interest loans. The sheer magnitude of these loans was not disclosed, but found by an audit forced through Congress by the head of the finance committee, Ron Paul. It's easy money at its worst. It punishes savers and rewards speculators.

ZIRP is maintained by interest rate swaps. These are derivatives contracts agreeing to purchase prior bonds at full face value, should the interest rate rise. Previous lower interest bonds lose value very quickly when the current rate rises. If the US ten year rate rose to a sensible 7%, then the swaps would be triggered. The cost to the big five US banks would exceed $30 trillion and possibly go much higher. $100 trillion is not impossible. ZIRP must be defended, but buyers have fled the scene. The Fed has bought over 70% of US long bonds since mid-2011. All other buyers are buying in for only one year or less. They can exit at any time. So, the big banks have transformed risk and maturity – some short term income matched against a sudden, huge potential loss, which can happen at any time and will sit like a lit bomb on the books for years. And these positions keep getting multiplied to maintain the low T-Bond rates.

There is no escape. If the 10-year Treasury rate rises above 2%, the banks will be totally insolvent almost immediately. They will cover it over and try to push the rate below 2% again, but if it stays above long-term, the strains will become enormous.

To detail this a bit, here's a hypothetical example: MegaBank sells short $100 billion in T-bills, 1 and 3 month short-term instruments, at almost zero percent interest. People are still buying the very short term ones because it's a safe place to keep big money which is highly liquid. The banks then buy $100 billion in 10 year bonds at 1.75. They get the interest differential without having to put up any of their own capital, which of course banks always like. Unfortunately, they have transformed maturity from short term to long term. They have to roll over the existing T-bills every few months and add $150 billion new ones to support the unceasing 10-year bond buying, or the whole thing blows up right on the off-balance sheet. If T-bill rates rise, they have to short bonds (borrow money from mister market) at rates higher than the 10 year investment they are holding. Quite suddenly, all the big banks are upside down on some very, very large positions. $1.8 trillion a year adds up fast. The US banking complex is trapped within its own policy.

ZIRP also makes the economic price structure completely off-base. Cheap money drives up asset prices, but does so on an unsustainable debt basis. Bubbles invariably blow up, then pop. Due to the grind of inflation, savers are punished by low returns or driven into equities. Quantitative Easing, aka money printing, has equally bad effects. It also creates inflation, but in a double-down way. Aside from money printing going into the economy and pushing up prices, much more money goes into speculation, rather than into manufacturing where the rewards are lower. As industry declines, fewer goods are chased by more money. Banks do not lend, they gamble. Gambling winnings are much higher and losses are absorbed by the government and, ultimately, the citizenry. That is the essence of moral hazard. Why not risk it all if you can win big, but can't really lose?[30] The non-productive financial sector has grown from under 10% in the 1950's to over 30% of the US economy today.

The ratings agency got in on the deal. They were customers of the funds that wanted to market toilet paper as triple-A. If they told the truth, the funds went elsewhere to get the stamp they wanted. So they lied to stay in the river of money. There was, and still is, dump trucks full of propaganda about the solvency and viability of the big banks, the prominent funds and the system as a whole. And gold takes the opposite side of that trade. So the machine turns its guns on that enemy.

Confidence in the system is failing and risk is going to the moon. When sovereign defaults, such as by Greece, Spain and Italy begin, the positive feedback mechanism cranks into high gear. Institutional money gets defensive. It all gets parked at the central bank. Further, the southern banks have already posted all their good and medium collateral to borrow money. They only have post-it notes left to borrow hundreds of billions against – and nobody wants it.

During 2008, it came out that GSax was leveraged 333 to 1,[31] JPMorgan at 52 to 1, and even so, they still wanted to do away with the fractional limit. That's why people who study it often refer to the fractional reserve requirement as a Ponzi scheme. A Ponzi scheme requires a growing pool of new investors to pay off the old ones. The need for new capital eventually goes parabolic. The bond complex of the US is the biggest Ponzi scheme in the history of the world. The need for new funds will soon overtake the ability of the Fed to monetize in any realistic manner, now that foreigners are dumping T-Bonds, adding to the stress. Hyperinflating the money supply will fail as the complex tears itself apart. More and more fixed income investments will be forced into the sucking maw as legalized measures push pensions and 401(k)s into the Treasury complex. Congressmen are discussing such ideas now and they have been implemented in distressed countries. These forces will take investment capital from elsewhere and severely damage the economy.

On June 13 and 14, 2013, the Fed bought several billion of 10 and 30 year bonds *before the Treasury sold identical instruments*. This is called monetization – printing money to pay off debt – and price fixing. The Fed purchase drops the yield on them before the sale and does it in such size and scope that the monetization is essentially out in the open – if only the media would report it. The general public is left in the dark, giving foreign investors and insiders a head start as they cast about for means to leave the sinking ship.

The Fed bought 61% of all government debt in 2011.[32] But it gets worse when the data is analyzed. Operation Twist was intended to flatten the yield curve. The yield curve is the yield rate of Treasury measured by bond duration – shorter term bonds tend to have lower interest rates. The 1 month T-Bills are hovering around 0%. People still buy them as a place to park big money, but keep it liquid. Operation Twist bought long-term (mostly 10 year T-Bonds) and sold short term (1 year or less) T-Bills. This is the classic transformation of maturity trick, just mentioned above. And even if it is the Fed doing it, it still only makes the problem worse. Obviously, selling short-term debt to buy long-term debt forces the institution to sell multiples of the buying. In other words, the purchased assets are on the books for 10 years, but the sold assets have to be rolled every single month – a rate of at least 10 times. And more short term assets are added each month, making the position more and more imbalanced.

The monetization also needs to perpetually increase because of the rising deficits and because legitimate buyers have left the building. At the same time, the tracks of it need to be hidden, but this is becoming more or less impossible. Only the public, which does not really pay attention to anything, can be deluded for long periods. Real investors cannot. Even the sleepy retirement and pension funds managers are waking up.

Operation Twist forces the timeline into an awful compression. As the huge Asian pools convert long-term securities to short-term securities, their average maturity gets shorter and shorter. This means that much more debt rolls over per month/year than previously. This compression will take a year to be created. When it unwinds, the effect may destroy the US currency and bond complexes. In other words, China, Japan, and other big US instrument holders can cash in all their debt – several trillion – in a year or so. At that time, the Fed will have to turn all the debt into dollars to roll it over. Existing investors don't want it – freshly created money will have to fill the bill. The defense mechanisms will be incredible to see. It appears that Operation Twist was designed for the Fed to purchase every 30 year bond ever issued. This is not a trivial matter – it is a cornerstone of the global monetary system. By monetizing it, global cheap money – the US kind – will begin moving very quickly. And quickly moving oceans are called tidal waves.

All this debt compels governments to devalue the currency and reduce its real value. Devaluation means more currency must be printed, of course, and that allows more debt to be repaid rather than defaulted. Of course, a devaluation also makes the holdings of savers worth less – unless they are very skillfully invested. Overseas investment has a lot of appeal when the dollar gets dropped. But it puts both governments and citizens in a tricky spot. Governments cannot announce a planned devaluation because all the money would leave the currency, sparking a massive psychological, then real, inflation – a devaluation before the devaluation. Usually, governments warn the well-connected elites, who can then preserve wealth (theirs, at least) and actually increase it. Ben Bernanke told a group of banking CEOs about the nationalization of Fannie Mae a few days early. They profited enormously from the illegal tip.

The citizens are basically on their own. Somebody has to take the devaluation hit and since the citizens are holding the currency, they're the ideal candidate. So those who understand the game front-run by getting out of the currency and into something that holds value. That's why gold and silver are so attractive. They have held monetary value for 5000 years, 30 times longer than any currency existed. And all of those devalued during their existence. No fiat currency has ever been stable. Only precious metals have. It may appear that PMs are quite volatile, but very long-term charts show an extremely stable pattern. This stability is being attacked by the monetary powers – detailed extensively in the Metals Trading, Manipulations and Theft section – to scare investors away.

The chart from the IMF (Figure 13 below) shows something very interesting on closer inspection. First, the IMF claims that 16% of these safe assets will become unsafe in the next few years. That's a lot and it's not clear which ones these will be. (See Figure 13 below.) ]That leads to the second point. It is clear that in the IMF's view, the single safe asset that will remain so is gold. This chart tells the whole story of truly safe assets. All other assets on the chart are debt. All other assets are subject to currency problems, counterparty issues, loss of faith by the creditor, monetization or outright default. Gold is the only asset that is unequivocally safe. The only risk is it can be stolen, but as shown here and elsewhere, that risk is in everything. It's called the price of safety. When the paper burns, true money will look a lot better.

Unfortunately, the IMF is the worst oppressor when it comes to monetary policy. Under Article 4, Section 2b of the organization's Articles

**Figure 13**

**Safe Assets by percentage**

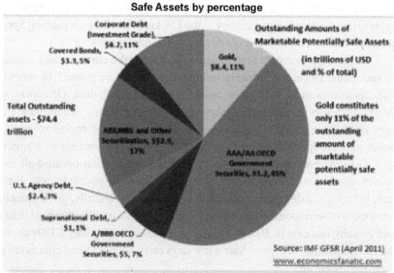

Source: IMF GFSR (April 2011)
www.economicsfanatic.com

of Agreement, member nations are prohibited from linking their country's currency to gold. Gold is well understood to have a stabilizing influence on a nation's economy – damping both booms and busts. Since stabilization is the IMF's stated goal, this policy is highly questionable. The not-so-hidden agenda of the IMF is to keep the globe in the fiat currency spiral.

Meantime, the game must continue, no matter how bad the referees are. The Fed has its own committee for (perhaps illegally) propping up the paper markets. It's been discussed for years by numerous analysts and is called a conspiracy theory on the mainstream media. The Exchange Stabilization Fund (ESF) is quite real. It keeps appearing wherever markets are manipulated. Its managers' moniker is the 'Plunge Protection Team.' The PPT allegedly supports the prices of stocks by buying the stocks, especially in the wee hours when they are thinly traded. They can also buy future options as a cheaper approach. At any rate, one of the most telling pieces of evidence comes from the Fed's website – see Figure 14.

**Figure 14**

**Average Cumulative Returns on S&P 500 Index on
Days before, of and after FOMC Announcements**

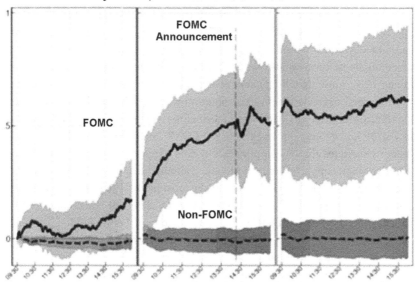

The Federal Open Market Committee makes an announcement about monetary policy eight times a year. Every time it does, the market lifts. Figure 15 below shows where the S&P 500 would be without those eight periods: *trading at less than half the present value.*

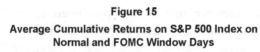

**Figure 15**
**Average Cumulative Returns on S&P 500 Index on**
**Normal and FOMC Window Days**

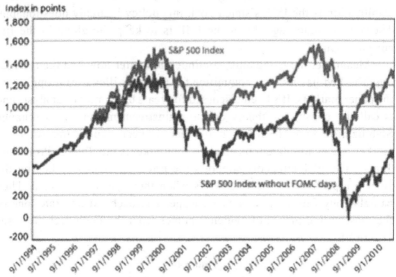

Figure 15 compares the average returns on S&P on normal and FOMC window days – day before, day of, and day after announcements. On normal days, returns are pegged at zero. On the three day window, they accumulate to .65% on average. According to the Fed report, "we show that since 1994, more than 80 percent of the equity premium on U.S. stocks has been earned over the twenty-four hours preceding scheduled Federal Open Market Committee (FOMC) announcements (which occur only eight times a year)—a phenomenon we call the pre-FOMC announcement "drift."[33] The paper concludes that it is a puzzle why this happens. Indeed it is, because without illicit support of printed money, it should be impossible. As Occam's Razor says, the simplest explanation is the most likely. The ESF is supporting the market by purchasing equities and futures. The ESF was started with funds from government theft of the people's money. Public holding of gold was declared illegal; it was taken in by the Fed, and repriced 40% higher. The full tale is in the central banking section, below.

Much of this market levitation comes from algorithm trading. The stock market has increased its trading activity by more than a hundred-fold in the past few years. It isn't legitimate traders hunting for volatility – it is high frequency algorithms. These computers do a number of things, but mainly they trade not just to reap returns from tiny movements of vast holdings, but also with each other to keep the market propped up artificially. They now comprise 80% of the trading market. That makes it impossible for normal traders to function. Market analysis no longer works. Value investing, Warren Buffet and general public style, is dead. Goldman Sachs was caught front-running the orders. Their software saw the bids before anyone else. It bought and sold within milliseconds, shaving risk-free pennies on millions of shares every day. It's illegal – so the government stepped in to protect GSax. The whistleblower was labeled a criminal and the story went away with no other prosecutions.

Algorithm trading is also called high-frequency trading. HFT systems search the live stream of quotes to find tiny arbitrages in bid-ask spread. These exist as differences in the electronic network before they are synchronized. The differences do not exist for more than a few thousandths of a second, so the searching computers have to be very fast. This arbitrage skews the market dramatically, making tiny technical indicators the driving trend rather than fundamentals. This trend divorces investment from connections with fundamentals, and thereby any purported meaningfulness as a measure of the well-being of the economy

The value investor cannot win in this game. That's partially because most of the value money is drained out in billions of tiny grabs. It may seem like a half a penny per share is not worth the concern, but when billions of trades take that half a penny a day, it adds up. And that is money taken away from the value market by the rapid speculative market. It's like betting the bathtub will fill up with the drain-plug that has a hole.

HFT traders have no positions open at the end of the day because they trade, not according to value, but according to market direction. As such, they push the market much further in any particular direction than would otherwise occur. Because they perpetually cull the market for consistent small returns, their Sharpe ratio (measuring reward to risk) is thousands of times higher than buy and hold investors. HFT trading is a very good deal, if you can afford the technology. However, even more money can be made if that risk is evened out, so the traditional investors are taking it on by spreading it among themselves. This type of trading has been happening since 1999, with large market share since 2004 or so. The public never knew until *The New York Times* published a story on it in 2009. It's an interesting point because most people assume that things aren't true if they've never heard of them – things like the suppression of the gold price.

Nasdaq, for example, has a loophole that allows certain traders to see the orders ahead of the rest of the market. When a slow set of traders wants to buy in without tipping the market, they gradually ramp up the position. But the HFT computers spot the first anomaly and buy up the shares ahead of time, knowing the trade is on. The machines flash and retract bids thousands of times a second, trying to find the highest price point. They sell a tiny offering at $30.00, then $30.10, then $30.20 until they get to $30.80, and it doesn't get hit before the retraction. The retraction is to see if the slow money wants to buy at that price. If it does, then the 'algos' (HFT software) jump higher to test the next price. When a bid is not matched, they fall back and sell at the maximum the 'whale' will buy at. They have found the hidden information – the other sides' highest buy point and they dump 50,000 shares at that price. It's illegal because it uses the advantage of frontrunning (buying shares in advance  due to awareness of a soon forthcoming much larger purchase) to take away the other side's only trading advantage – proprietary data, internally generated data that contains technical or other information controlled by a firm to safeguard its competitive edge.

Most orders should get filled at below the bid price in a fast moving stock with an aggressive bidder. The way it used to work was the bid was a maximum limit and the order would be filled to agree with the market. Most of the order would not necessarily be filled at the limit price. Now the algos tease out the limit price, buy up the lower offerings by frontrunning, then cram 98% of it through at the bid limit. The dumb money – mutual funds, mostly – always pays too much, feeding the machines. There are rules in place to prevent this from happening, but it is one of the primary profit sources for the big banks these days, so don't expect much action on that. The Tabb group estimated HFT profits at $21 billion in 2008. If most people cannot get a fair trade, the markets sacrifice their integrity.[34]

The daily number of trades on the market has increased by thousands of times. It's led to the flash crash phenomenon. The *crash of 2:45* on May 6, 2010 dropped the Dow Jones by $600 in 3 minutes. It was a total drop of $1000 for the day, the largest in history. The market quickly recovered. The cause was HF trading. The traders accumulated a mere 200 contracts in the e-mini futures market, but traded an astounding 27,000. It was called a hot potato, as the algos swapped enormous positions back and forth. Some S&P 500 companies traded at one cent per share. Some companies went to $100,000 a share. Some traders put out stub orders – way out of the price range and not meant to be filled – with the intent of choking the system. This creates an imbalance in the orders, some quite delayed. The computers can see the orders before they hit on multiple exchanges. They try to manipulate an arbitrage (simultaneous price differential) between different exchanges. They also buy or short sell shares – frontrunning. If there's a big sell order, they short-sell ahead, driving down the price, then buy the shares back at the bottom of the sell limit. HFT trading was integral to the flash crash.

No one knows specifically why the flash crash happened or, more likely – those who know aren't telling. With these kinds of anomalies, somebody made a lot of money at somebody else's expense. Probably a number of market makers got creamed. At any rate, the event is clearly market manipulation, whether by accident or hidden design. It's another part of the shadow bank system and all the big banks are doing it.

Billionaire and hi-tech investor, Mark Cuban, calls HF traders the "ultimate hackers." They are trying to exploit the trading platforms, using software to outsmart software. It is a recipe for disaster. The argument that HFT narrows spreads and provides liquidity is absurd. The liquidity must already be there for HFT to function in a market. And bid spreads are meaningless to investors – they only matter for traders. To say this is a legitimate function is to say the stock market favors traders over investors.[35] Indeed, one HF trader expressed serious concerns that algorithm terrorism could create global havoc.

Knight Capital endured a crushing self-induced cardiac event. They lost half a billion dollars in minutes. It was, apparently, a software error. The company was set to release its exciting new market making software, but during tests, the software went live and began trading stocks that Knight was not making markets (providing liquidity) for. Knight was the largest market maker in small cap stocks. Equity owners took a steep hit as the market dried up. The companies also lost access to capital markets.

According to Charles Hugh Smith, the market is rigged in multiple ways. HFT trading skims profits on millions of transactions. The PPT prevents the market from falling below certain levels and gooses rises from time to time. Dark pools – invisible exchanges of stocks – trade massive shares off the normal, transparent markets. All of these activities occur without general public knowledge. Short of an open knowledge of critical market operations, the average investor cannot win. The titanic skimming operation is officially sanctioned, but the means are not available to most investors. Eventually, Smith claims, the system will crash. When HFT trading hits a big momentum play to the downside, it will accelerate the momentum – that's how it functions. The Fed will be unable to buy in to stop the massive selling. Its pool will be overwhelmed.[36]

There are a host of reasons why the stock market and the entire system is essentially a wealth transfer mechanism from the middle class to connected insiders. Figure 17 shows an amazing reality. Basically, the standard investment strategy for the middle class is death by a thousand cuts.

Jeffrey Boyd is the CEO of Priceline. He received options for the stock of several hundred thousand shares as part of his compensation. He exercised these options at $20 to $30 per share. Options, of course, are not exercised at market prices, but at pre-agreed prices. These insider shares are created when the options are exercised, as if they were new shares. When options are exercised, the buyer gets the shares at the option price, not the market price. He can then sell them at the market price. When Boyd exercised the options, he was able to sell the new shares into the market at more than $550/share. This

**Figure 16**

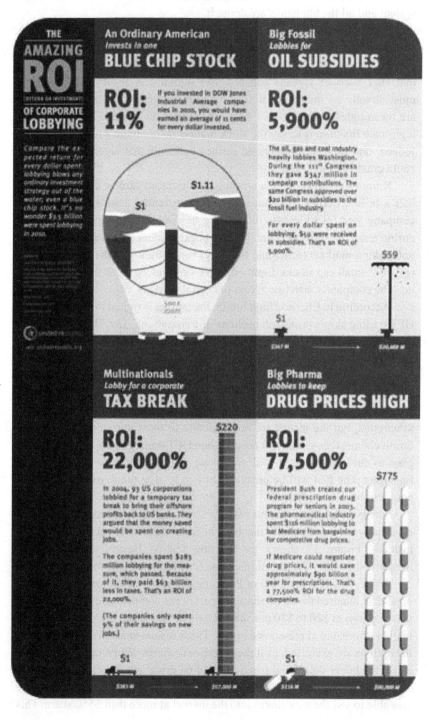

2000% windfall put $120 million in his pocket. The Priceline stock began tanking soon afterwards. It was the second time this had happened. Priceline went to a high of $960/share in the early 2000s. Then, after some option exercises, it fell to $6. About 20% of the ownership is from Vanguard, Fidelity and other 401(k) funds. Financial advisory companies used retirement monies to unload insider stocks – up to a billion – on Priceline. The funds inflated the value of the stock from $300 million to $30 billion, by encouraging the public to invest in this company. In other words, after inflating the value of Priceline stock, they then sold off private stock options at that price, draining off the public investment. As the saying goes, the stock market transfers money from Main Street to Wall Street.[37]

Urban lingo has the phrase OPM – other people's money. Banks have developed the art of using OPM to the utmost degree. It should really be called other people's assets because they would hardly stop at mere money. The technique is called rehypothecation. Rehypothecation (and it's out of control younger twin, 'hyper-hypothecation') tells you all about the moral direction and free reign of bankers. It facilitates the slow strangulation of the middle class.

Hypothecation is simply the use of an asset as collateral. Rehypothecation is the use of client assets by a brokerage or financial firm as collateral for the firm's purposes. The client takes the risk and the firm gets the reward. Title is still owned by the original party, but it is 'hypothetically' controlled by the lender. While clients can be compensated, most clients are unaware of the procedure and their assets are used without their knowledge or gain. Of course, it's in the fine print, but that's seldom clear. Usually, the practice is used against the client – equities are borrowed for short sales against the securities, driving the price down. It begs the question – who owns the assets in a default scenario, the client or the entity with collateral pledged to it? Collateral has no meaning except to secure a loan in the case of default. If your stock is collateralized (without your permission or knowledge) for MS to borrow money from JPM, then you can actually lose your assets when MS hits the skids and 'The Morgue' collects its collateral. This happened with MF Global and PFG Best. Numerous investors got skinned. We'll return to that in a bit.

Rehypothecation has different limits in different places. In the US, 140% of the collateralized loan value can be loaned against. In the UK, there is no limit. Client collateral can be used again and again to finance more speculation. London is the banker's paradise for a very clear reason. Rehypothecation is very profitable, so all the big houses set up a London office to milk the cow as hard as possible – relocating client assets without their knowledge to the UK. Half the shadow system was based on rehypothecation by 2007. It was not on balance sheets for several reasons. Not being cash, it didn't have to be there. But it was a good cash substitute and a great way to make money. This surged up capital to earnings ratios – a hidden way of looking stronger. It looked as if companies made very high returns for capital, but it hid the massive leverage being used in order to do so, which if included in the calculations, would have completely changed the ratios.[38] It's not pretty either. Up to four times leverage can be and is based on awful collateral. Even Reuters printed, "Considering that re-hypothecation may have increased the financial footprint of Eurozone bonds by at least four fold then a Eurozone sovereign default could be apocalyptic." That's why Greece is being bolstered, but when Spain, Portugal and the much larger Italy begin to topple, no force may be able to hold it up. In a default, the underlying bonds will be worth precisely zero and the leverage goes to infinity on those bonds. The shadow system is a house of cards.[39]

Before Lehman collapsed, its collateral was about $1 trillion, while the rehypothecation was about $4 trillion. Afterwards, hedge funds balked at the risk and put clauses limiting or preventing their funds being used in such a manner. Now only 'muppets'[40] – average investors who don't know better – have their assets put on the block.

Singh and Aitken showed that rehypothecation played a central role in the 2008 crisis and subsequent deleveraging. This led to a drying of credit

**Figure 17**

**SEC Lenders - Lending and Reinvestment Flows**

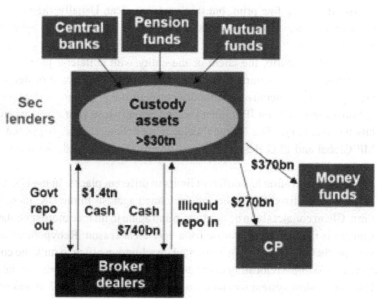

and disappearance of lending between banks and in the general economy. Markdowns on collateral – called 'margin spiral' – can rapidly get out of hand. Most of the asset backed mortgage instruments lost up to 90% of face value in months. The shadow banking system was much larger than previously understood – leading to a distorted, under-evaluation of systemic risk. Rehypothecation allows for pretty shady accounting. Multiple companies can list assets though their ownership of these is shared, unlike on-balance sheet assets.[41]

Figure 17 shows the real threat. The entire system rests on $30 trillion in assets. Out of these are created an endless chain of hyper-collateralized assets that are just more debt and promises. When any part of this flow is seriously disrupted, and it will be, global contagion and banking crisis will follow. The system will see increasing problems with increasing frequency and eventually an uncontrollable implosion. Such a real world event happened in 2011.

MF Global was a derivatives (options, futures, etc.) broker and a primary bond dealer for the US Treasury. This is an important point. Primary dealers are among the most scrutinized of financial companies. They are supposed to be very conservative in operation, extremely stable, and possess very high integrity, guaranteed by the regulatory authorities. This company was officially rated triple gold star, completely immune to any solvency and liquidity issues. And yet, MF Global was highly leveraged, very risk-prone, and engaged in a number of unscrupulous practices. Clients, including subsidiary clients, lost billions. The lesson is clear: the auditing system is broken. All parties failed in their duties.

Why the checks and balances system failed is less clear. It was either incompetence or willful deception. Those scrutinizing are some of the highest paid accounting firms in the world. Either they attained their position through years of incompetence, or it was a show of one-time incompetence, or they were deliberately and well-paid to do exactly what they did – cover up MF Global's financial black hole. How many more MF Globals are out there?

In 2008, the company was fined $10 million for inappropriate trading activity, and blamed it on a 'rogue trader,' a recurrent scapegoat in the modern financial world. Liquidity concerns tanked the stock price, then MF Global was fined another $10 million for bad risk management. The company rehypothecated big-time, betting the farm on the prospect of Greek default on its debt. Greek debt was very high-yield. The firm took out credit default swaps on the bonds, probably hoping for a subsequent massive payout by the swaps contracts upon Greek default. But its timing was bad and the hyper-leverage dove-tailed with market concerns – liquidity disappeared for MF Global. And the Greeks failed to default. To maintain the appearance of solvency and liquidity, MFG dipped into the customer till. Segregated accounts are (were) considered sacrosanct. It was a line even the banks wouldn't cross. If they did, the system would have been further exposed as hopelessly corrupt. Taking customer funds without asking is simply stealing, even if the intent is to return the funds. It's no different than lawyers dipping into client trust funds. On October 31, 2011, the company admitted that $891 million in customer funds was transferred to cover huge losses, including an odd $175 million transfer directly to JPMorgan. The true amount is not well-disclosed, nor is the length of time over which the malpractice occurred. The amount was later adjusted to 'at least $1.6 billion.'

MF Global was using a complicated internal and external trade. Its London branch was doing a repo with the New York branch taking the other side – the reverse repo. A repo is a short-term sale with an agreement to buy back later. Repos are supposed to fund short-term liquidity needs, but they also allow for funny accounting games. The company used a fiction – an internal repo to maturity – to game the regulations. It was a simple one to spot, but the regulators ignored it. In this case, it was done to provide a booked profit to make the business look more solvent. But the trade had a two-day shortfall in the window before maturity when the bonds were sold externally. This, combined with the default risk, put an unendurable liquidity crunch on the business. This became public knowledge, investors withdrew funds, lenders pulled back, and the death-spiral sank the ship, disappearing billions in client funds.[42]

Analyst Chris Whalen calls it outright theft. Clients lost gold, bonds, currency and other assets. HSBC even filed suit against JPMorgan over $850,000 of its gold held from MF Global. MF Global seems to have been pledging client gold – the ultimate backstop asset – against its creditors' claims. There would be no lawsuit between two such entities otherwise. This leads to a nasty potential revelation. If one is doing it, usually they all are. Again and again, the existence of common practice has been proved – like in the LIBOR rigging. The question is to what extent the GLD and SLV exchange traded funds (HSBC is the custodian) are backed by physical gold. The metals can be rehypothecated to more than their market value. They may have multiple claims on them, and given the wording of the funds, the clients will be last in line. These funds are the biggest privately held stocks of silver and gold in the world. We'll look at this in much more detail in the manipulation section.

Lehman and Bear Stearns were larger than the MF Global crisis. Customers were made whole in both cases before any other proceedings. That this did not occur with MF shows the extent of systemic strain at this point. Customer accounts are now needed to feed the beast. It exposes the problem in public view. Trust is beginning to fall off the cliff, despite the efforts of the mega-banks to avoid it. They need the money to stay where it is – on their ledgers – to keep leverage issues from upending their balance sheets. It's proof of desperation. And, in a footnote of corruption, the customers are being charged storage fees on their stolen metals – otherwise they forfeit any settlement claims on them in future. Meantime, the prices of the metals dropped precipitously, so the cash settlement was far less. And naturally, the assets were frozen, preventing the legitimate owners from selling them.

Commingling of funds is the ultimate crime in brokerage activities. No one was prosecuted. Ann Barnhardt closed down her financial firm based on the handling of MF Global, with the following letter, edited for brevity:

> Barnhardt Capital Management has ceased operations…
> **I could no longer tell my clients that their monies and positions were safe in the futures and options markets – because they are not.** And this goes not just for my clients, but for every futures and options account in the United States. The entire system has been utterly destroyed by the MF Global collapse.
>
> The futures markets are very highly-leveraged and thus require an exceptionally firm base upon which to function. That base was the sacrosanct segregation of customer funds from clearing firm capital, with additional emergency financial backing provided by the exchanges themselves. Up until a few weeks ago, that base existed, and had worked flawlessly.
>
> Jon Corzine STOLE the customer cash at MF Global. …[Regulators'] reaction has been to take a bad situation and make it orders of magnitude worse. Specifically, they froze customers out of their accounts WHILE THE MARKETS CONTINUED TO TRADE, refusing to even allow them to liquidate. … The risk exposure precedent … has destroyed the entire industry paradigm.
>
> …MF Global is almost certainly the mere tip of the iceberg. The Chicago Mercantile Exchange did not immediately step in to backstop the MFG implosion because they knew and know that if they backstopped MFG, they would then be expected to backstop all of the other firms in the system when the failures began to cascade – and there simply isn't that much money in the entire system. **In short, the problem is a SYSTEMIC problem, not merely isolated to one firm.**

> ...The futures and options markets are no longer
> viable. ...The system is no longer functioning with
> integrity and is suicidally risk-laden. The rule of law
> is non-existent, instead replaced with godless, criminal
> political cronyism.[43]

1.42 million ounces of silver went missing in the scandal – vaporized funds, the mainstream media called it. But it went somewhere, to someone. It was stolen. The bad bets, Jim Willie explained, put pressure on the Commodities Exchange, inc (hereafter referred to as Comex). People wanted actual delivery of their silver futures contracts. JPMorgan could not fulfill these contracts legally – using their own metal instead of allocated metal stored for clients. "JPM increased the amount of silver in their registered vaults by precisely the amount that was supposed to be delivered ... JPM effectively averted both a Comex default and a European Sovereign Debt implosion."[44]

On December 12, 2011, HSBC filed a lawsuit to prevent an MF Global client from taking delivery on physical gold and silver from the Comex. The metals were doubly owned, confirming the critics' claims. It's difficult to sort out what really happened – probably by intent – but it may have gone like this: MF Global lost precious metals it was supposed to deliver. JPMorgan apparently was being hammered by margin calls on a number of derivative bets that were getting out of hand. Their reserves were scraping bottom. The silver and gold futures calls for delivery had put the bank in a tight squeeze. They held on to the MF Global metals that were supposed to be delivered, putting them instead into their own account.[45]

JPMorgan is also serving as trustee for the case in spite of their notable conflict of interest – they have liens on substantial assets. This conflict of interest is a further spit in the eye of the clients. "Evidence mounts," Jim Willie explains, "that JPMorgan simply converted 614k ounces of MF Global client silver into JPM licensed vaults." They moved 613,738 eligible ounces into their vaults on Nov. 18. After waiting a week, they changed it to registered. Two definitions – eligible means that it meets quality standards for good delivery but is still owned by a private party. Registered means it is available for delivery to satisfy a futures contract. All the silver they held for others soon after the MF Global collapse was also converted to JPMorgan ownership.

On Oct. 31st, MF Global publicly filed for bankruptcy. The CME announced that about 1.4 million ounces of eligible silver had vanished from the client holdings at MF Global, of which 627,182 was from banks outside the cartel. It was the first deposit of any quantity into their silver vaults in half a year for JPMorgan. Total futures contracts (covered later) are many times the deliverable amount of silver available. The Comex itself is probably approaching a default. They badly needed silver to meet futures deliveries, which are rising aggressively. However, since early 2013, Comex vaulted silver has risen significantly.

One trader, whose account was vaporized, said the freeze came because of stock positions with impossible counterparty risk. To save a few hundred accounts, the holdings of 35,000 commodities customers were literally stolen. Customer account receipts were immediately confiscated at the beginning of the investigation. This made it very difficult for them to prove their asset claims. The claim was that the money was "missing" and could not be found. US regulators accepted this even when it was shown to be a lie. Richard Heis, an administrator of MF Global's UK division, said, in the US, the claim is "nobody knows where the money is. We know exactly where the money is."[46] Some analysts claim the regulators are throwing up a dust cloud to protect the perpetrators, letting the clock tick until the statute of limitations expires.

The 2005 bankruptcy reform legislation[47] elevates derivatives above all other asset classes in a bankruptcy. This puts the banks (holders of 99% of all derivatives) above any other asset holder. In a rehypothecation scenario, the innocent public is pushed underwater and loses. Considering derivatives tower above all other assets by volume, the danger is extreme. In a true derivative havoc situation, no brokerage-held asset would appear to be safe – MF Global proves it. People would do well to examine the fine print in their pension and 401(k) contracts. If people have cash in an investment account at Morgan Stanley, for example, it means that when the firm goes Lehman, that cash can be used legally to pay off MS's exploded derivatives. There is even a clawback provision. If the client removed the funds in the weeks beforehand, MS can reverse the transfer.

When Bank of America took over Merrill Lynch, they brought a freakish $53 trillion in derivatives onto their balance sheet. By moving that and a pre-existing position ($77 trillion) from the investment to the commercial side, they put it on the FDIC's insurance list. According to the Market Ticker, it's an "armed financial nuclear device... daring anyone to tamper with it." All banks have the same type of massive systemic risk, deliberately booby-trapping their balance sheet. This is commingling of funds on an extreme scale. The firewall between a bank's investments and its client deposits is gone. The public will bes held hostage in any ensuing chaos. Bank CEOs, the Ticker claims, lie with impunity about the risks. The warning is very clear – "you could lose everything in your bank and investment accounts – every single dime."[48]

The Chicago Mercantile Exchange (CME) is a non-governmental regulatory body in charge of overseeing MF Global and other such brokerages. Top management wrote a public letter in July, 2012. The group was "appalled by the recent misuse of segregated funds." In order to reinstate customer confidence, they proposed revised regulations, including unannounced audits of segregated funds, daily and bi-monthly reporting and electronic confirmations of segregated funds, and CEO guarantees of procedures. "CME Group is committed to making whatever changes are necessary to strengthen customer protections, restore confidence in the futures industry and ensure the effectiveness of these critical markets."[49]

Unfortunately, the CME had reneged on this mission even before the letter. They had an agreement to make investors whole as part of their mandate, but refused to do so. CME probably had the money, but according to the organization's Chairman, Terry Duffy, it would set a $185 billion precedent. In other words, expect more MF Globals, beyond the CME's ability to backstop.

The Peregrine Financial Group (PFG Best) repeated the MF Global scenario. The Commodities Futures Trading Commission (CFTC) and other regulators checked out Peregrine Financial and found it in fine shape in January, 2012. A subsequent investigation found fraud that extended back several years. It turned out that an account listed as holding $225 million only held $5 million. CEO and owner, Russel Wassendorf, attempted suicide over the debacle with a gas hose to his car. Thousands of clients lost money when their claims were illegally put behind the counter-claims of other banks. Again, JPMorgan is in the mix – this time holding the Forex transactions. Segregated accounts were raided, the funds 'vaporized.' Someone got them, of course. All customer accounts were frozen. People could not access their own positions, except to do some selling.

It's happened before. The National Futures Association signed off on audits of Sentinel Management Group a few weeks before the firm failed in 2007. As people's assets had been rehypothecated, Bank of NY Mellon filed suit for $312 million to be paid before depository clients. The suit was settled in August, 2012, in favor of BNYM. The clients lost. The suit sets a pretty frightening precedent – financial firms in bankruptcy can use client funds to pay off their debts. They can legally post client money as collateral and mingle client funds in emergency situations. Barnhardt posted a strident appeal to people to get over their "normalcy bias…get your money out now!"

# Endnotes

| | |
|---|---|
| 1 | Aaron Task, "SEC Dropping Lehman Case: Where's the Outrage?", yahoo finance. May 25, /2012. |
| 2 | Many Wall Street executives says wrongdoing is necessary: survey. Reuters, July 10, 2012. |
| 3 | "The Rotten Heart of Finance", *The Economist*. July 7, 2012. |
| 4 | "The Big Losers in the Libor Manipulation", George Washington blog on zerohedge. July 3, 2012. |
| 5 | "Paul Craig Roberts on the Real Libor Scandal and Bond Market Armageddon",. Capital Account, Russia Today. July 16, 2012. |
| 6 | Bill Gross, "Beware Our Shadow Banking System", CNN Money, November 27, 2007. |
| 7 | Shadow Banking Economics and Policies, IMF. December 4, 2012. |
| 8 | "The Many Ways Banks commit Financial Fraud", George Washington Blog on zerohedge, July 3, 2012. |
| 9 | The Scam Wall St. Learned from the Mafia. Matt Taibbi. Rolling Stone. June 21, 2012. |
| 10 | Azam Ahmed, "JPMorgan's role in Power Market comes under Scrutiny", *The New York Times Dealbook*. July 3, 2012. |
| 11 | Rajeev Syal, "Drug money saved banks in global crisis, claims UN advisor", *Guardian* UK. December 13, 2009. |
| 12 | Ed Vulliamy, "How a big US bank laundered billions from Mexico's murderous drug gangs", *Guardian* UK. April 3, 2011. |
| 13 | Laura Marcinek, "Biggest U.S. Banks Curb Loans as Regional Firms Fill Gap". Bloomberg.com, June 26, 2012. |
| 14 | "77% of JPMorgan's Net Income Comes from Government Subsidies", Washington's Blog. July 1,/2012. |
| 15 | "Europe's Neo-Feudalism. Interview with Michael Hudson", Keiser Report, July 7,. 2011. |
| 16 | Jerome Corsi, "Whistleblower explains ABC's of Money Laundering", WND. February 23, 2012. |
| 17 | Jerome Corsi, "Banking Giant HSBC a 'criminal enterprise'", WND. May 8, 2012. |
| 18 | "JPMorgan complicit in Vatican Money Laundering.", Silverdoctors.com, July 6, 2012. |
| 19 | Bernie Madoff was not involved in the mortgage scandal. |
| 20 | "Countrywide whistleblower reveals rampant mortgage fraud – everyday business", fedupusa.com July, 2012. |
| 21 | Jim Pupluva, "Credit Crisis the Result of Greatest Financial Crime in World History", Silver Bear Café, September, 2011. |
| 22 | GAO audit of Federal Reserve, 2011. |
| 23 | Rob Kirby, "The Greatest Hoax ever Perpetrated on Mankind", June 17, 2012. |
| 24 | Tyler Durden, "The biggest financial company you have never heard of", June 10, 2009. |
| 25 | Tyler Durden, "MF Global collapse may have apocalyptic consequences", Zerohedge, December 2011. |
| 26 | Jim Willie, Hat Trick Letters, 2012-2013. |
| 27 | Dallas Federal Reserve Annual Report, 2011. |
| 28 | Orderly Liquidation of a Failed SIFI: JPMorgan Chase. Harvard Law School – confidential report, March 2012. |
| 29 | "Second act of JPM-CIO fiasco", Zeroedge.com, May 31, 2012 and Mark Mitchell, 2009 report. |
| 30 | Jim Willie, Hat Trick Letter, May, 2012. |
| 31 | Leverage can be calculated in a variety of different ways. Also, market conditions and company actions can drastically change it in short order. The essence of high leverage is sudden change in that leverage. |
| 32 | "Fed buying 61% of US debt", *Wall Street Journal*, March 28, 2012. |
| 33 | David Lucca and Emanuel Moench, "The Pre-FOMC Announcement 'Drift'",. Federal Reserve Bank of New York. July 11, 2012. |

34      Charles Duhigg, "Stock Traders find speed pays: in milliseconds," *The New YorkTimes.* July 23, 2009.

35      Mark Cuban: "High-Frequency Traders Are the Ultimate Hackers", *Wall Street Journal*, June 26, 2012.

36      Charles Hugh Smith, "A Common-sense View of the Stock Market", Of Two Minds website. August 10, 2012.

37      Brother John F., "Silver Update 80812 – Busted Trust", Youtube.

38      Hypothecation. Wikipedia.

39      Chris Elias, "MF Global and the great Wall St re-hypothecation scandal", Reuters. December 7, 2011.

40      Greg Smith, "Why I Am Leaving Goldman Sachs", *The New York Times* Opinion page. 3/14/2012.

41      Manmohan Singh and James Aitken, The (sizable) Role of Rehypothecation in the Shadow Banking System, IMF working paper 1072. 7/2010.

42      Yves Smith, "The Real Bombshell in the MF Global postmortem", Naked Capitalism, June 5, 2012.

43      Ann Barnhardt, "BCM has ceased operations", Barnhardt Capital Management. 11/17/11.

44      "MF Global Lawsuit puts Pressure on JPMorgan: Bullish signs for silver as Comex rehypothecation exposed", Silver Vigilante. June 5, 2012.

45      Jim Willie, "Exposure of Banker Corruption", July 5, 2012.

46      Kit Chellel, "MF Global's U.K. Administrator KPMG Says It Knows Where Clients' Money Is", Bloomberg. December 16, 2011.

47      Bankruptcy Abuse Prevention and Consumer Protection Act, 2005.

48      Karl Denninger, "Let's Make the Clawback Risk Real", Market Ticker. December 6, 2011.

49      Terry Duffy and Phupinder Gill, CME Group letter, July 23, 2012.

# 5

# PHYSICAL GOLD

Gold is called aurum in Latin and takes the periodical symbol, AU. Most pure metals are silver to white in color. Gold is one of the few with a yellow color. It is the 79th element, between platinum and mercury, with silver above and roentgenium below. The atomic weight is a beefy 196.96. It melts at 1064C and boils at 2856C. Gold is extremely stable chemically, but not inert. Nitric acid dissolves silver and other metals, but not gold. The expression 'acid test' means to test for gold with nitric acid.

Gold is the most ductile and malleable of all metals. One ounce can be stretched into a wire reaching 5 times the height of Everest or hammered into an 81 square meter sheet. It can be beaten thin enough to be transparent and the passing light is greenish-blue because it reflects yellow and red. It's useful in spacesuits because it reflects infrared. Most new gold supply goes into investment and jewelry. About 10% goes to industrial uses.

Precious metals are weighed in the Imperial Troy system, not the normal avoirdupois system. A troy pound is slightly less than a conventional pound and a troy ounce is slightly more than a conventional one – 1.09/1. Twelve troy ounces make a troy pound.

The alchemical symbol for gold was a circle with a dot - ☉ - the Chinese symbol for the sun. In an interesting connection, gold is thought to have been formed in supernovas because of its large atomic number. It was present in the early, molten earth where it sank to the center. Later, the crustal gold was brought up by asteroid impacts. If the theory is correct, the earth's core could contain many times the amount of surface gold.

The current value of all above-ground physical gold is about $7 trillion (at $1200/ounce). All the gold ever mined to date weighs 170,000 tons – 5 billion ounces. It would fit into a cube 20 meters on a side. It readily combines to make alloys, conducts heat and electricity extremely well, is lustrous and quite dense. A cubic meter weighs 19,300 kgs. The largest gold bar in the world is in the Toi museum of Japan and weighs 250 kgs.

One of the only metals found in nugget and flake forms, gold was probably the first metal discovered. Egypt was the first civilization to smelt it in 3600 BCE and in 1200 BCE they invented the lost wax technique which is still used for jewelry. In 610BCE, the Lydians (now Turkey) minted the first trade coins from electrum, a gold-silver alloy. The Chinese created a square gold coin in the same period, called a ying yuan. The Chinese currency is called the Yuan today. After conquering Persia, the Greeks took the gold hoard. Meanwhile, they began the practice of alchemy, trying to turn lead into gold. In 58 BCE, Julius Caesar paid off Roman debts with gold from the Gallic war, then instituted the first widespread gold-based currency. Hydraulic mining techniques greatly increased extraction rates. Fourteen hundred years later, King Ferdinand conquered South America to get its gold. The Aztecs valued it for its own sake, but found little utility in it, and called it 'excrement of the gods.'

Gold mining may be around 7000 years old. Methods are varied, but come down to two, hydraulic and rock. Hydraulic methods – panning, sluicing, rocker boxes and the like – run water through a sieve and separate out the gold. Rock mining supplies vastly more gold. It is underground mining and open pit. The largest gold mines are actually copper mines – gold comes as a byproduct. The main detrimental effect is the wide use of sodium cyanide to extract ore.

Gold is found in lode deposits dispersed in rock, and in alluvial deposits from hydraulic action. The oceans contain 15,000 tons of gold, but it is so evenly dispersed as to make extraction economically unrealistic. The alchemists were correct. Gold can indeed be synthesized. There are a number of methods, but all use either particle accelerators or nuclear reactors. The accelerator knocks protons out of liquid mercury, leaving gold and lower atomic weight metals. The reactor method leaves behind radioactive gold. Both methods create gold that is hundreds of times more expensive than natural gold.

A number of cities began or exploded from the search for gold. Johannesburg came into being due to the largest gold deposits ever found. San Francisco ballooned in the 1850s gold rush. The Yukon territory saw an amazing 100,000 people flood into it in the 19th century. The world's deepest mine is the South African TauTona, at 3777 meters. South Africa has produced 50% of all gold ever mined. In 2008, China overtook it as the world's largest gold producer.

Most gold mines have from 1-5 ppm gold. At least 30 ppm is required to be visible by the naked eye, so most gold in mines is not visible. The cost of mining gold was about $544/ounce in 2010, with a wide variation. Gold mine supply was 83,850,000 ounces in the same year. Supply is declining while price rises – a very telling phenomenon.

The problem is known as peak gold, and it applies to most extractable commodities, including oil. All the peaks are interconnected and impact the price in a number of ways. According to capitalist theory, an increase

**Figure 18**
**Forecasted world production from gold mining likely to decline**

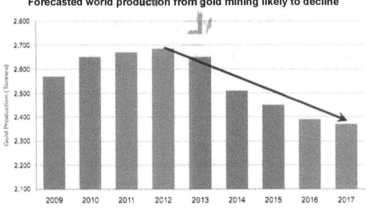

in demand will cause an increase in supply. But this fails to account for a decrease in the actual existence of a commodity. We seem to be hitting maximum extraction from our current methods. Open pit mining has become incredibly aggressive, with ore quality declining by around 90%. Ore grades were once 20 grams/ton. Now they are below two.

There are a number of methods to refine gold. The purest is the Wohlwill electrolysis process, but it is too complex to use in large scale. The Miller process is the most common and uses chlorine to dissolve and extract gold from the ore.

Gold gave rise to the very idea of money as a store of value and currency as a medium of exchange. By the 20th Century, every major country was on the gold standard, except China. Today, governments and central banks list 31,000 tons of gold on their books. Fort Knox, with atomic bomb proof vaults, 300 tanks and 30,000 soldiers guarding it, lists 4581 tons. The Federal Reserve Bank in New York has a vault on the bedrock 80 feet below Manhattan where 6718 tons are listed on the books. Some analysts question whether all the gold is actually there.

Gold is repeatedly invoked as a metaphor for good qualities and principles. The golden rule, golden mean, and golden ratio are philosophical symbols for ethics and mathematics. It represents love, compassion, integrity, justice, power, wealth, optimism and other good things. It is used for many prestigious awards – the gold medal, Nobel Prize, golden globes, emmies, etc. Crowns and wedding rings are gold – it symbolizes unbroken union, vows, and the spiritual element of commitments. Many positive expressions rely on gold – good as gold, golden boy, you're golden, and a heart of gold, for example. And of course, to central bankers, it is a "barbarous relic."

# 6

# CENTRAL BANKING
# AND THE FEDERAL RESERVE

*It is well enough that people of the nation do not understand*
*our banking and money system, for if they did, I believe*
*there would be a revolution before tomorrow morning*
—**Henry Ford, founder of the Ford Motor Company**

### Fed and US Central Banking History

The contentious history of the US engagement with central banking (CB) is not taught in public schools. That's unfortunate, because it explains a lot about the directions the country takes and certain features of the national mindset. The first attempted central bank was the Bank of North America, established in 1782 by the first Treasury Secretary, Alexander Hamilton. It ended three years later when the state of Pennsylvania revoked its charter for "alarming foreign influence and fictitious credit."[1] The public found that the bank was controlled by European interests.

Hamilton next created the First Bank of the United States, again with European backing. The fight was difficult. John Adams was against it. Much of the Revolutionary War was fought around issues of national sovereignty over the currency. A government-issued currency is built into the Constitution, which was ratified the same year as Hamilton's bank began operations. The First Bank was far more restricted than are today's. Its charter was for only 20 years. It was forbidden to buy US bonds or issue currency/incur debt greater than its capital. It was not a public bank, as its name might suggest, but a private for-profit corporation. Inflation was 72% during its first five years, creating broad spread alarm.

Thomas Jefferson hated it. "I believe that banking institutions are more dangerous to our liberties than standing armies,"[2] he said. An elegant misattribution has frequently been appended to this:

> If the American people ever allow private banks to control
> the issue of their currency, first by inflation, then by deflation,
> the banks and corporations that will grow up around [the

banks] will deprive the people of all property until their
children wake-up homeless on the continent their fathers
conquered.

Jefferson and Madison insisted, on Constitutional grounds, that the
government should issue coined money and not bills. They also objected to the
centralization of power and loss of trade for the states. But Jefferson primarily
objected to Hamilton, whom he saw as a venal power grabber. "Hamilton's
financial system had two objects ... to exclude popular understanding ...and
as a machine for the corruption of the legislature."[3] Hamilton won and his
central bank was established. When the charter expired in 1811, however, it
was not renewed.

The bankers did not give up. The Second Bank of the United States was
chartered in 1816, predicated upon the War of 1812, and the resultant debt and
inflation. The bank was known to be corrupt and used its power for gain over
non-chartered banks. The bank became grievously overextended by issuing
credit far beyond its capital. A boom period led to a real estate bubble, oddly
similar to recent history.

The Second Bank also functioned as a commercial bank, giving it a gross
advantage over competitors. All federal funds were deposited there, so its
working capital was multiples that of any other bank. It did not set monetary
policy or regulate the banking system, and it did not have a monopoly on
bank-notes – luxuries the modern Federal Reserve possesses. However, the
federal government would only accept Second Bank-notes for payment of
taxes. It was also exempted from all state taxes. Like the previous two banks,
the majority of stock was owned by foreigners.

The director during whose tenure the bubble arose was sent packing. His
replacement chose to shrink the money supply by calling in loans, causing a
collapse in real estate. He also cashed in many state bank notes for their gold,
putting them out of business. A depression ensued.

Nicholas Biddle took the reins and managed it more skillfully. A period
of national prosperity followed. However, the bank grew too big and began
creating de facto monetary policy. It was able to restrict economic growth by
pulling gold and silver away from smaller banks.

Enter Andrew Jackson and his War on the Bank. Jackson had lost a lot
of money when the backer of paper currency he received on a land deal went
bankrupt. He liked specie – gold and silver coins. He didn't like paper money,
he didn't like credit, and he definitely didn't like the Second Bank of the
United States. "You are a den of vipers and thieves," he told them. "I intend
to rout you out, and by the eternal God, I will rout you out."[4] For Jackson, the
bank's centralized power destroyed states' rights, and was unregulated. The
unique privilege of the institution led to inflation.

In 1830, a senator and the US paymaster dueled to the death over the issue. When Senator Pettis verbally abused the bank president, Biddle's brother (the paymaster) attacked him in a hotel bed while ill. Pettis challenged and Biddle accepted. They dueled on Bloody Island, Illinois on August 27 at short range. Both died from the wounds in days.[5]

When the charter went up for renewal in 1832, four years before expiry, Jackson vetoed it. He went on the offensive, ordering all federal funds withdrawn from the bank. He had to replace the Treasury Secretary twice before Roger Taney would actually remove the funds. Congress never confirmed his appointment, but Taney went ahead with his job. Jackson deposited the money with various state banks in an attempt to strengthen and broaden local economies and decentralize power. Accused of monarchical tendencies by the wealthy, Jackson was actually the father of populism.

Richard Lawrence tried to assassinate Jackson because of his war on the bank. He thought that Jackson's war had dried up the money supply and led to the loss of his job. (Later, Lawrence claimed to be Richard 3rd and was institutionalized as insane.) Because both of Lawrence's pistols misfired (and were proved to be in good working order), the incident was mythologized into an Act of Providence – Jackson's war on the bank was divinely protected.

As a union of soft and hard money advocates, the coalition that arose against the Second Bank is relevant. Both groups were united against excess federal power, but agrarian and working class citizens mistrusted banks and paper currency. On the other hand, soft money speculators wanted state banks to have greater ability to issue currency. They wanted a laissez-faire, unregulated economy, and the Second Bank was in the way, with de facto regulations. The two forces were tactically united against a common enemy, but divergent in monetary policy. Ironically, the long victory fell to the soft money advocates. Private state banks were more freely allowed to issue their own currency.

Despite serious opposition, Jackson won. The Congress voted not to renew the charter in 1834, based on Jackson's popularity due to this issue. The bank became a standard bank, then failed in 1841.[6] Jackson made the bank war a national cause. To this day, he's still a hero to many in the sound money community.

From 1837-62, only state banks were allowed, leading to a 30-fold increase. Their notes had to be backed by some percent of specie. They circulated below face value and were short-lived, five years on average. This wildcat banking dominated the 'free banking' era.

The Civil War led to creation of the National Banking Act. National banks had higher standards and reserve requirements. They were required to accept each other's notes at par. They also had to purchase government Treasuries. This funded the ballooning war debt. The number of national banks surged to 1500.

In 1881, President James A. Garfield said, "Whoever controls the volume of money in our country is absolute master of all industry and commerce ... and when you realize that the entire system is very easily controlled, one way or another, by a few powerful men at the top, you will not have to be told how periods of inflation and depression originate." Two weeks later, he was assassinated.

Not long after, Democratic candidate, William Jennings Bryan, gave his famous Cross of Gold speech, igniting public anger against the bankers. "The money power denounces as public enemies," he said, "all who question its methods or throw light upon its crimes." The Wizard of Oz was a thinly veiled allegory about the national debate.

Banking and liquidity conditions led to the panic of 1907. That year, a speculative environment prevailed. Bucket shops churned through junk stock. A number of banks funded a bid to take over United Copper. When the bid failed, there was a run on the banks. Regional banks withdrew funds from the New York ones. The large Knickerbocker Trust went bankrupt and the contagion really struck, causing a 50% drop in the stock market. Though J.P. Morgan is historically credited with saving the day by providing the banks with needed liquidity at interest, not everyone agrees with this version.

Upton Sinclair's *The Money Changers* was a roman a clef, a novel with real people disguised as characters. The banker, Waterman, stands in for Morgan. People loved Waterman for his largesse, but he was actually loaning interest-free government money for personal profit. Waterman caused the bank run by creating then sabotaging a huge, interlocking deal which he knew would cause a panic run. Waterman's bank then paid for the government they wanted, using profits to place their people in the Treasury. Today it's called 'regulatory capture,' when an industry controls the governmental oversight body. When these industries hit the wall, the Treasury would bail them out with government funds. But meanwhile, businesses closed, millions lost employment, and a severe contraction followed.[7] Sinclair's story-line captured the fate of many people. The crisis had been deliberately manufactured for private empire-building by James Pierpont Morgan.

The bankers used the panic of 1907 as a pretext for reinstating a central bank. The public was extremely resistant. George Earle gave voice to the general opinion. Central banks were bad policy because they destroyed freedom. In the beginning, such 'dictatorial powers' worked well and could offer great benefit. But in the long run, centralization of power moved to selfish ends.[8]

G. Edward Griffin exposes the Fed in his 1987 book. He calls the Fed a failure and a deception. The value of the dollar has fallen 97% since the creation – hardly protecting the value of the money. It's a cartel with abusive pricing and unfair taxation to benefit the elites rather than the public purse.

It's a totalitarian organization, Griffin charges, which promotes wars and destabilizes the economy.[9]

In 1913, the bankers won a victory that is now a hundred years old, the passage of the Federal Reserve Act. It was done in the most devious manner: at the close of the season, in a special session announced after most of the Congress had left for home over Christmas. Only a few members attended the session, which lasted from 1:30am to 4:30am. All those present during this clandestine session voted in favor of the Act.

Jekyll Island is now infamous in sound money circles as the birthplace of the Federal Reserve. In 1910, emissaries from the US's most powerful banks took a late night journey on a private railcar to the island. Senator Nelson Aldrich, head of the National Monetary Commission, joined them. The meeting was totally secretive – no one's last name was mentioned in order to keep the serving staff in ignorance. Warburg, Strong, Vanderlip and Aldrich were there, but their last names were not. The meeting was in response to the public outcry for monetary reform. The bankers' strategic plan was to create an illusion of public service with a radically different underlying reality.

Bankers were in awful repute. No reform bill drafted by them had a hope of passing Congress. As central banks were not wanted by the public, their creation was named the Federal Reserve System, as if it were a public entity. It was (and still is) owned by private corporations who profit from it. The President appoints the Board of Governors, but the 'Advisory Council' exerts tremendous power, possibly even decision making authority. Those Council members are not revealed.

Congress has the Constitutional power 'to coin money and regulate the value,' so the Federal Reserve is not really constitutional. Congress has regular meetings with the Governors, but has no legal authority over them. Congress can only question and try to expose their actions. In the years before passage of the Fed, five million dollars from the banks was spent on propaganda efforts to 'educate the people' through a consortium of professors. The Aldrich plan and the Federal Reserve Act were presented as opposing measures, but they were not really different. The eventual plan was the Federal Reserve Act. A series of dog and pony shows were put up to make the public believe that Congress was protecting their interests, but the Act placed the issue and control of US currency into private hands.

The true leadership of the Federal Reserve was addressed by historian Eustace Mullins. The Board of Governors meets four times per year with the 'Advisory Council,' selected strictly by the bankers, whose members remain anonymous. Their council is 'non-binding,' but the entire premise of the system was secret control. The power structure was cloaked in the boring dress of administrative tedium, the verbiage designed to put people to sleep. But Charles Lindbergh saw it more transparently. "The Federal Reserve Board and the Federal Advisory Council administer the Federal Reserve System as its head authority, and no one of the lesser officials, even if they wished, would dare to cross swords with them."[10]

Woodrow Wilson, the sitting President at the creation, was only allowed one appointment to the Board of Governors of the Fed. Wilson, it seems, was an able politician in certain regards, but a novice in economics. He fully supported the inception of the Federal Reserve, and paid a heavy personal price for that act. His ubiquitous quote is included here because of its importance.

> The growth of the nation, therefore, and all our activities are in the hands of a few men. We have come to be one of the worst ruled, one of the most completely controlled and dominated Governments in the civilized world – no longer a Government by free opinion, no longer a Government by conviction and the vote of the majority, but a Government by the opinion and duress of a small group of dominant men... Some of the biggest men in the United States, in the field of commerce and manufacture, are afraid of somebody, are afraid of something. They know that there is a power somewhere so organized, so subtle, so watchful, so interlocked, so complete, so pervasive, that they had better not speak above their breath when they speak in condemnation of it.[11]

Wilson openly acknowledged that US democracy is dead and the system fell to a monetary tyranny.

During the 1920s, the Fed expanded the money supply by 60%. Margin loans for speculation were encouraged. Then the banks called in huge numbers of margin loans in October, 1929. No one knows why, but the coordinated activity was a boon for the top banks – especially JPMorgan. Speculators were forced to sell to cover them, taking losses in a cascading pattern. The bankers cleaned up, buying the distress price stock. The Fed contracted the money supply by $8 billion, an enormous amount during this time.[12] Ben Bernanke even acknowledged that Fed activity caused the Depression by sharply contracting the monetary system.

It's not much of a secret anymore that the Federal Reserve is a private corporation, owned by member banks. The President appoints the Board of the Fed, but it's for a 14 year term and he gets a short-list of nominees to appoint from – the list is only one person long for each appointment. By this little ruse, they claim that the Fed is a 'quasi-public institution.' Three years after its creation, the first federal income tax and the IRS came into being. It is responsible for issuing the nation's base money supply and for regulating the bank's expansion of that money. The Fed also sets interest rates. Part of its mandate is to control inflation and prevent economic volatility. Given the situation outlined in the opening chapters above, its success in either is highly doubtful. The dollar has lost 97% of its value since the Fed arrived.

The Fed makes its public/private status deliberately opaque. In media statements and the like, representatives imply that it is a governmental agency without saying so outright, to avoid blatant lying. However, the litmus test for truth is in court, where perjury is a serious offence. "Each stock is owned by the member banks, 100% privately," senior Fed council, Yvonne Mizusawa, testified in federal court.[13] Bloomberg exposed more details of the charade. "While the Fed's Washington-based Board of Governors is a federal agency subject to the Freedom of Information Act and other government rules, the New York Fed and other regional banks maintain they are separate institutions, owned by their member banks, and not subject to federal restrictions."[14] While the Fed has a Board of Governors, which is part of the government, the private advisory council really pulls the strings. The status is critical for many reasons. Bloomberg went to court for information about the enormous loans made by the Fed during the 2008 crisis. The Fed claimed that Freedom of Information Act requests were not relevant to their operations because they were not a government entity. Since this body controls the US (and world reserve) currency, the information affects not just every American, but every nation on the globe. Their actions matter a great deal and, many argue, transparency with such a mighty power should be mandatory in a nation which purports to be a democracy.

That secrecy-in-the-open is an integral part of central bank operations. Even as head of the House Committee on Finance, Ron Paul said he could find out more about CIA operations than about Federal Reserve operations.[15] To follow central banker speak is an act of unspeakable tedium and an exercise in jargon-laden esoterica. The Bank for International Settlements (BIS), for example, is the Central Bank of central banks. Though it assumes global regulatory status, the BIS is solely owned by the Federal Reserve and the Banks of England, Switzerland, Italy, Holland, Germany, and France. Hardly anyone knows this information or precisely why the BIS exists or what it does. But the question, as always, is 'who controls who?' It's almost impossible to tell who is in charge. The BIS is intended to consolidate the various central bank powers and bring them into a unified focus of activity to promote their owners' best interests. Of course, a self-regulating industry cannot be forced to serve the public good. The BIS is immune from any taxes, from the oversight of any governments, and its members enjoy a very high diplomatic immunity in most nations.[16] They are above the law.

While it might be valid to say that the Federal Reserve is a private corporation and not part of government, it could also be said that it is the actual government, while elected officials are merely the public display of that government. Most politicians are not in power to serve the public good. They are there because they crave power. Real power deploys a twofold methodology of carrot and stick or guns and gold. Dominion stems from force or capital. Capital is the more powerful for a simple reason – soldiers must be paid. And soldiers cannot take over capital, since they haven't the slightest idea of how to manage it or how it works. Capital is the true power. The Fed and other central banks have total control over the issue of financial capital.

Looking at it from a historic perspective, gold and monetary historian Ferdinand Lipps claims that the two most damaging events of the 20th Century were the creation of the Federal Reserve and the abandonment of the gold standard. A gold standard, he explained, enforced fiscal discipline. A profligate nation would find its gold shipped out to balance its trade deficit. Gold creates a stable monetary value. If prices rise, gold leaves the country. With less money, prices decline and gold returns. The balance is kept. The people love gold; politicians hate it. They must live within their means.

The Byzantine Empire had 800 stable years as the center of global trade under a gold standard. There was no monetary devaluation and no mass debt. The 19th century saw relative peace, stable currencies, and growth without inflation. The 20th has seen steady long-term inflation, many individual hyperinflations, the worst wars in history, genocides, mass starvation, enormous slums and "ultimately, the decline of civilization." The gold exchange standard introduced in 1922 led to an immediate inflation – because it allowed reserves to be in dollars, pounds, or Swiss Francs as well as gold. Thus the reserves no longer held their value. The looseness of the gold exchange standard (versus a true gold standard) allowed for the sloshing liquidity and boom that crashed the global economy in 1929.

When Nixon abandoned the gold-dollar exchange once again in 1971, all bets were off. Military adventurism was no longer restricted. A gold standard would have made the many subsequent US wars impossible, curtailing its ability to finance them. Instead, the global economy funds US debt enabling the US to conduct wars to retain its hegemony over it.

Lipps contends that gold is under assault by money powers,, showing how gold rises in Europe and every day is smacked down at the market open. Gold is not an asset for speculation, Lipps argues, but a 'political metal.' As it is in absolute conflict with profligate money creation, it must be kept down to sustain the fiat currency cartel. A serious and fast rise in the price would threaten the entire foundation. Since it cannot be pushed down indefinitely, the cartel is trying to control the speed of its rise, to prevent a breakout.

There is a worldwide war of monetary devaluation with a huge printing spree being undertaken by all countries against a backdrop of a moribund dollar and bankrupt United States. Negative real interest rates and a casino stock market are worsened by mountains of debt and the disappearance of central bank gold. The middle class is being destroyed by the monetary ruin, the wealth divide is going to unbelievable levels and political turmoil is rocking the world. A Kondratieff winter – global economic decline – is setting in. As Lipps puts it, there are "subtle relationships between freedom, money, intellect, war, peace and gold." Behavior was better, more honest, under a gold standard, because the monetary system was honest. It enforced a better moral compass. With no limits on government expansion or behavior, with no limits on monetary excesses and greed, morality is disappearing and that – unlike the infamous tax cut pretext – is indeed having a drip-down effect. In fact, a moral man works against himself in a corrupt system. The police state, the welfare to forestall starvation or revolution (not necessarily in that order), the massive financial graft – none of these are possible under a gold standard. For Lipps, an ethical money leads to an ethical people.[17]

In 1933, Congressman Louis T. McFadden brought formal charges against the Board of Governors for the Federal Reserve on behalf of the American people, charging it with the criminal acts of conspiracy, fraud, unlawful conversion, and treason. It addressed how the Federal Reserve had fooled the American people into thinking it was a government institution when it was, in fact, a private one. He laid the "foisting of the 12 private credit monopolies" at the feet of European bankers. McFadden survived two assassination attempts before dying of intestinal flu.

Here's what the Fed's website says it is:

> The Federal Reserve System is not "owned" by anyone and is not a private, profit-making institution. Instead, it is an independent entity within the government, having both public purposes and private aspects.
>
> As the nation's central bank, the Federal Reserve derives its authority from the U.S. Congress. It is considered an independent central bank because its decisions do not have to be ratified by the President or anyone else in the executive or legislative branch of government, it does not receive funding appropriated by Congress, and the terms of the members of the Board of Governors span multiple presidential and congressional terms. However, the Federal Reserve is subject to oversight by Congress, which periodically reviews its activities and can alter its responsibilities by statute. Also, the Federal Reserve must work within the framework of the overall objectives of economic and financial policy established by the government. Therefore, the Federal Reserve can be more accurately described as "independent within the government."
>
> The twelve regional Federal Reserve Banks, which

were established by Congress as the operating arms of the nation's central banking system, are organized much like private corporations--possibly leading to some confusion about "ownership." For example, the Reserve Banks issue shares of stock to member banks. However, owning Reserve Bank stock is quite different from owning stock in a private company. The Reserve Banks are not operated for profit, and ownership of a certain amount of stock is, by law, a condition of membership in the System. The stock may not be sold, traded, or pledged as security for a loan; dividends are, by law, 6 percent per year.

The Fed's website description carries on for twenty tedious pages, yet no mention is ever made of its actual ownership – only a denial of such. A somewhat typical opposing view is as follows:

Although the Federal Reserve Bank claims not to be private as their website claims, they clearly operate under terms that no other "government institution" operates by. For example, they are not required to submit financial information and are not subject to IRS audits, nor do they even publish the amount of money they print to the American public. So given these terms it's hard to believe the Federal Reserve's claims that they are a government institution providing a genuine service to the American people. A commonly held position not mentioned on their website is that The FED is a privately owned central bank. Central banks are supposed to implement a country's fiscal policies. They monitor commercial banks to ensure that they maintain sufficient assets, like cash, so as to remain solvent and stable. Central banks also do business, such as currency exchanges and gold transactions, with other central banks. In theory, a central bank should be good for a country, and they might be if it wasn't for the fact that they are not owned or controlled by the government of the country they are serving. Private central banks, including the United States FED, operate not in the interest of the public good but for profit.

The FED is the only for-profit corporation in America that is exempt from both federal and state taxes. The FED takes in about one trillion dollars per year tax free! The banking families listed above get all that money. Forty cents in every dollar of US taxes.[18]

The New York Fed is owned by foreign interests, some say. Being the most powerful branch by far, New York sets monetary policy for the country, so the claim is doubly serious. The Fed's power is incredible. If it is owned by foreign interests, then it amounts to a loss of sovereignty over the US currency – more or less a stealth conquest. But do the claims have any merit?

It's not possible to ascertain ownership of the Federal Reserve Bank of NY. It is a corporation, but not publicly traded. Shares are not transmissible. The SEC does not have oversight and has no power to compel the organization to reveal its ownership. However, to become a nationally chartered bank requires ownership of Fed stock within the home region. There are eight particular NY banks which must own stock by this criteria and which hold a strong authority within the central branch. However, the voting authority is not parceled out by amount of stock owned. All member banks get a single vote. The Fed is also somewhat distributed (on paper) as to its national powers. This makes it theoretically difficult for NY to control the entire works. However, the Fed is notoriously secretive. Ownership should be a matter of public record, but it is hidden. In a common critique, the NY Fed actually controls Fed activity and policy, but regional branches are created to give the illusion of a dispersed authority. These regional branches can (and have) sorely criticized Fed actions, but they do seem powerless to affect them in any significant way.

Dean Henderson put in a FOIA request to find out who the top stock-holders of the major banks are. His request was denied due to 'national security concerns.' According to researcher J. W. McCallister, eight families own 80% of the New York Fed – the real Fed. The families are the Goldman Sachs, Lehman, Rockefeller, Kuhn-Loeb (all in NY), Lazar, Warburg, Rothschild, and Israel Moses Saif families (all in Europe). These same families, through their banks, control most major global industries – oil, insurance, electronics, and food production.[19] The commercial banks nominally own the Fed, but have little direct authority, irrespective of their ostensible voting powers. Who does own it? No one has ever found out. Congressmen Wright, Patman and McFadden failed. In a legal finding, however, it was confirmed that "the Reserve Banks are not federal instrumentalities ... but are independent, privately owned and locally controlled corporations."[20]

Suppression of criticism is not unheard of, either. In 1955, German agents seized and burned 10,000 copies of Eustace Mullins translated book, *The Federal Reserve Conspiracy*. Why they did so remains unexplained to this day.

The Fed's public mandate is stable prices and maximum employment. Some claim a super-ordinate mandate – to protect the banking cabal. This seems probable since the Fed is owned and operated by its member banks. If their viability is threatened by fulfilling the official mandate – which mission will win? Will the banks commit seppuku to save the real economy? Unlikely. Since the Fed's inception, the dollar has declined over 95%, the economy

Figure 19
Declining Value of the U.S. Dollar (USD)

has seen a series of booms, busts, crashes, asset bubbles, and bank runs that almost never happened under a gold standard, and unemployment has been far greater, as well, culminating in the nosebleed rates happening today – if one looks under the hood of the manipulated jobs reports.[21]

The entire operation is said to be illegal by many analysts because fiat money may be unconstitutional. Article 1, Section 10 says "no state shall make anything but gold and silver coin a tender in payment of debts." The Constitution also gives any rights not enumerated to the states, not the Federal government. The government is not granted the right to issue or mandate unbacked fiat currency. Federal Reserve notes are unconstitutional. They should probably be illegal, but this has never been tested in court.

The secrecy and power-lust stems in part from Montagu Norman. This unusual man controlled the Bank of England as Governor for 24 consecutive years (1920-44) and was called the currency dictator of Europe by the Wall Street Journal. He despised democracy and governments in general, feeling them a menace to private banking. He was prone to extreme paranoia which he held in abeyance, but it colored his outlook profoundly. He thought of his life as a secretive, undercover operation against the army of sound money advocates. He traveled tens of thousands of miles every year in disguise as 'Professor Skinner.' He presided over the steep decline of British monetary power, seeing it moved to Basel, Switzerland. There, he felt, private banking was beyond the reach of government interference. The creation of the Federal Reserve just prior to this allowed Norman to ally with Benjamin Strong, the first head of the Federal Reserve. That said, the two men were not, themselves, the real power – they were merely agents of the powerful private bankers.

Carroll Quigley, a Georgetown history professor, wrote an insightful expose of the Federal Reserve and the surrounding cartel called *Tragedy and Hope*. Feudal economic history has gone through multiple stages beginning with agrarian feudalism where concentrated aristocratic wealth led to trade. Commercial capitalism marked the second stage. Demand increased and better production led to industrial capitalism. Profits increased and financial capitalism arose from the expansion ability. This led to cartels in the fifth stage, monopoly capitalism. The privileged sought to retain and expand their privately owned power, while the public attempted to use the government to curtail that power. Each stage is accompanied by a depression because the old powerful interests try to retain power at the cost of suppressing the general wealth and the new system.

Because of the powerful tie of self-interest to economic activity, Quigley continues, capitalism tends to fracture itself. It may benefit or harm society, depending on the approaches, aims, and methods of the participants. This led to a fractionation of the various groups into merchants, traders, consumers, labor and bankers. The first activities were open and obvious, but monetary movements were not so. Bankers' interests moved in opposition to the rest of society and they enhanced this opacity to deliberately mystify the public. Indeed, they used it to very destructive, though profitable effect:

> By the middle of the stage of financial capitalism, however, the organization of financial capitalism had evolved to a highly sophisticated level of security promotion and speculation which did not require any productive investment as a basis. Corporations were built upon corporations in the form of holding companies, so that securities were issued in huge quantities, bringing profitable fees and commissions to financial capitalists without any increase in economic production whatever.
>
> Indeed, these financial capitalists discovered that they could not only make killings out of the issuing of such securities, they could also make killings out of the bankruptcy of such corporations, through the fees and commissions of reorganization. A very pleasant cycle of flotation, bankruptcy, flotation, bankruptcy began to be practiced by these financial capitalists. The more excessive the flotation, the greater the profits, and the more imminent the bankruptcy. The more frequent the bankruptcy, the greater the profits of reorganization and the sooner the opportunity of another excessive flotation with its accompanying profits.[22]

Written in 1975, the above describes the events of recent years quite accurately: finance capitalism was already off in a world of its own, with its own modes of operation and rewards divorced from or even antithetical to real production. Over the centuries, this broader evolution of capitalism led to fractional reserve banking and ultimately to central banking, via the route of financial capitalism. The Rothschild dynasty, able to move monarchies, sat at the pinnacle of this movement with the house of Morgan, a late-comer, in second place. These dynasties had modern characteristics, separating them clearly from industrialists. They were international, integrated into government, vested into bonds and not commodities, devoted to sound money (at first) in the form of a gold standard, and highly secretive in their operations and government influence.

Their relation to sound money is very interesting. The bankers lent money as gold in the form of certificates. They disliked inflation as it reduced the value of the money lent out. Their loans thus had lower value at collection. In a deflation, the loans increased in value. But deflation is a powerful force – it provides a huge disincentive to producers, so the bankers could not deflate willy-nilly. They only used it to consolidate power – buying distressed properties cheaply. They had a difficult conundrum to face, however: their practice of loaning money out was inherently inflationary. In order to do business, they had to push the system in the opposite direction than they desired. But without loaning money out, they would have no income.

So the bankers convinced business and government of two key axioms. They were: 1) money had to be based on gold, and 2) politicians could not be trusted with issuance of the currency so bankers were thus the logical choice to control the currency system. "It was necessary to conceal," Quigley continues, "or even to mislead, both governments and people about the nature of money and its methods of operation." The bankers actively sought, as a policy, control over their respective governments through currency control mechanisms – especially the government bond markets. Economic favors and financial backing in politics were highly useful, as well. Of course, they still are.

History cannot be understood without an understanding of money and how it is created. This is the brute fact of central banking. For centuries, the scam has been to create a powerful central bank, then control it through seemingly subservient, private investment banks. These family banks mostly converted to public, share-issuing banks in the mid-twentieth century for reasons of liability protection. Morgan, Rockefeller, Lazard and so forth did so – only the super-secretive Rothschild bank remained private. This relieved them of the requirement to issue financial disclosures to the public.

These men, Quigley found, aimed "to create a world system of financial control in private hands able to dominate the political system of each country and the economy of the world as a whole. This system was to be controlled in a feudalist fashion by the central banks of the world acting in concert by secret agreements arrived at in frequent private meetings and conferences. The apex of the system was to be the Bank for International Settlements in Basel, Switzerland, a private bank owned and controlled by the world's central banks which were themselves private corporations."[23]

## World Central Bank History

> *Minting money and creating currency must be*
> *the sole monopoly and right of the Governor.*
> *Therein lies all power.*
> — Po-Chu-I (Chinese sage, 9th century)

Sir Josiah Stamp was president of the Bank of England in the 1920s and the second richest man in Britain. "Banking was conceived in iniquity," he famously said, "and was born in sin. The Bankers own the Earth. Take it away from them, but leave them the power to create deposits, and with the flick of the pen, they will create enough deposits to buy it back again. However, take it away from them, and all the great fortunes like mine will disappear, and they ought to disappear, for this would be a happier and better world to live in. But if you wish to remain the slaves of Bankers, and pay the cost of your own slavery, let them continue to create deposits."[24]

Central banking hails back to 1649 when Netherlands Central Bank financed Oliver Cromwell's brutal and repressive takeover of England. Cromwell fell to Charles II, but he in turn fell to another banker puppet, William of Orange. William issued a Royal Charter for the Bank of England to his backers and borrowed a newly existing "national debt" of £1.25 million. The supportive bankers also received the immense power to collect taxes from the citizens in order to pay that debt. Private goldsmiths were compelled to store their gold in BoE vaults and were no longer allowed to make gold certificates. Et voila: the Central Bank was born. Bankers now had government sanctioned monopoly control over currency.

Analyst Eustace Mullins goes deeper and connects it to the Rothschilds in particular.[25] When the economy collapsed in 1857, Rothschild Bank rescued a single company, the slave trader, Peabody and Co., for a million pounds, perhaps more – around half a billion today. This was not a business loan – it was a buyout. Rothschild owned the company, in essence if not fact. It bought securities for pennies on the dollar, then watched the market climb back up. Peabody's successor was Junius S. Morgan, father of the man himself. The name Peabody and Co. was changed to Junius S. Morgan in 1871 and to J.P. Morgan in 1895.

The Rothschild connection is interesting, for it's considered a story of power-lust without any regard for ethics. It's also important for this book, because Mayer Rothschild dictated the ideology of modern banking in 1773. Mayer Amschel Bauer was a Frankfurt goldsmith. He changed his name to Rothschild in reference to the red shield marking his place of business.

Not all of the history that far back is verifiable, but certain aspects are quite credible. Rothschild called together other powerful goldsmiths. He convinced them that by banding together, they could steadily gain control over world finances. What follows is a condensed version of William Carr's list of points as read by Mayer Amschel Rothschild. It's included here not because it's thoroughly verified, but because it provides a simple ideological framework for a Machiavellian control of global finances. It would work, if implemented skillfully, and it informs much of the actions of bankers that extend to this day.

1) Law is merely force that is hidden, thus nature teaches that power is right. No other ethics exist.
2) Political liberty is a concept, not a reality. By promoting 'Liberalism' the public would gladly give up freedom for a false ideal.
3) Gold had superseded the might of monarchies. Rulers had to have capital – and that was the real power wielded by the goldsmiths, collectively. By manipulating the visible powers, they could rule in secret through financial means.
4) Ethical rulers should be displaced because ethics was a lack of ability, leading to weakness. Therefore, any means was permissible to attain as much power as possible.
5) Right comes from power. Morality is merely an abstraction.
6) Secrecy is paramount. The methods, actions, wealth and connections must not be known by the public until the bankers' power became invincible.

Mayer Rothschild did exist of course, and his heirs did amass incredible power. The remainder of the Rothschild history is fairly well established. The bank of Rothschild is an actual bank and to this day has massive holdings, deep ties to all major markets and broad government penetration. Because the bank is a private company, it has no obligation to disclose holdings or financial status. No one knows how much they own or what they do.

By the next generation, Nathan Mayer became the wealthiest man on Earth – perhaps in history, with a net worth equivalent to almost half a trillion dollars today.[26] Brother James amassed a 600 million franc fortune. Only Louis XIV was wealthier and not by too much. James had £150 million more than all European bankers combined. The name Rothschild meant power. It was a lesson well-taught by Mayer Rothschild to his offspring – money's function as a medium of exchange or store of value was not its primary one. Mayer discovered a profound truth that today eludes most of the masses. Money is the best tool for political control. And the greatest power of that tool lay in the ability to create and enforce acceptance of a currency. The power belonged to the Rothschild dynasty through the Bank of England.

Still that power was in its early years. Citizens were aware of the potential abuses of it. The Bullionist Controversy, a forgotten but pivotal point in the early history of the Gold Wars, was the first real test of banker power. In 1797, fear of French armies landing on the shore of England prompted a bank run. People withdrew gold until an emergency edict disallowed 'for a period of one month' removal of specie from the Bank of England. That month lasted 24 years.

The central bank was in a long cold war with the regional ones. Most banks provided full convertibility, but before a 1765 law prohibiting it, Scottish banks had a suspension clause to prevent an assault by cartels on their gold. In a fractional reserve system, a large cartel can (and often did) accumulate a large stock of a bank's notes, then cash them at once. Any bank without full ability to convert would become insolvent and declare bankruptcy. The Scottish policy prevented this. The attendant events demonstrated two things: banks can be viciously predatory and gold was the make or break asset. This is another reason banks have tried mightily to dismiss it from the financial system.

At this time the BoE was not officially a central bank. Its position made it a de facto one, however. Monetary theory was woefully behind monetary mechanics. There was no understanding of flexible exchange rates versus commodity money, or central bank to standard bank interrelations.

The Bullionist Controversy years saw two periods of high inflation and a consequent debate about restoring currency convertibility into gold. At the time, there was no such thing as a consumer price index. Inflation was based on general public sentiment about rising prices, taking into account some factors like wheat, gold price, and the exchange rate. A pamphlet by a businessman explained the issue to the general public – over-issue of notes was the problem and it led to inflation. Convertibility into gold checked the bank's self-interested desire to over-issue. This was called the Bullionist position.

Anti-bullionism (BoE defenders) arose quickly. They explained the problems as due to a poor wheat crop driving up prices through imports and forcing down the exchange rate by extra imports. Their second cause was payment of subsidies to allies in the war against France. These explanations became stock-in-trade defenses. Later, they would be groomed into more sophisticated forms and given the names "cost-push inflation," and "the transfer problem." Next, they blamed the over-issue of notes on the country banks. Finally and most importantly, they put forth the Real Bills doctrine of proper monetary policy.

Real Bills was a method of cash flow. When a debtor owed money to a creditor, the creditor could get advance money, at a discount, from the bank. The bank later collected from the debtor and, for the service of the advance, took its cut. Hence the discount in the advance from the principal. (Example: A owes B $100 in October. B gets immediate $95 loan from bank. Bank collects $100 from A in October.) Then the process repeats and occurs throughout the economy. Defenders of the BoE claimed that the bank operated quite strictly in this fashion. Since the supply and demand were both there, the bank merely facilitated cash flow. Therefore it could have no possible impact on inflation. This core defense has been used again and again and is still put forward in more convoluted from today. It is the primary pledge of bankers – 'we only serve the needs of the greater economy.'

The Bullionist response came from banker, Member of Parliament, and anti-slavery crusader Henry Thornton.[27] Thornton's work was a masterpiece of economics, easily transcending all other documents in the Bullionist controversy. Oddly, it supported the BoE position post-1797, but took a definitive Bullionist stance. It laid out arguments that still live in the gold standard debate. He agreed with the bad harvests and the balance of payments problems of the anti-Bullionists. Then he put forward a ream of well-constructed procedures, including means of tightening credit and reserves, as the way to suspend specie payment without incurring inflation. The country banks creating inflation argument was well-refuted. Any over-issuance leading to inflation could come only from BoE.

The BoE, he explained, would have to suffer through a gold drain from a temporary balance of payments problem, knowing it would be corrected later. Further, the bank should exert more credit into the economy, strengthening the flow of business without suspending convertibility into gold. This would force the bank to have quite high reserves, as there would be a foreign drawdown and an expanded credit supply, but that was why a central bank existed. Stability was its function and it had to operate by a much higher standard than a typical bank. He did hedge and defend the bank's actions in suspending payments in this particular case, but only on a temporary basis.

Thornton's middle road approach ended at a discussion of the Real Bills doctrine, which he tore to shreds. The Real Bills doctrine was deceptively incomplete by not including the terms of the agreement. An artificially constrained interest rate could lead to an excess issuance of notes by eager borrowers and to price inflation. (Note that the critique strongly applies to today's zero interest rate policy by the Federal Reserve.) The proper course was a controlled increase in bank-notes, striving to match real economic growth so as not to cause inflation. Thornton eventually changed this 'friendly critic' position, deciding that the BoE was untrustworthy. The suspension of convertibility had gone on for far too long though it was only meant as a temporary measure.

David Ricardo penned some important arguments, thoroughly rejecting all anti-Bullionist premises. No balance of payments was a problem – the market would clear itself. In the event of overprinting, notes would be tendered for bullion and prices would remain stable. The House of Commons joined in on the side of the Bullion Report. The Real Bills doctrine was deemed nonsensical. The 1810 report urged the return of convertibility at 1797 rates, even though it was wartime and this would entail strong deflation. Thornton agreed.[28]

Ricardo had the final word. His position dictated monetary policy in England for the next century. "A currency may be considered as perfect, of which the standard is invariable, which always conforms to that standard, and in the use of which the utmost economy is practiced."[29] It is highly questionable whether the Federal Reserve and other central banks ever practiced this 'economy,' from its creation until the 2008 crisis. It is clear that they have utterly disposed of the idea since then.

**Fed Policy**

*Some even believe we (the Rockefeller family) are part of a secret cabal working against the best interests of the United States, characterizing my family and me as 'internationalists' and of conspiring with others around the world to build a more integrated global political and economic structure – one world, if you will. If that's the charge, I stand guilty, and I am proud of it.*
**– David Rockefeller,** *Memoirs*, **page 405**

The Federal Reserve has its own police force. After 911, they were granted far broader powers. Before then, the Fed police force only had jurisdiction on Fed property. Afterward, they were equivalent to all other Federal officers, anywhere on US soil. Their mandate is "to protect and safeguard the premises, grounds, property, personnel, including members of the Board, or any Federal Reserve Bank, and operations conducted by or on behalf of the Board or a reserve bank." The Federal Reserve is "independent of the government," which leaves an open question – is it legal for such an entity to have an official federal police? Is it in the best interests of society for a legal police force to serve a private enterprise instead of the general public?[30]

The Federal Reserve has an explicit mandate on its website. In typical banker fashion, they massaged the text into an opaque pile of jargon seemingly designed to cause reader arrest due to tedium. Here is the short version:

> By conducting open market operations, imposing reserve requirements, permitting depository institutions to hold contractual clearing balances, and extending credit through its discount window facility, the Federal Reserve exercises

considerable control over the demand for and supply of
Federal Reserve balances and the federal funds rate.[31]

The three tools to conduct monetary policy: Open market operations,
purchases and sales of U.S. Treasury, and federal agency securities—the
Federal Reserve's principal tool for implementing monetary policy. The Federal
Reserve's objective for open market operations has varied over the years.
During the 1980s, the focus gradually shifted toward attaining a specified level
of the federal funds rate (the rate that banks charge each other for overnight
loans of federal funds, which are the reserves held by banks at the Fed), a
process that was largely complete by the end of the decade.[32] The discount
rate is the interest rate charged to commercial banks and other depository
institutions on loans they receive from their regional Federal Reserve Bank's
lending facility—the discount window.[33] Reserve requirement – the amount
of funds that a depository institution must hold in reserve against specified
deposit liabilities.[34]

During the tenure of the Federal Reserve, the country has largely
prospered. The desire for FRNs in the world has been mostly strong for a
hundred years. The economy became the largest in the world, coveted for its
ingenuity and respected for its quality. Though that declined after 1970, the
nation still enjoyed prosperity. The Fed's goal of maintaining the dollar as
reserve currency was in fact beneficial for the people. It's impossible to say what
would have happened without a central bank. There is, of course, no reason
why the government could not have managed the currency itself or indeed, as
current circumstances prove, to think, as bankers contend, that government
would be more profligate than they have been; nor does government appear
to be so very vulnerable to public pressure to spend on public well-being, as
contended. In actuality, at least such spending would have brought a far greater
share of the prosperity to the people. It might have cost the role of world reserve
currency, however, leaving the people to have less overall – as will certainly
be the case today, with the economy so dependent upon it. Other countries'
central banks do not have the same excuse.

A key question arises: what happens when the interests of the privately
owned Federal Reserve move in direct opposition to the interests of the US
citizenry? What happens when central banks' interests worldwide are in direct
opposition to public interest?

This divergence in interests is happening now. It has occurred briefly in the
past – as evidenced in the Long-Term Capital Management (LTCM) collapse
and other national financial problems. The 2008 bailouts were clearly not in
the public interest, though they were advertised as such – as a way to get the
credit supply moving again. It failed because the banks were given money, but
not required to loan it out. They were scrambling for solvency. As their asset

base crumbled, their reserves more or less vanished because of the leverage. They had nothing at all. When liabilities exceed assets, you are insolvent. When cash flow cannot keep up with expenditures on top, you are bankrupt. The government prevented the major banks from failing with the lie that they were necessary to keep the productive economy rolling. In fact, they now are the biggest drain on the productive economy because all the money goes into keeping them afloat. And it's getting worse.

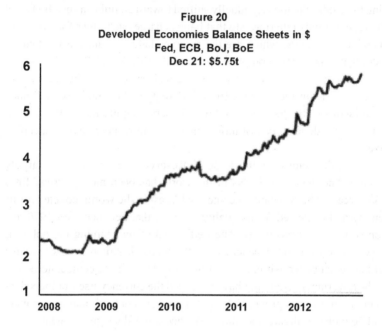

**Figure 20**
**Developed Economies Balance Sheets in $**
**Fed, ECB, BoJ, BoE**
**Dec 21: $5.75t**

Figure 20 above shows a tripling of central bank balance sheets in Europe, the US, and Japan. Adding assets to balance sheets comes from purchasing them. This adds to the money supply. Additionally, it serves to bail out banks from their bad assets – now on the balance sheets of the central banks, making them the ultimate bad banks. Because they can print money at will, they are only technically insolvent. If these assets were marked to market, they would be worth next to nothing. No one would buy them, even if they had the money. On the liabilities side of the equation, the CBs have the creation of the money used to buy the assets. This money should be retired when the assets are sold. But insofar as the CBs bought the very worst assets to save the banks, the assets are worth far less than 50% of the price paid. You could say the CBs foolishly paid full book value for them, if you wanted to assume that they were both stupid and on the public's side. If these assets were offered for sale, they would promptly lose 80-90%. So the CBs created $4 trillion, but could only retire $1 trillion or so in the event of full liquidation. Translation: all the developed economy central banks, too, are crushingly insolvent. The next event will be bankruptcy. For a central bank, true insolvency comes when it destroys its currency. History has established that currencies have stress limits. They fail when too much pressure is put on them. People panic and abandon them.

The world has never been in a situation where all the major currencies are simultaneously inflating. Typically, there has always been the safe haven of another currency. When France destroyed its currency in the 19th century, the British Pound was able to absorb much of the stress. Safe currencies were always gold-backed. Nowadays, many CBs are working in unison, simultaneously inflating their fiat currencies. There is no safe haven. Even the Swiss have a public policy to sell as many Swiss francs as necessary to keep the currency at 120 to the Euro. Big money is steadily and quietly moving into physical gold because there is no gold-backed currency.

The Federal Reserve's overt mandate – to stabilize the nation's economy – has now openly diverged from its covert, but obvious mandate – to create profit for its owners and ensure their survival. The banks are simply too big and too deep in the hole to contribute positively to the real economy anymore. They drain away true wealth from the producers and savers. The dual mandates are now in direct opposition. Even a cursory analysis reveals which one the Fed has chosen to serve. It is trying to maintain a stable economy for as long as possible, but only in support of the banks. If the economy really tanks, especially in a global sovereign debt crisis, the banks will fail, too.

While this seems like a unified purpose, it is not. If the banks were allowed to fail, the economy would quickly recover. The central banks are maintaining the economy in a short-term, steady decline in support of the banks, whereas they claim to be maintaining the banks long-term, in support of the economy. They are destroying the economy and the fallout will be far worse. History shows again and again that a short intense recession flushes out the bad debt. The parasites are allowed to fail and no longer drain the productive economy, which quickly recovers. When this has been allowed, the pain is only a few years and the recovery comes. Iceland is the best current example.[35]

When recycling debt higher and higher through bogus mechanisms is tried, the result is Greece – promising a grinding descent of a decade or longer and a long, flat low afterward with no strong recovery. Overwhelming debt is an economic yoke around the world's neck, being perpetuated by the central banks in service of major banks struggling for survival. They should all sink or swim without help. Savings, checking, and CD holders should be made whole, even by printing money. Everyone else – bondholders, stockholders and other investors in the institutions – should go to the sharks. That is the risk of investing and due diligence is the responsibility of the investor.

The real problem has been around in potentia since 1971, when the gold standard was severed and fiat currency became the global reality. The situation was managed until the 1990s, when the Reagan spending ramp-up had to be dealt with. Clinton turned a surplus by the questionable method of borrowing Social Security funds for the general budget. Social Security is a separate fund, paid into by workers during their working years. While accounting gimmicks had been used before then, the Clinton administration exhibited a new level of mastery in that area. Hedonics, substitution, core inflation and other shell games were used to hide the inflation from the general public.[36] This managed to mask the increasing deficit spending from the balance sheet.

The Bush years put deficit spending back on the table as official policy. Cheney claimed that the mandate given by voters allowed them the right to run much higher deficits. Excess spending is great for current administrations, because it allows short-term economic boosts while deferring the problems to later administrations. It's one of the greatest problems faced by elected governments with term limits. Alan Greenspan agreed with Cheney, and turned on the money creation spigot full blast, pushing interest rates into the basement. The housing bubble ensued and the much larger Treasury bubble and general credit bubble has followed it. All this money creation has put the Federal Reserve complex in a lot of difficult straits. Maintaining the spiraling Treasury complex – as outlined in the shadow banking section – has become a near impossible tightrope walk. The complex is wildly out of balance with huge, top-heavy derivative positions. Yet putting more fiat currency into the system shakes up the big money, which is rapidly losing confidence in the Fed's ability to maintain a strong US currency. Those funds – national reserves, sovereign wealth, hedge funds, and non-Western banks – are piling into gold. So are citizens of many nations. The physical gold has been drained from Western mega-banks.

The extreme loss of gold risks moving the banks beyond insolvency into actual failure. Without the solid, value sustaining anchor of the last real asset, the mountain of paper is lit. Morgan Stanley, for example, faced a debt downgrade from Moody's – A2 to Baa2 – barely investment grade. MS has big interest rate swaps like JPMorgan, but hasn't the breadth or size to weather the storm. When their rates hike, their borrowing costs go way up – nobody wants paper that's already on fire. Worse, investors leave in droves, ratcheting up the leverage.

The government is holding the show together. On June 13, 2013 Jamie Dimon showed up to a Senate Banking Committee hearing sporting a pair of cufflinks with a message. They bore the Presidential Seal and he intentionally got them on camera. The message is open to interpretation, but speculation includes a few possibilities: The administration will protect the bank; the presidency is in the JPM pocket; or the big banks are the government. And how much difference is there, really, between these three? It's important to remember that JPM is probably the largest stakeholder in the Federal Reserve.

**Figure 21**

**Assets of the Federal Reserve System - 1945 to 2012**

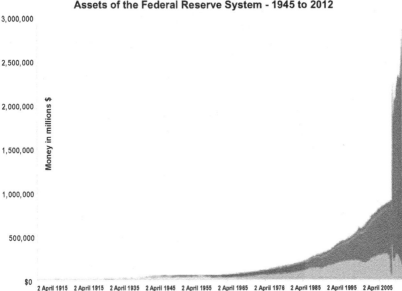

Within all this monetary creation, MOPE – management of perception – figures prominently. The Fed is in inflate or die mode. Without massive monetary creation, the mega-banks are all hopelessly illiquid. They are insolvent either way – their real assets cannot be sold for enough to cover even a fraction of their liabilities. Monetary creation has the perverse effect of increasing the insolvency because no bank counterparties exist and the sums are far too great for any other entities to engage with. The banks are now simply too big to survive. Like a whale bigger than all the fish in the ocean combined, they cannot find enough to eat.

When gold rises and especially when it hits new highs, all bond and credit assets lose value in real time. They must address such issues as negative real interest rates and ongoing currency devaluations. In such an environment – as at this writing – no bonds of any kind provide a safe home for capital. Bond traders, often with enormous portfolios, know this. According to analyst Chris Laird, a gold price rise of 25% would require a bond discount of 25% to remain attractive. That's because bond traders are sophisticated and know that gold is money. And sovereign bonds have almost no yield at this point, because any nations with yield on their bonds are aggressively devaluing their currency, meaning that a 5% yield on a bond facing a 6% devaluation is worth less in real terms at expiry, even though the nominal value has risen. The yield is negative. When gold hits new highs, it serves as the real benchmark for bond values. So if bonds don't move with respect to currencies, then a gold rise of X% equals a bond discount of X%. This is how bond traders see their world.

The consequences are pretty big. Pimco manages $2 trillion – a 25% discount is worth $500 billion. It's not play money. The big funds will turn away investors because they can't get yield on those huge portfolios. The giant bond funds, being slow-moving and without a place to park their financial tanks, will become liabilities.[37]

For Fed policy, this means that they nonetheless have to figure out a way

**Figure 22**

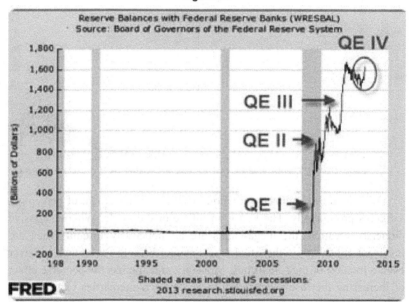

to keep money flowing into the big bond funds since they are major investors in the various nations' debt portfolios. They also want to keep the canary – gold – from giving away the systemic failures. The unspoken policy seems to be to keep the game churning and manage perceptions for as long as possible, even as the wheels fall off – maintain the charade. As long as there is sufficient liquidity (sloshing money) the giant zombie banks can shuffle along. But politically, this plays very badly. People don't like to see the banks getting trillions of dollars while Main Street is left to starve. The general economy relies on continual loans from the banks to continue non-financial economic activity – production and the like. But the banks aren't loaning money. Primarily because they can't. They're scrambling for short-term funding and profits. Low interest borrowing and short-term speculation (like high-frequency trading, derivatives, and shorting commodities) is where the money is.

Consequently, the Fed has to lie. Rather than understanding that the banks are strapped, the public thinks they're flush, because the even more worrisome systemic dimension of the problem is being concealed. Nobody at the top wants to see salvation policies from and for the bottom start gaining traction which might put paid to the one percent. Bernanke has to claim that propping up the big banks is the only way to save the economy from disaster, when in fact, the big banks are sucking up all available financial capital, and starving the real economy.

The players all know how the system works, but keep silent because the mechanism benefits them so heavily. The Rothschild brothers helped create it and said so in an 1863 letter to New York associates:

> The few who understand the system will either be so interested in its profits or be so dependent upon its favours that there will be no opposition from that class, while on the other hand, the great body of people, mentally incapable of comprehending the tremendous advantage that capital derives from the system, will bear its burdens without complaint, and perhaps without even suspecting that the system is inimical to their interests.[38]

The Fed's monetary policy decisions are not subject to executive or Congressional approval. Because the Federal Reserve operates in secret, has no actual oversight (though mandated by law), and is not audited, there is no accountability for their actions and the harm it may cause. However, since it operates on such a large scale and largely in public view, the policies are not difficult to piece together. Analysts decipher banker speak and match it against Fed actions to get real policy. In 2011, Bernanke claimed an end to quantitative easing. In 2012, we saw QE3 followed in less than two months by QE4. The Fed is desperate; otherwise they would not be acting so overtly.

QE is risky – it can go either side of the intended result. Either it over expands the money supply, causing inflation and possibly hyperinflation. Or, banks who hold the base money do not multiply it by lending into the general economy out of fear of debtor defaults, collapsing balance sheets and their own insolvency; they keep it pocketed as capital reserves in a defensive strategy. This is what seems to have happened, leading to the general anguish that Wall Street is bailed out and Main Street is hung out.

The GAO audit of the Fed tallied a lot of black marks against the organization. Fed members were allowed to hold stock in bailed out companies – a clear conflict of interest. When a dizzying array of these emerged in the process, the Fed waived its already weak requirements addressing the issue. The Federal Reserve's Internal Audit department simply ignored all impropriety.

To say nothing (as it did) of the small matter of $16 trillion created and loaned at 0% interest to the banks. There is another name for a 0% loan – a gift. If the "borrower" never owes any interest, what's to pay back?

These are among the many problems flowing from perpetual quantitative easing. Now traders and economists are taking opposite sides. More QE is poison, the traders think, but the economists, with job security in mind, are backing the Fed. At some point, the Fed will fail altogether, and QE will spiral the real economy down much faster than a true laissez-faire flush-out. The returns of stimulus are diminishing, but the problems are escalating. Soon, the entire game of modern economics will be exposed as a total deception..

The entire policy is intended to reflate the pile of moribund assets. Unfortunately, it relies on the perpetual creation of more phantom assets and debts to push up those already failing. A system cannot be reflated by creating an ever-increasing pile of broken balloons. The Fed is up against the hopeless job of cleaning up a toxicity trap with more toxic assets. The gap is only widening. Fund manager David Einhorn put it very well:

> It's very hard for economists with models, with very limited sample sets and empirical data to understand [that we've gone beyond the point of monetary policy diminishing returns.] I think you wind up with a different view from people like me in the real world who aren't just trying to figure out what do the models say, but how do people actually behave.... if the Fed loses control, if the Treasury loses control ... these scare people ... companies defer long-term investments in the country because they are worried about significant tail risks these very aggressive policies are creating.[39]

## Endnotes

1    Goddard, Thomas H. (1831). History of Banking Institutions of Europe and the United States. Carvill. pp. 48–50. From Wikipedia – Bank of North America.
2    Letter to John Taylor, May 28, 1816.
3    The Complete Annals of Thomas Jefferson, Round Table Press, 1903.
4    Andrew Jackson, to a delegation of bankers discussing the recharter of the Second Bank of the United States, 1832.
5    A.W. Moore, Bloody Island. Illinois early history. Ibex Archive online.
6    Second Bank of the United States: a Chapter in US Central Banking. Philadelphia Fed, Dec. 2010.
7    Upton Sinclair. The Moneychangers, 1908.
8    George H. Earle, "A Central Bank as a Menace to Liberty", 1908 essay.
9    G. Edward Griffin, "The Creature from Jekyll Island – a Second Look at the Federal Reserve System", American Media, 1994.
10   Charles Lindbergh, "Why Is Your Country At War?", 1917. Quoted from Mullins.

11    *The New Freedom: A Call for the Emancipation of the Generous Energies of a People*
      (New York and Garden City: Doubleday, Page & Company, 1913

12    "41 Facts about Central Banks no longer taught in US schools", The Prudent Investor.
      November 15th, 2010.

13    c-spanarchives.org/clip/3668281, January 11, 2010.

14    "AIG Trustees Should Answer to Taxpayers, Not Fed, Towns Says, Mark Pittman",
      James Sterngold and Hugh Son – May 12, 2009.

15    Ron Paul, interview with Mike Maloney. 2007.

16    Beat Balzli and Michaela Schiessl, "The Man Nobody Wanted to Hear: Global Banking
      Economist Warned of Coming Crisis", July 8, 2009.

17    "Gold Wars: Military Conflicts, Gold and Currency Crises" June 2004 speech at
      University of St. Gallen.

18    Greg Hobbs, "What is the Federal Reserve Bank (FED) and why do we have it?",
      Novebmber 1, 1999, www.john-f-kennedy.net/thefederalreserve.htm.

19    Dean Henderson. "The Federal Reserve Cartel: The Eight Families", June 7, 2012.
      Global Research.

20    *Lewis v. United States*, the U.S. Court of Appeals for the Ninth Circuit.

21    Walter John Williams of shadowstats.com unpacks the deceptive measures of the dif-
      ferent government unemployment statistics, showing that unemployment is over 20%
      if measured in traditional ways.

22    Carol Quigley, *Tragedy and Hope: a History of the World in our Time*, Quigley, Car-
      roll. GSC and Associates, 1975, from Chapter 20.

23    Quigley, ch. 9.

24    Silas Walter Adams, *The legalized crime of banking and a constitutional remedy.*
      Boston: Meador. 1958, p. 13

25    William Guy Carr, *Pawns In The Game*, privately printed, 1956. Quoted from Mullins.

26    The 10 Richest People in the World of All Time, Money Stock Tycoons. from *Forbes
      Magazine*/Wikipedia.

27    Henry Thornton, *An Inquiry into the Nature and Effects of the Paper Credit of Great
      Britain,*1802.

28    David Laidler, Highlights of the Bullionist Controversy, 1999 http://economics.uwo.
      ca/people/laidler_docs/highlightsof.pdf.

29    David Ricardo, "Proposal for an Economical and Secure Currency", in P. Sraffa (ed.)
      1816. supra Laidler, p.19.

30    http://en.wikipedia.org/wiki/Federal_Reserve_Police.

31    The Federal Reserve System: Purposes and Functions. Board of Governors of the
      Federal Reserve System. 2005.

32    FRB: Monetary Policy, Open Market Operations. Federalreserve.gov. 2010-01-26

33    FRB: Monetary Policy, the Discount Rate. Federalreserve.gov. 2011-07-19.

34    FRB: Monetary Policy, Reserve Requirements. Federalreserve.gov. 2010-10-26

35    http://www.guardian.co.uk/business/economics-blog/2012/aug/21/iceland-debt-relief-
      lessons-eurozone

36    Covered in the inflation section.

37    Chris Laird, "Why the Bond Markets Fear Gold Now", Prudent Squirrel. January 11,
      2013.

38    John Sherman, Rothschild executive, letter in support of proposed National Banking
      Act. June 25, 1863.

39    Tyler Durden, "David Einhorn Explains How Ben Bernanke Is Destroying America",
      zerohedge.com, October 25, 2012

# 7

# INFLATION, DEFLATION, DISINFLATION, STAGFLATION AND HYPERINFLATION

*Keynes without uncertainty is like Hamlet without the prince*
—Hyman Minsky

The global economic situation cannot continue as it has. Something has to give. Major problems are on the horizon. The economic situation is presently so unbalanced that soon one of the 'flations will move out of control – inflation, deflation, hyperinflation, stagflation or biflation, all of them bad. This section explains those topics, how they come about, and how likely they are. Some will happen, at least nominally, for a time – others already are. Thus the important questions are the severity and the consequences.

First, a few words on the setup and why some dire occurrences are inevitable. Aside from the conditions already explained, the US fiscal situation is beyond any hope. The federal deficit is actually a mirage – things are much, much worse than the $1.1 trillion deficits typically put forth. The Treasury puts out the true government shortfall after the media numbers. They use Generally Accepted Accounting Principles, not the cooked numbers put out for the public.

The federal deficit is actually $1.3 trillion for 2012. But when the unfunded obligations are added in (shortfalls in Social Security and Medicare), the number is $5.3 trillion more. That was the additional amount needed for 2012 to fund future obligations – $6.6 trillion shortfall in total for a single year. It's 42% of national GDP, making the worst banana republics look like prudent savers. Total obligations are $85 trillion, over 5 times the officially advertised debt.[1] Also, five times the official GDP. Remember: these are the official government numbers, not any third party ones. The government is telling everyone, in the open but without trumpets, that the fiscal situation is hopelessly insolvent. The media fail to report the real numbers. Even worse, the backstopping of the Pension Guarantee Fund, FHA and the Post Office are not included, nor are numerous bailout obligations for nationalized entities.

When a country hits GDP to obligations of over 100%, it's considered irreversible, headed for implosion. Only its world reserve currency status has allowed the US to continue faking it this far. GDP and taxation cannot possibly cover this, no matter the time frame. The government cannot squeeze additional revenue out of the private sector. The balance has been attained and maximized – increasing taxes will reduce revenues by damping economic activity.

At some point, soon, the government will be unable to meet these various obligations by taxing and borrowing. It is already monetizing significant amounts of debt through the Fed. Most of that activity is hidden and shuffled, but too many years of this and holders of US instruments get fatigue from falling returns and rising risk. There are no new investors and old ones want to divest. Printing money is the only option. Further mechanics of how this destroys the economy are covered in other sections. Here we simply look at how these forces play out against each other – deflation, the natural tendency of a fractional reserve system – versus inflation, the central bank's efforts to push it the other way. Quantitative Easing programs have steadily increased to the point where, at this writing, they are currently monetizing $85 billion per month of Treasury and bad mortgages. Monetization is inflation.

In situations of general economic deterioration, demand collapses, profits disappear, businesses fail and jobs vanish. Parabolic budget deficits in excess of $1 trillion require huge printing. Threats to the dollar from inflation can come from many potent macro-economic forces and situations which may loom in the future:

- Monetization. To protect mega-banks, the Federal Reserve is printing massive amounts of money, affecting the credibility of the currency.
- Economic systemic collapse. Another round of banking crises and failures would strain the budget and Treasury to the point of foreign abandonment.
- Failed Treasury auction. This would send a wake-up tremor throughout the bond world, bringing out global bond vigilantes – traders who force more honest interest valuations by speculating against manipulation – and causing nations to dump Treasuries.
- End of reserve currency status. If the world no longer needs dollars for oil or trade, the endless supply of dollars will have a far more difficult time finding a home.
- There are virtually no positives for the dollar. Political instability, terrible trade gaps, inflation, government insolvency, financial systemic fissures, ultra-low interest rates and Quantitative Easing

are all major dollar negative forces that are steadily worsening.[2] Inflation is issue #1.

## Inflation

> *By a continuing process of inflation, governments can*
> *confiscate, secretly and unobserved, an important*
> *part of the wealth of their citizens*
> **– John Maynard Keynes.**

Inflation, every economist knows, is a tax. It is a hidden tax, because people do not lose money, per se – the money they have loses value by a process known as Seigniorage, wherein the issuer of a currency assigns it a much higher face value than the cost to produce it. The issuer gets the difference. By inflating the supply of money, the monetary issuer is able to acquire tangible goods and services in exchange for the cost of paper and the printing process. Not even that, when the process is digital. Loans under a fractional, fiat system are a form of seigniorage granted to banks. They are allowed to create money (thereby inflating the supply) and make their money by charging interest on that.

But the inflation tax, per se, is the value transferred from holders of cash (middle class) or credit (bond investors) to holders of value objects (gold, art, real estate) or debt (government and so forth). Governments can spend money at current value, before it inflates prices – since it causes that inflation. It thus gets new inflated money at value before that inflation hits and lowers existing (savers') money. Savers are effectively taxed by the loss of value in their holdings. If the government does it slowly, then the public never notices.

It's called the 'illusion of money,' and it fools people at an intuitive level. People measure in nominal terms – number of dollars – rather than purchasing power. All governments rely on this confusion in their citizenry. People do not comprehend inflation. If a hypothetical choice were posed to people – receive a 2% pay cut with no inflation or no pay cut and inflation is 4% – most would choose the latter, even though it meant they lost twice as much. People simply do not understand the real value of money.

Typically, a 5% annual inflation rate has been carefully managed (though control is now being lost). At this rate, returns to the creators of money and to the government are maximized without the public becoming upset. This means that a saver loses 5% of his income, leaving only 95% value at year's end. This also applies to money saved from previous years. Any money left in cash for 50 years would be 95% diminished in value – this is the hidden tax that forces people to constantly seek returns on saved money instead of simply having enough for retirement.

Inflation is usually considered to be a monetary phenomenon. If more currency enters circulation without an increase in the supply of goods, then more money chases the same or fewer goods. Inflation is inescapable if more money is spent on the same amount of goods – it is mathematically definitive.

Looking back to the 12th century, economic historian, David Hackett Fisher, found a recurring cycle to economic systems – a variable and volatile inflation with enormous wealth disparities culminating in total collapse.

> Food and fuel led the upward movement. Manufactured goods and services lagged behind. These patterns indicated that the prime mover was excess aggregate demand, generated by an acceleration of population growth, or by rising living standards, or both. [1990s to mid 2000s]. Eventually, prices went higher, and became increasingly unstable. They began to surge and decline in movements of increasing volatility. Severe price-shocks were felt in commodity movements. [2008 oil price shock]. The money supply was alternately expanded and contracted. Financial markets became unstable. [2008 and after scenario]. *Government spending grew faster than revenue, and public debt increased at a rapid rate. In every price-revolution, the strongest nation-states suffered severely from fiscal stresses*: Spain in the 16th century, France in the 18th century, and the United States in the 20th century ...Wages, which had at first kept up with prices, now lagged behind. Returns to labor declined while returns to land and capital increased. The rich grew richer. Inequalities of wealth and income increased. So did hunger, homelessness, crime, violence, drink, drugs, and family disruption.[3]

All of this is happening, much as Fisher describes. Along these lines of increasing volatility, an alarming thing happened in June, 2012. The Shadow Banking system liabilities re-inverted, becoming smaller than conventional banking. The SBS liabilities first became larger than the traditional system's liabilities in 1995. Then in 2008, the liabilities reversed in the SBS and began to decline. In July, 2012, they crossed the line below the traditional system's liabilities. Why does it matter? It indicates that the SBS is undergoing a slow-motion debt deflation scenario – largely by getting out of that side of the business. That's why all the new money created – in the tens of trillions – has not entered the Main Street economy. The systemic liabilities have declined by $6 trillion from $21 to $15 trillion – a 30% drop with enormous numbers. Figure 23 shows very clearly when the credit bubble popped. This is one big

Figure 23
Shadow Bank Liabilities vs. Traditional Bank Liabilities (SBN)

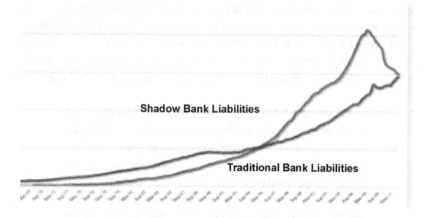

reason the economy will remain in recession. No new credit is being created. The SBS is deleveraging by market forces – the credit bubble is over.

According to the NY Fed, this is critical. The SBS functions as an inflation buffer. It performs all the traditional functions of credit transformation – liquidity, risk and maturity – but does so without any deposits. That lack of deposits prevents the shadow money it deploys from leaking into the general economy. It just drives up asset values and creates new debt-based assets. "The entire rickety shadow banking system is based simply on the good faith and credit that rehypothecated assets, converted into liabilities, and so on (think repos and reverse repos) courtesy of fractional reserve credit formation (recall rehypothecation), are valid and credible sources of liquidity." That functions in an expanding environment, but is a serious disaster in a contraction. As the SBS instruments mature and are cashed out, liquidity is taken out of the system since these credit instruments function as money in themselves.

Around the end of the Great Depression, banks moved from a deflationary to inflationary policy – by a thoroughly self-interested process, of course. They sought a greater sphere of control, but that could only come about through stock ownership in corporations. This created an inherent conflict. The transformation of maturity problem forced them to use short-term funds (customer deposits) to issue long-term assets (stocks). The system only worked if they could quickly liquidate the stock holdings at high values. But large stock liquidations caused stock prices to fall quickly, especially instituting panic selling and the like. But, according to Carroll Quigley's research, the banks also found the system to be highly deflationary. The deflation occurred because of the gold standard, which limited the supply of sound money and thereby the pace of technological innovation, which was rapidly increasing the real wealth.

Financiers solved this problem by separating ownership from control, primarily through distributing corporate stock to large numbers of people, shareholders, or "the owners". Public buy-in allowed for a few persons to control vast amounts of other people's capital. The system further moved towards monopoly control through industry cartels and the separation of control from ownership. The creation of monopolies and cartels allowed businesses to restrict production and artificially inflate prices.[4] From that system, shadow banking arose, putting overwhelming control in the finance sector, which roundly abused it through an ocean of synthetic investments.

The problem? The Fed has to create more and more 'flow' money to prevent systemic collapse. That money is rising in the conventional depositary system – which can leak into the general economy and quickly in a bank run. As the SBS continues to deleverage, the depositary base will rise. Within a few years, at current rates of movement, the depositary base will double from $10 to $20 trillion. And with it, monetary inflation.[5] Price inflation follows.

Another mode is called demand-pull inflation. If the stock of an item decreases without demand decrease or if demand increases but stock stays flat, then demand will increase the price – like diamonds. This is the sleight of hand illusion created by market leaders like Apple where the good sells for far more than competitors or normal cost plus profit. Demand-pull is not typically true inflation because it only applies to specific sectors, and therefore does not impact all prices in the economy as a whole. If people spend more on i-phones, they spend less elsewhere because the overall supply of money did not increase.

There is also cost-push inflation. When the availability of resources declines, especially of energy and raw materials, then the cost of manufactured products naturally rises. Manufacturers cannot operate for long at a loss, so if steel goes up, then cars become more expensive.

Generally inflation relates to increases in the money supply more than to scarcity. If it comes about with an increase in population – more people need more money and they typically increase the supply of goods by increasing the work-force – it will not lead to inflation. However, central banks tend to create money at a far faster rate than population increases, as they favor facilitating opportunities for profit over stable monetary management, so we see a steady multi-decadal roll of inflation.

The velocity of money – how many times it changes hands – is an important factor in inflation. If people spend money faster, this increases the amount of money spent without actually increasing the money supply. In this book's argument, velocity is more a mass-psychology phenomenon, speeding up in relation to trust in currency, desire to get investment returns and to profligate consumer spending habits. Currently velocity is very low for a number of reasons but mostly due to the amount of new money that is parked in the reserves of banks that aren't lending. However, plenty of new money is leaking into the general sphere, largely due to massive government deficits. The expanding money supply is thus causing the current inflation, not velocity. Increased velocity, I argue later, is the main mechanism for hyperinflations.

Massive money printing (QE) results in a 'rising cost structure' without a compensatory increase in wages. The prices of commodities, durable goods, energy, and food all go up from speculative pressures but wages don't go up. People's income stagnates, dwindling in real terms. Industry suffers from plummeting consumption. Jobs vanish, incomes decline more. Pensions and savings cannot earn money in a zero interest environment. Savers and retirees have less disposable income. More money is printed to stimulate the economy, continuing the cycle of decline. Without an industrial base, an economy cannot grow. It can only burn up.

During inflations – currency and price – governments try to mask the results. They game the statistics. The US government is the reigning master at this ploy. Walter John Williams of Shadow Government Statistics (http://www.shadowstats.com) has been the chief unmasker of these ploys. The official Consumer Price Index (CPI) runs inflation at about 2% or so. However Williams, in 2013, claims inflation is knocking at 10%. He has solid data to show why. He merely uses the government's methods from 1980. There are quite a few inexplicable differences in these.

The CPI no longer measures the requirements to keep to a certain standard of living or increases to normal expenses. Deceptions are used to keep social security payments lower and to artificially inflate GDP to paint a false picture of economic recovery. This also makes real wages look better since nominal wages are deflated by the CPI to normalize them. A lower inflation rate produces less deflation on wages, so they seem stronger. But the truth of the situation emerges nonetheless in the fact that now most families need two workers to maintain their standard of living, while in 1970s, they only needed one.

CPI now measures 'core inflation.' This reversal of sense term means inflation excluding food and energy costs. The logic – food and energy are volatile and skew the 'long-run' rate of inflation numbers. This is ridiculous, of course. The long-run numbers would smooth out any volatility over time and any increases in food and energy would be properly incorporated into the data, and besides, food and energy are the most critical consumer items. Along with shelter, they are the only true human requirements for physical existence. It is ludicrous to use any inflationary measure which ignores such essential items.

Inflation once measured a fixed basket of goods – some food, some gasoline, rent, and some non-essential items. There were no substitutions or changes in size or weighting within the index number. That changed in 1990.

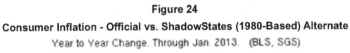

**Figure 24**
**Consumer Inflation - Official vs. ShadowStates (1980-Based) Alternate**
Year to Year Change. Through Jan. 2013   (BLS, SGS)

— SGS Alternate CPI, 1980-Based     — CPI-U

Published Feb 21, 2013                                    shadowstats.com

Politicians put forward the idea that substituting 'hamburger for steak' would result in a more accurate inflation measure. If people switched to hamburger, it was argued, they had merely substituted beef in one format for beef in another. Geometric weighting was also introduced, lowering the amount of any basket item that rose in price, on the assumption that people would then buy less. Accordingly, as far as CPI was concerned, instead of a 12 ounce steak going up 10% in price, it went down in size by 10%, keeping the inflation rate unchanged. It was lousy political cover for the change, but no one cared at the time. It only affected the cost of living adjustment for social security.

Weighting has become absurd. Health insurance is gauged at 4.3% inflation from 2008-12, even though all companies show rates going up by 25%.[6] Even then, it's weighted as a tiny 1% of the basket, far below most people's expenses for health insurance.

Next came hedonics – downwardly adjusting inflation by a fuzzy measure of product improvements. If the price of vehicles went up 30%, then the addition of new gadgets (whether desired or not) were used to lower the inflation rate to meet targets. There may be some logic to it, but the price adjustments are non-quantifiable and arbitrary product changes are often marked as hedonic improvements to lower inflation numbers.

Inflation is further disguised by the dollar index. The dollar is measured against a basket of other currencies, but if all currencies are being depreciated simultaneously, there will be no decline in the relative measure of any particular one. However, in terms of real goods or gold, it will buy less. A true currency index would definitely factor in gold at 25% minimum.

One point is so critical, it deserves special mention. Inflation must be subtracted from GDP to get an accurate number for GDP. That's because if the nominal economy grows by 2%, but inflation is 5%, then all the purported growth and more simply reflects monetary increases. No productive increases or unit sale increases have occurred. In this scenario, the productive economy has contracted, not expanded. Leaving aside the issue of whether perpetual economic growth is good or even feasible, the question remains if it is in fact occurring. If the statistics are doctored downward by the government, then GDP growth is lower by the difference of true inflation to CPI. The numbers are clear. GDP is in steady, vigorous contraction.

**Deflation**

> *You cannot borrow your way out of debt*
> **– Daniel Hannan**

Deflation is more or less the opposite of inflation. Money becomes more valuable. In a sense, deflation has happened in the computer industry for almost 20 years. Computers have become less and less expensive because of improved processing techniques, mechanization, in-built knowledge and economies of scale. This is essentially cost-push deflation – the manufacturers have made computers very inexpensive and made many of them. Measured in gold, we are in a true global deflation. Everything has been going down in value relative to gold for 12 years running.

Fear of deflation has become extreme. Portfolio insurance is at peak levels. Institutions are worried about debt defaults and money supply collapse. It's a difficult journey between inflation and deflation. The past few years saw $10 trillion in global money increases – the fastest rate in history in both absolute and percentage terms. The ECB has swollen its balance sheet to unbelievable levels; as of June, 2012 it hit 30% of European GDP. All of this is to fight deflation.

Fed chairman Ben Bernanke has openly asserted an anti-deflationary policy on any number of occasions. In 2002, he said,

> sustained deflation can be highly destructive to a modern economy and should be strongly resisted. Fortunately, for the foreseeable future, the chances of a serious deflation in the United States appear remote indeed, in large part because of our economy's underlying strengths but also because of the determination of the Federal Reserve and other U.S. policymakers to act preemptively against deflationary pressures.[7]

Preemptive action means printing money. Monetary expansion has a brief beneficial period during each iteration, but is subject to an extreme law of diminishing returns. After a few cycles, the process goes almost entirely negative. It does decrease volatility during the printing, Artemis Capital claims, but when the expansion stops, volatility goes crazy. High volatility is good only for very short-term traders. Long-term investors – the public, pension funds, etc – get crushed. In such a scenario, the best bet is to buy hard assets, commodities, and energy, and get out of the paper markets. Take the long view.

True deflation is what central banks fear – a more broad-scale currency contraction. At this point, people, businesses and governments become insolvent. They can no longer pay off the increasing debt-load. A burgeoning global default on the loans leads to banks being forced to write off a significant amount of bad debt. When a bank is paid off for a loan, the principal pops out of existence. The bank must nullify the principal. It is not allowed to create money and regard that asset (the loan) as still in existence when it is paid off. It can only keep the interest. They must do so whether the loan is paid or written off. In a deflation, everyone is looking for money to pay off debts. There's not enough of it, so money becomes extremely valuable. Prices decline because people hold on to money rather than buying things.

The main debate currently is whether the economy will run toward deflation or inflation – will the fractional reserve brute market force (deflation) overcome the unlimited monetary creation powers of the Fed (inflation)? As Figure 25 shows, there have been no deflations since 1950 and no deep or sustained ones since 1930. But the conditions are far more extreme now, and analysts make the case that deflationary forces will strike quickly and

**Figure 25**
**U.S. Historical Inflation Rate**

overcome the CBs power to work against them. This seems unlikely, however, since Central Banks can create and dispense money in unlimited amounts in hours, and they definitely seem inclined to continue doing so.

In a deflationary spiral, businesses lose money due to lowering prices, then they fail. People lose their jobs and have less money to put into the economy, causing businesses to further lose revenue due to decreased sales. More businesses fail and the cycle continues. The cycle is horrendously amplified by massive debt. As prices fall, money becomes more valuable and people hoard it. The largest corporations and banks suck in all the money they can to survive – they are so badly leveraged that each drop in the debt markets (especially housing) causes seismic faults in their balance sheets and reserves. Because they are so large (more than half the economy) and so powerful, they dry up available currency in the general economy by not loaning it out again, once they have taken it in. This makes money needed to pay off debts, and just to survive, more expensive and harder to obtain, again exacerbating business failures.

Deflationists argue that Japan is a modern example of a deflation and that this fate awaits the US. Since 1990, prices in Japan have supposedly been in decline, causing economic havoc, because the banks have huge bad assets and won't lend. But it's not true – Japan has not experienced a sustained deflation. Prices have gone up and down, but on average, they are the same as in 1990. They've been flat. Japan has deflated for brief periods, but always seen a moderate inflation afterward to balance it.

**Figure 26**
**Annual Inflation Rate (%) - Japan %**

In the US, according to Austrian theory, the 1930s saw a deflation – a money supply contraction – caused by 9000 banks failing. Depositors' funds vanished with them. The FDIC was created in 1934 to make depositors whole and protect the banks from a run by eliminating the fear. Since then, the money supply has never again contracted.

The two causes of deflation of concern here are debt deflation and credit contraction. Debt deflation is described above. Credit contraction is when banks will not lend. In the current situation, bank balance sheets are so bad that they need to increase reserves defensively. Reserves are not loaned out because the fractional leverage is already very high from massive debt failures – they need reserves just to remain solvent as more debt goes bad. Moreover, in an ultra-low interest rate environment, there is lower profit but without diminished risk on loaned money, so banks have less incentive to lend. Instead, they have been given a risk-free 'carry trade' on US Treasuries. They can borrow enormous amounts from the Fed at 0.25% then reinvest in US Treasuries at 1-3%, or in Fed accounts at 0.5%.

Deflationists argue that the Fed cannot force banks to lend – it can only lend them money and hope. This is patently false, even absurd. Banks have enormous amounts on deposit at the Fed called excess reserves, on which the Fed pays a small interest. In fact, it's a scam in favor of the banks. This never occurred before the 2008 crisis, but now it is policy. Banks pay the Fed 0.25% for the money, then loan it back for a slightly higher interest rate. The banks are guaranteed risk-free profits for not lending. All they need to do is borrow enormous sums – and they have. To spur lending, all the Fed needs to do is charge the banks to keep the money in a Fed account rather than paying them for doing so. They can simply raise the rates until the banks have to start loaning in order to avoid losing money. Central bank activity is fighting debt deflation primarily by propping up the banks, then fighting inflation by preventing them from lending. But their activity does not lessen the credit contraction deflation, it worsens it. The Fed is lying about using QE to try to get the economy going again; that is only a ruse to give money to the banks while hanging Main Street out to dry. Routine deflation is not a real concern to central banks, because they can overrun it any time they want. The elephant in the deflationary room is shadow banking. This is the *true* deflationary threat.

Shadow banking creates credit without the bother of depository backing. Hence, rather than being inflationary, it is deflationary in a crisis, and gruesomely so. Liabilities and assets are increasingly indistinguishable – they can be switched around on the balance sheet (often they are not even on the balance sheet) with deceptive accounting intent, but without violating the rules. Banks can expand credit with willful abandon, without even the fiat restraints. Each level of the credit 'hierarchy' or each new subset of the shadow system pushes up the nominal amount of credit funding flowing through the system. By being constrained within the shadow system, it is non-inflationary – the 'money' cannot really escape into the tangible world of commodities and physical stuff. That's because it primarily exists as inter-bank promises and asset values – not as liquid capital. The SBS does create massive deflationary pressure, however. Credit is also debt and must be repaid or defaulted. Counterparties can get cold feet and call in short-term paper and the shadow system is mostly short-term paper. This has been the number one con-game of the Federal Reserve. They have 'brought' these assets onto their balance sheet – read – they created money to buy them at face value rather than market value. This keeps the banks, however temporarily, from having a capital crisis that reveals their fundamental insolvency. Liquidity is provided in spades. Considering how deep the hole is, no amount of liquidity can reverse the massive insolvency, but it can mask it for quite a while. And it has.

This is where the Fed is banging its head on the floor. By QE, the Fed is reflating the conventional side of the system, where inflation is a short hop away, because of the need to expand the Main Street money supply through loans. Unfortunately, the shadow system is running scared. The Fed's monetary push is being used to deleverage the other side of the system. And the gap between shadow and conventional is growing. Analyst Tyler Durden showed that the gap shortfall since the Lehman collapse grew by $300 billion during the most aggressive part of QE. The Fed stepped up its fallacy with $85 billion in QE, going into the conventional system. For now, the inflationary genie is held in check by the shadow side's deleveraging. The big players know that the hugely controlled system currently in play cannot be sustained. They are getting out, unwinding the system piece by piece. Soon enough, the new money will seek a new home. With loss of faith in bonds, currencies, shadow liabilities, stocks and all sorts of paper, the managers will move the newly created money into hard assets – oil, gold, land, etc.[8] When that happens, the next and most destructive threat of all will really come into play.

## Hyperinflation

*The surest way to overthrow an existing social order*
*is to debauch the currency*
*– Lenin*

Hyperinflation is supposedly impossible in the developed world where money velocity is extremely low. But this ignores the emotional component of velocity that comes into play very quickly when arising from fear. The argument also ignores the weight of history. Strong economies have hyperinflated. Velocity is low in part because so many countries hold such enormous reserves. Japanese, Chinese and other large reserve portfolios take money out of the supply, in essence, but not out of their velocity calculations. If that money moves quickly and publicly, other big money panics. Prior to the famous Weimar hyperinflation, Germany's currency base doubled with no corresponding inflation. Then suddenly hyperinflation took off. Prices rocketed by 20 billion times, doubling almost every 24 hours. Gold beat the hyperinflation at 1.8 times the average rate. Anyone who held gold saw their real net worth increase steadily.

When the question of currency extinction arises, the knee-jerk response is that the US dollar is immune. Few know that the nation has already burned up two other currencies in hyperinflations, the Continental and the Greenback. One can add the Confederate dollar to the list. The average lifespan of a fiat currency is 40 years. The current Federal Reserve note turns that age in 2013.[9]

The 'safe haven status' for the US dollar fell under serious threat with the increasingly desperate QE efforts from 2010 onwards. This marks the psychological beginning of the end for the buck. Panic selling of the dollar can happen without warning. The Fed and ECB will no doubt stand ready to defend it, buying dollars with other currency reserve stashes. This defense can continue for a very long time – traders are the ultimate setters of exchange rates and none wishes to cross swords with the central banks. However, a nation willing to take a large loss on dollar holdings could conceivably crash the dollar willfully. A concerted attack by Eastern nations would be devastating, though it is unlikely in the near term. They might even improve their situation by balancing these losses against a store of gold. Another trigger scenario is repudiation of the petrodollar standard by Saudi Arabia, though in the government's increasingly vulnerable position, this seems unlikely. The appearance of hyperinflation will be marked by a plunge in the dollar index and a rapid move to dispose of dollars and Treasuries.

According to fiscal and currency expert, Walter J. Williams, hyperinflation has been baked in since 2006 or so. Originally, he put the terminal date around 2018, but with Fed actions since the 2008 crisis, he has moved the outer limit for hyperinflation to 2014. His analysis is highly informed and detailed.[10] The numbers are credible, based on analysis of government shenanigans. His prediction of hyperinflation, given ongoing Fed activity, is highly probable, but the timing may be off. A lot depends on foreign actions, especially those of China, Russia, and OPEC. At any rate, the government is trapped. It cannot work its way through the fiscal debt, impossible obligations and parabolic deficits without massive printing or direct default. There are no other options. No government given this choice has ever defaulted – it has always tried to print its way out, unwinding its debt via destruction of the currency.

Hyperinflation has different definitions. Cagan's is the most generally accepted: a monthly inflation rate over 50%. This is pretty staggering, becoming a 13,000% annualized rate. A $10 meal would cost $1300 at year's end. A far lower rate – 100% annually, doubling prices – would feel like hyperinflation to most people. In such a case, a gallon of gas would rise from

$5 to $40 in three years. The International Accounting Standards Board cites several conditions in its definition, among them a 100% cumulative inflation over 3 years. In any case, in a hyperinflation, the rate of inflation continually increases and actually accelerates. As a country moves into hyperinflation, it might go from 15% to 35% in one year, then 50%, then 100%, then to a 1000%. At this point, the inflationary trend – the destruction of currency value – seems unstoppable.

It's widely agreed that at least 55 countries have experienced hyperinflation since 1900. It's a real threat. Hyperinflations frequently follow wars, severe crises, and deep social unrest. While they initially often stem from government engagement in foreign wars or need to service debt in the teeth of declining tax revenue, once hyperinflation has taken hold, it is exacerbated by government need to provide for the sheer survival of the people.

Some theorists consider hyperinflation to be merely a difference in degree of inflation. This is erroneous. Inflation is a monetary phenomenon – increasing ratio of currency to market items. Hyperinflation is a mass psychological phenomenon – repudiation of the currency. When the public knows the value will decline rapidly, they seek to fully divest of currency in exchange for objects of real value. In a slight inflation, people will hold onto large volumes of currency as legitimate savings. In a higher inflation (10-20%), people will instinctively feel that monetary savings are a losing proposition, but will not fully and instantly divest. They will invest in stocks, real estate and other instruments, then imagine their nominal increase is a real increase. They will still gauge wealth in terms of the currency. In a hyperinflation, people panic and dump. Inflation is generally tied to supply of currency, and hyperinflation is tied to velocity of currency.

In hyperinflation, when people get paid, they immediately go to the store to buy things – they are dumping the money as fast as possible. Turnover of the currency goes up by hundreds of times. In severe cases, employees get paid twice a day. They rush away to spend the money on their lunch break. The process seldom continues for long. People cannot live this way – it's too anxiety-ridden. Their struggle for survival effectively becomes a repudiation of the currency, as they are forced to seek ways around losing out on their salaries' swiftly declining value. An employer who can pay employees in a stable currency will become the employer of choice. A merchant who has a reliable barter system, alternative currency or a hard currency will instantly rise in prestige. Smart merchants are inclined to accept only precious metals, other stable currencies, barter, or direct labor for their goods. They will no longer accept the national paper. Governments typically respond with Draconian price controls and mandates to accept national notes. Shelves go bare instantly because merchandise cannot profitably be sold at such prices.

Stores operate at a loss until they fold because the money they receive is below operational costs. People resort to black market solutions. Supply chains are broken – no one wants to sell into a failing currency from outside. Producers with long wait times for payments go bankrupt.

All of this decimates real tax revenues, creating an ever-worsening fiscal problem. Unable to borrow or tax, the government prints money to cover its deficits. As the largest buyer in the economy, the government then pushes inflation ever higher. A destitute government can trigger hyperinflation in such a way. Tax revenues and investors become increasingly unavailable. The government must print the money to cover the unbelievable shortfall. The government then spends this money directly into the economy, driving up prices everywhere. An overwhelming feedback loop arises where the government must print more and more money to cover the inflationary death-spiral it has created. But this printing only causes prices to rise further. In the case of the US, the situation is exacerbated dramatically by huge entitlements, massive military spending, and enormous debt. The US government spent about $3.6 trillion on budget with a corresponding off-budget amount. That makes the government share of GDP over 30% without producing anything.

Virtually all models of hyperinflation blame excessive government borrowing and spending for it. Most models calculate a tipping point for government expenditures. There are many expenditures such as social security, medicare, pensions, military budgets and so forth that are not denominated in currency but set as target goals. When the combination of debt load, deficit spending, borrowing costs, and money printing accumulate to drive these costs up more than printing of money can accommodate, the government cannot improve its fiscal position. In other words, cost of operations will inevitably increase more than money created and spent because the government is driving inflation faster than it is increasing spending. Thus it falls further and further into hyperinflating deficit and debt. Simultaneously, it destroys the national wealth and standard of living. The next step is typically massive social unrest, followed by extreme changes in governance. Many credit Hitler's rise directly to the German Weimar hyperinflation.

It's important to realize that the actual supply of money in a hyperinflation does not increase nearly so much as the rate of inflation. There may only be an increase of 1000% in bank issued money, but the velocity increasing by the same will turn inflation into 1,000,000%. In the case of Zimbabwe, inflation became 22 quadrillion percent annually. Hungary experienced the highest inflation rate ever after WWII: 42 quadrillion percent monthly. Prices doubled every 15 hours. Governments simply cannot print the money fast enough to front-run inflation. As inflation reaches a critical tipping point –

typically north of 50% annual inflation – velocity increases dramatically. In a stable economy, the money supply turns over 2-3 times a year. In a hyperinflation, the money supply can turn over 2-3 times each day.

There are about 120 currencies in use today. Over 600 have disappeared, 156 from hyperinflation. Of the others, most vanished from military take-over, phase-out into another currency, revaluation, or renaming. After these latter events, most currencies fail within 20 years.[11]

It's useful to include a few lessons from past hyperinflations. The Weimar inflation is the most cited. After World War I, Germany had huge debts for war reparations. Initially, the country experienced deflation, which lasted for almost two years. Money velocity was low, the economy was performing, the currency was among the world's strongest. When it turned around, inflation was normal for a brief time, then hyperinflation struck with a vengeance. One person said it happened "like lightning ... The shelves in the grocery stores were empty."[12]

In 1791, France experienced a hyperinflation. Mobs raided Paris groceries. The state blamed merchants for the rising prices and imposed price controls. Trade halted. Food disappeared. High taxes rose further. Capital fled the country and the poor were abandoned. Price controls led to restrictions on sales of gold and silver, enforced by six years of imprisonment. Anyone taking the French *assignat* (the failing currency) at a discount could be fined heavily. In 1794, if someone asked which medium of exchange they preferred – paper or gold – before the sale, they could be put to death. The deteriorating situation ended in flames when the nation burned the *assignats*. In France's previous hyperinflation, John Law had made the use of gold and silver as currency illegal as well as ownership of gold itself. He closed the border to those leaving with PMs just before the fall of the French currency. Nations in desperate currency straits often clamp down on access to or holdings of precious metals.

The stock market is hitting new highs even as businesses fail from hemorrhaging losses and unemployment climbs the wall of worry. The coinciding of stock highs with a massive recession -depression even – is a clear sign of looming hyperinflation. There is another old warning signal of impending fiat failure. Most hyperinflations feature a disappearance of the coinage. As the metal in the coins begins to exceed the nominal value of the coin, their issuance ceases. Only paper notes continue to circulate. During the Roman hyperinflation, the coins were gradually debased by removing the silver content. The US has switched from copper to zinc for pennies. The metal in the nickel coin is worth seven cents (and is being removed). Smaller coinage is being taken out of circulation. It may seem less important, but when the penny disappears, mark that date down. Hyperinflation may be near.

Other 'flations

*Fragility rises on long-term trend,*
*with increasingly severe financial crises*
*– Hyman Minsky*

There are a few other 'flations. Though it sounds obtuse, the simplest is disinflation. This is merely a reduction in the inflation rate. If inflation ran at 10% in one month and 9% the next, there was a 1% disinflation. Disinflation is not deflation; it is still inflation, unless the disinflation exceeds the total inflation rate. Disinflation, if validly measured, indicates greater control over the inflation rate by the monetary creators.

Of more import is stagflation. In the 1970s, stagflation was *the* fear. Most people talked about it, but few understood it. In a sense, it's quite basic – rising prices, slowing economy with falling employment and lagging wages. Stagflation was thought impossible, until it happened. Rising prices were believed to spur production and hence job creation. More money creation was believed to be a panacea for a sluggish economy, and a consequent bout of inflation was a sensible price to pay. Economists were wrong – returns on printing declined quickly. It turns out to be more complicated. More money is just more paper. It is not more wealth and soon enough, the public understands this.

Stagflation is very intractable once it gains a hold. The tools for lowering unemployment contradict the tools for tightening inflation. Stagflation is politically measured by the so-called Misery Index: inflation plus unemployment.

It can arise from supply shocks in widely used essential goods, especially oil. When oil hit $150 in 2008, prices soared at the same time that economic activity contracted. Energy intensive businesses that were undercapitalized failed. Think of the auto makers. The key danger is a huge price rise for producers which cannot be easily passed on to consumers.

The second cause of stagflation is poor policy. If the Fed prints too much and the cost of labor is non-competitive (because the Chinese work for a lot less), then industry contracts while the money supply increases. Stagflation can also emanate from changes in the relative value of currencies, often from forex (currency exchange) markets, leading to severe price rises.

The above are more conventional ideas. The more hard money Austrian school finds stagflation to be solely caused by excess printing. Because the first ones to receive money (banks/financiers) benefit from it most by having increased purchasing power, and because those later in line (manufacturers/ labor) are the true producers, money creation destroys productive capacity by weakening the producer's position in the capital chain.

In truth, the current economy will experience multiple phases, with some deflation, inflation, stagflation and possibly culminating in hyperinflation. Meantime, and from a more gold-based perspective, the current experience might more accurately be termed *schizoflation*. In some sense schizoflation, also called biflation, is always happening in real terms. As money moves from one sector to another, the sector losing funds experiences deflationary pressures and the sector gaining funds experiences inflationary pressures.

The current circumstance of debt saturation will create a predictable printing response. The increase in currency and debt will make biflation a powerful force. Necessary items – food, energy and so forth – are rising because of printing pressures. Big-ticket, debt-encumbered items are dropping because of lower purchasing power from recessionary and job loss conditions combined with unwillingness to take on more debt. It's a double hit for the middle class who still buy food and energy, and whose savings are mostly in paid off houses and bonds – debt-tied instruments that lose value. We will see meaningful deflation in debt encumbered assets (houses, cars, capital equipment, businesses), collectibles (baseball cards, old coins, postage stamps), paper assets (stocks, bonds, derivatives), and unnecessary items (left-handed potato peelers, chrome wheel rims, Christmas sweaters) and severe inflation in food, commodities, and precious metals. David Korowicz explains in more detail, by invoking the rising energy costs as lynchpin:

> High oil prices feed back into the economy through reduced economic activity, increasing pressure on discretionary income and rising defaults. This is an accelerator of debt deflation dynamics. In discussing this we need to be clear about the definitions of inflation and deflation. Often, inflation and deflation are defined in terms of rising and falling prices. These are secondary effects. One can have rising prices in a deflationary environment. In this study, inflation and deflation are a rise or fall in money + credit relative to GDP [meaning – if printing outpaces production, that is inflation]. Debt deflation, even without rising food and energy prices, leads to reduced discretionary ... Rising food and energy prices, because they are at the heart of non-discretionary expenditure, lead to further squeezes on discretionary spending, credit issuance, and the ability to service debt. Thus economies are caught between vice-grips of debt deflation arising from credit over-expansion, and the rising costs of its primary needs. This reinforces a debt deflationary spiral.[13]

Food is incredibly correlated to this cost because food production costs are almost entirely energy driven. As oil becomes more expensive and scarce, food will follow. As food is inelastic in demand, it will soak up more and more of people's money, drying up discretionary spending. This leads to civil unrest, beginning in poorer countries. Biflation is very punishing for a society and leads inevitably to social unrest.

## Endnotes

1    Shadowstats.com
2    Walter Jon Williams, No. 445: SPECIAL COMMENTARY – Review of Economic, Systemic-Solvency, Inflation, U.S. Dollar and Gold Circumstances, Shadow Government Statistics. June 12, 2012
3    David Hackett Fisher, *The Great Wave: Price Revolutions and the Rhythm of History*, Oxford University Press, 1996, pp. 237-238,
4    Quigley, ch. 9.
5    Zohan Pozar, et al. , Shadow Banking. Federal Reserve Bank of NY staff report #458. February 2012 revision.
6    Walter J. Willialms, "Hyperinflation Special Report", Shadowstats, 2012.
7    Benjamin Bernanke, Federal Reserve Board meeting, November 21, 2002.
8    Tyler Durden, "The Fed Has Another $3.9 Trillion In QE To Go (At Least)", Zerohedge. com, September 23, 2012.
9    See the Petrodollar section for details
10   Williams, Hyperinflation special report, 2012.
11   Mike Hewitt, "History of Fiat and Paper Money Failures: The Fate of Paper Money", rapidtrends.com.
12   W.J. Williams, supra Shadow government statistics. Jan. 25, 2012.
13   David Korowicz, "Trade-off", June, 2012.

# 8

# METALS TRADING, MANIPULATIONS AND THEFT

*Those who manipulate this unseen mechanism of society*
*constitute an invisible government, which is the*
*true ruling power in our country.*
—**Edward Bernays**

The multi-century war against gold and the attempt to replace it with fiat currencies was quite overt until the mid-1960s. Totalitarian governments, communist governments and Western governments alike all outlawed gold ownership at different times in order to enforce the use of a paper currency. People were given no choice. In former times, gold was simply forbidden for the public when it threatened the government-sanctioned currency. That tactic is too blunt for the modern world. Now, they have turned gold into just another currency, or even degraded it to a commodity. At least that's the attempt. It has worked since 1980. The two primary techniques are propaganda (smearing gold), and the centuries old method of creating fractional gold – purporting to sell gold via paper instruments – creating a synthetic supply. This changes the equation from gold price = money supply/physical gold – to gold price = money supply/(physical + paper gold). The amount of paper expansion thereby is stunning in itself, but the creative methodologies are the real prize.

Beginning in the 1930s with the gold exchange standard, there was a decades-long process of demonetizing gold using increasing sophistication and propaganda. Even in 2012, owners were called traitors to their country, because "civilized people don't buy gold," at least according to Warren Buffet's partner.

When gold was re-legalized in 1975 in the US, propaganda shifted. Instead of a monetary basis, gold was rebranded a 'commodity.' It became simply another speculative investment like wheat or oil. What could not be enforced through laws was accomplished through re-education. People were trained to believe that gold was not money. In so doing, they lost all clear understanding of what money actually is. It's a peculiar irony, in a society that prides itself on capitalist ideals, the extent to which money remains a mystery, even though it's a fairly clear subject. The understanding of it has been deliberately muddled and obfuscated to protect, not the public interest, but the interest of elite controllers.

Even within this mode of thought, gold is a good investment because the competition has high risk. Ten year bonds have duration risk, land and fine art have liquidity risks, currency has devaluation risk, and the stock market has many pitfalls. Only short-term Treasuries present a viable alternative for the big investor. But the return on these is appalling – 0.2%. This is well below inflation, meaning the investor's value is slowly eroding. Real interest rates ultimately drive the gold market. When they are negative, meaning money cannot find a return in the market, gold tends to rise.

**Figure 27**
**Gold & US Real Rates**

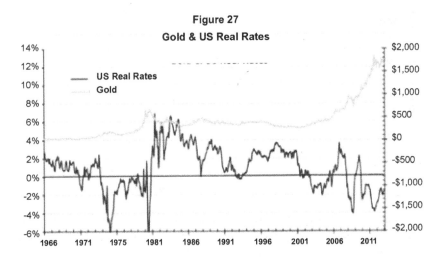

One of the strongest reasons for suppression of PMs is to make the dollar look good. Gold is the canary in the coal mine. If it rises too much and too fast, this is typically due to high inflation or negative real interest rates. Negative real rates occur when interest is less than inflation – loans become cheaper over time in real terms. In other words, if inflation is 8% and you can borrow money at 3%, then borrowing money to invest in a commodity basket will pay 5% each year after paying the loan. The investor gets paid to borrow money. Since 2000, for example, gold has increased by an average 16% per year (silver boasts 20%). It would have been a winning investment (as of January 2013) to borrow $100,000 long-term at 6% and buy gold – $400,000 profit. (Silver would be twice the profit). Negative real rates don't occur in free markets – no one would loan money only to get less of it back in real terms. Negative real rates occur from central bank manipulation and lead to economic problems in the long run.

The rule of Gibson's Paradox states that gold will rise by 8 times (2% minus the real interest rate). Real rates are the nominal interest rate minus inflation. Nominal rates are near zero (for banks borrowing from the Fed), so real rates are negative – over 3% at this writing. For the formula, that's 8*(2%-(-3%))=8*5%=40% price rise per year predicted. Of course, that assumes gold is in an unmanipulated market. That is the financial controllers' fear

**Figure 28**
**Gold YoY vs Real Interest Rates (since 1978)**

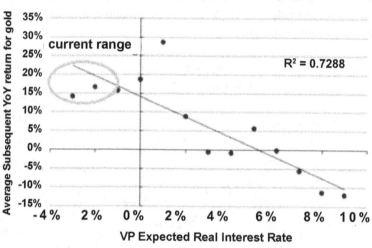

– that gold will leap upwards, drawing in investment, drying it up from elsewhere and exposing the rolling failure of the fiat regimes. So gold must be held in check. They admitted it long ago. "Central banks," Alan Greenspan said in Congressional testimony, "stand ready to lease gold in increasing quantities should the price rise." This leads to the need to keep the price down. While they have been more successful at this in 2011-mid 2013 than in years previous, there are downstream consequences. Artificial suppression leads to blow-off rises where the suppression cannot be contained. The suppression cannot continue indefinitely for numerous reasons – rising public awareness, shrinking supply of physical, and powerful interests allied to release the price. The physical supply is the real key.

The techniques of suppression are many, and growing almost daily. But this proliferation of technique does not indicate better control – it indicates desperation.

The price suppression appears to have taken on a much more short-term goal – to facilitate less expensive default. Paper gold trades can be settled in dollars by a declaration of *force majeure*, standard clauses in contracts that exempt the fulfillment of obligations due to the interference of an unpredictable, overwhelming force. If the trading entity cannot come up with the underlying instrument (physical gold or silver), they may have no choice but to settle in (declining) dollars, Euros, or British Pounds. The short squeeze has become tight. If a strong player manages to enforce delivery of an amount greater than the Comex or London Bullion Market Association (LBMA) has or can get, then default is inescapable. Unconfirmed rumors circulate that it has already occurred. Some speculators have received a 25% premium on futures contracts in exchange for not applying for delivery. Being a lucrative trade, the speculators would not want to blow it up by going public. But the system cannot tolerate this damaging give-away indefinitely.

This section takes an in-depth look at some of the many mechanisms for gold price suppression. Many exist, and perhaps not all have been discovered by investigators. Just to give a taste – propaganda, gold swaps, gold leasing, shorting, allocated theft, rehypothecation, multiple sales, unallocated pools, Central Bank sales, smackdowns, timed interventions, margin calls, regulatory obstructions, blocked investigations and even war are used. Together, these techniques suppress the price, increase the supply, generate volatility and frighten investors away.

## Propaganda

*The CIA owns everyone of any significance*
*in the major media.*
~ **William Colby (former CIA Director)**

In "The Great Gold Bust," *Time Magazine* announced that gold had "about as much luster as a rusty tin can." That was in 1976, when it was at the bottom before a 400% rise. A more accurate sentiment came from *Business Week*: "For several thousand years, the world has thought of gold as money. For several hundred years, it has lived on paper credit and still thought of gold as money. It will take some adjustment to think of paper money as the only money and gold as just like pork bellies."

For a time, they were right. In 1999, *The New York Times* headlined "Who Needs Gold when we have Greenspan?"announcing the death of gold as money. Then the gold bull began, from 2000 going on and on. In 2004, smack in the middle of the current gold run, the *Financial Times* printed a screaming tirade against gold, proclaiming "the barbarous relic, as Keynes called it, is crumbling to dust...fetishization of the shiny metal... [it's] a lingering anomaly...Gold is on its way out as an investment." Gold rose 50% in the next two years. Forecasters have gotten gold wrong 7 years in a row.

**Figure 29**
**Gold Kept Rising Despite Analysts' Forecasts**

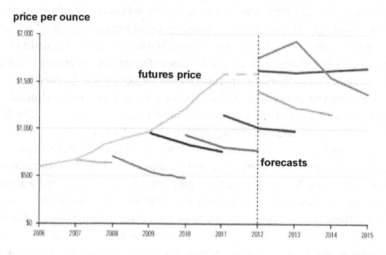

"Media manipulation currently shapes everything you read, hear and watch online. Everything," a *Forbes* magazine article stated, ironically following it with the headline "Why gold's long bull market may be history." We should definitely pay attention to the first article about media spin. For example, Nancy Grace did a major hit on gold buyers, calling them "lonely, rich white guys," several times. Her guest compared them to stalkers. Most recent propaganda is more cautious than this. "Gold dips to 6-month low as Bernanke says U.S. economy is improving," investing.com posted. The implied link is not established – a common media gambit. The article coincided with the (hostile to the US) G20 meeting on February 15 of 2013. "Has the Anti-Gold Rush Begun?" *Barron's* posted a week later, when options betting on GLD to decline a tiny $1, increased. These pieces are targeting investors with money. Kitco, a notoriously bearish gold retailer, let go of Jon Nadler, its gold perma-bear. Nadler had predicted a fall to $1000 for several years running after repeatedly predicting gold would never pass $1000, even predicting a drop to $300. Kitco cannot be considered a bastion of good sense – it has applied for at least 4 bankruptcy extensions while other gold retailers are announcing record profits.

The propaganda aims to scare people away from gold, John Embry claims, making it seem that people sell it during crises. They don't, but the paper markets get very choppy for a number of reasons – mostly manipulation for suppression and profit.

"For real people and policy makers whose job it is to care about real people, gold is irrelevant," *Business Insider* tells us, assuming most policy makers care about people. *The Telegraph* worried over gold in a March, 2013 report. Apparently, anonymous investors are "piling into equities," and out of gold. "The increasingly lonely-looking figure keeping the faith amid all this is John Paulson." George Soros, the article says, has cut his GLD holdings by 60%. Though Soros made no comment, the assumption is he's a gold bear. Strangely, he retained a $100 million stake in GLD. Soros bought much lower and may have simply chosen to take his 15% profit – normal institutional practice. He also moved the money (and more) into a bet against the yen, netting a billion dollars on the trade. In fact, his fund still holds almost half a billion dollars in gold and gold miners. That article was much ado about nothing. In fact, it's the dollar-centric view that's causing confusion. Even as these sentiments were written, gold was hitting hyperbolic highs in the Yen because of Japanese devaluation. (A year earlier, it was highs in the Euro.) This devaluation caused other currencies to rise and rebalanced the global gold equation – neither up nor down, but over to another currency. The media ignores the raging high in Japan, though.

Then a bombshell. When Cyprus went belly-up, the media announced it would have to sell 400 million Euros of gold to bolster the budget. Gold plummeted $85 on the news. Funny thing – the Cypriot government and central bank *had not discussed* selling their gold. Soon after, Reuters made the bizarre error that gold had "slumped to its lowest price in 30 years." They recommend London property, milk (even buying a farm), or Treasury bonds as safe havens.

In 2001, Jim Sinclair predicted $1600 gold by January of 2011. It hit the mark six months later. This was an awesome feat of prediction since in 2000, the metal was $250 / oz. Sinclair, a gold bull ever since, has done very well off the rise and been completely forthcoming about his opinions. He is anti-Wall Street. Executives, he claims with research to back it, are loading up on gold privately, while risking their companies publicly to be bailed out at the government trough. The accounts referred to are the Carlyle Group, known for high-level contacts and secrecy. Sinclair has been very active in the gold market for decades, even selling gold to wealthy Saudis during the 1980s. In spite of his experience, the mainstream media never invites him on to discuss gold. Though a few gold bulls appear on camera, no one who claims there is an active gold suppression gets mainstream airtime, no matter how prominent, knowledgeable or successful they are. Sinclair's latest prediction is $3500 gold by mid-2015.

Wherever you look in the mainstream media, it's claimed that metals prices are about to decline. No matter the news, good or bad, it portends a dark cloud for foolish gold investors. If QE is announced, the stock market should be able to ride it up, so investors should want to go there instead. If no QE is announced, the currency is not inflated, so there is no need for the haven of PMs. On good economic data, metals decline because of the enticement of profitable stocks. On bad data, they decline with stocks because of 'margin calls' and liquidation of gold for needed cash. Marginal data causes PMs to decline because 'gold does not pay a dividend,' like blue chips and bonds. These are some of the primary talking points of the media. In spite of this persistent dissuasion, gold and silver have enjoyed the longest and strongest bull market of any investment vehicle in history. Gold has risen from $250 to its current price and silver from $4, with anti-gold media spin nipping at the heels the entire way.

It's not just the media, either. The city of Houston (among others) has enacted new laws for buying gold. In order to combat jewelry thefts (the official line), store owners must get fingerprints and photographs from sellers of gold. This can be seen as a war on those who protect their wealth through owning gold. The growing desire to secure wealth against the ravages of out-of-control money printing is anathema to out-of-control government.

The negative stream produces occasional rich ironies. "The bull market for gold will not last," *SmartMoney* magazine predicted in 2004 when gold was at $422, "and anyone making gold the cornerstone of his or her investment porfolios is making a serious mistake." It has since tripled in price, making it hands down the best major investment in the world – except silver. *SmartMoney* admitted its mistake in an article, "Hits and Misses," where it announced it was going out of business.

The talking heads on the MSM (mainstream media) will pound the table with insistence that gold is a high-risk asset only invested in by nitwits. Perhaps they haven't seen the simple chart below. The chart is smoothed to

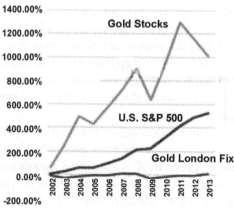

**Figure 30**
**Performance of the S&P500**
**v. Gold & Gold Stocks**
**2001-2012**

beginning of year prices. This removes the illusion of volatility that plagues gold's image. On a short-term timeline, gold is a yo-yo and silver is a nuclear yo-yo. But this is because of banker games to shake out the speculators and scare the public. This keeps the money out, the lid on the price and as much physical as possible in banker vaults.

Long-term trends are very difficult to argue with, however, and the trouncing of stocks by gold is only denied by someone painting the tape. It's impossible to understand how any competent financial advisor can call gold a bad or risky investment after it has been the best investment of the past 12 years. The S&P rose 9% over these years. Gold rose 524%. Are you smarter than a fifth grader? Because a ten-year-old can tell the right answer that 99% of the American public cannot. The message is clear: the establishment mouthpieces are simply lying, saying what they are told to say. They are not allowed to recommend gold. Neither are they allowed to even explain its obvious virtues. The lone dissenter is Rick Santelli on CNBC, who made a series of accurate points about excess amounts of paper gold in the ETF markets with nothing to back them up.

Goldman Sachs advised clients to sell gold and even short it in April, 2013. It seemed like good advice; after all, the metal dropped hugely soon after. Oddly, though, GS did not sell a single ounce of their good-size gold store during the drop. Most fund managers do not take their own advice. That's because it's no good.

Nobel Laureate Daniel Kahneman studied a group of portfolio managers' performance over a multi-year period. He was amazed to find that they had almost no variation between them in performance. All were well-diversified. All fared far worse than they might have by simply owning gold. That's because there is no real skill involved in financial advising. It can be summed up as: concentrate in rock-solid assets and hold them. Buy gold and silver and ride out the volatility. But no one would hire a person to tell them such a simple truth. They jawbone about stocks and good investments. Most clients seem to believe this fatal advice.

Financial advisors are not impartial. They make money by investing client money. They get a piece of each transaction, usually, which builds in an incentive to keep the money moving. Only trust an advisor who ties his income to a client's increase in value under his direction. Only then is the inherent conflict of interest overcome. This is why most advisors never recommend gold: no matter how much the client makes or how well his wealth is protected, the advisor gets nothing save a small initial fee. Anyone with such an obvious conflict of interest should not only be distrusted; they should be barred from doing business in such a manner.

Anti-gold propaganda merits an entire book, but much of the material would be more or less variations on a theme. Basically, the media post perpetual anti-gold articles and have done so for the entirety of the gold bull market. Most of the stories are about the poor investment qualities – it pays no return, it's high-risk, and it has no productive capacity. We'll end this section citing a few concerns raised by the rampant articles about the immorality of gold, Poor African children, NBC reported, have to dig for gold and are paid in bags of dirt; it concluded with the moral that gold investors should be ashamed for investing in such an unethical commodity, blaming an inert metal for child labor rather than the mining companies who exploit them. Gold can even be tied to terrorism! Al-Qaeda allegedly offered gold in payment for the assassination of a US ambassador. The story may not have been true. But no matter: a 'rumor' still serves to damage gold's reputation. Gold, we are to understand, is the medium used by those who wish to pay for morally despicable acts. Apparently, US dollars only serve virtue.

## Spot, Futures and Fixes

*Money changers have used every form of abuse, intrigue, deceit, and violent means … to maintain their control over governments by controlling money and its issuance.*
– James Madison

Propaganda is merely the first line of defense. The real ground war is fought in the spot and futures markets. The 'spot' price for gold and silver means the over the counter price sold on the London Bullion Market Association (LBMA) market. The price is called a 'fix,' an interesting word to consider. Once a day for silver, and twice for gold, the price fix is set based on contracts for delivery within 48 hours. The futures market is the reference for the spot market price. Once the fix is set in London, prices can converge from there. The fix is supposedly a mechanism for price discovery, a means to find out what the true price is. Of course, it can be used to manipulate the price as well.

Five banks presently set the fix – Scotia-Mocatta, Deutsche Bank, HSBC, Société Generale, and Barclays. Until 2004, Rothschild's Bank of London coordinated the fix in a very secretive manner. In a true market, there would be no need for the 'fix' at all. However, all London gold transactions flow from the daily spot fix. Since it is the largest market in the world, the fix price exerts the most influence over world pricing. The price comes by balancing each bank's buy-sell orders on the futures exchanges. When net bids match net asks, the meeting chair posts the fix. That the spot price is being opaquely controlled by closeted executives of major banks indicates there are obvious conflicts of interest and easy opportunities for collusive pricing. The system is so hidden that manipulation is difficult to demonstrate

– but that very hiddenness is already a cause of concern. Such a market is neither free nor transparent.

The Comex (Commodity Exchange, Inc.) is the US cousin of the LBMA. The Comex spot price is different, and in a sense, more transparent. It is still subject to manipulations, though of a different sort. The constantly fluctuating Comex spot is set by the 'most active month' trading. The critical closing spot price is set in the last two minutes of trading (1:30 pm) by averaging the highest and lowest trades during that time.

Though spot prices are derived from futures, the futures market is a bit different. As the name implies, it is a contract to deliver something in the future, usually a commodity, at a pre-arranged price. Futures markets were created for farmers to plan their crops. Frequently, they would overgrow because of a prior shortage that had led to high prices in a particular crop. Futures allowed the price to be set before the crop was planted, allowing farmers to plan better. When the futures price dropped to a non-profitable point, they would find a better futures crop to sell and then grow. This prevented a glut in some areas and an undersupply in others.

Soon other commodities producers were allowed to hedge against a falling price. A hedger must participate in the physical market and buys or sells a futures contract against that. If a small company needs a thousand ounces of silver every six months and is concerned about a price rise, they might hedge by buying some long futures contracts. This gives them price stability. A miner could sell a futures contract for, say, $100 per unit. This enables them to be sure that no matter where the price went, they could still produce at a profit. Whether the price goes down or up, they get no loss or reward. Speculators take the opposite sides of these trades, betting that the commodity will rise. If they expect a commodity to fall, they will sell. Someone must take the opposite side of a speculator's short sale. This means the speculative side of the market is actually far larger, since speculators take both sides of most trades to limit their risk. Currency traders also use the futures market to hedge (take an offsetting position).

Fewer than 2% of futures contracts terminate with any delivery. This goes to show how much of this market (and indeed our entire economy) is now given to speculation, rather than legitimate hedging. Speculators have taken over in every market because money overwhelms all other factors in commerce. Because of their size, traders now control the market. This is another huge downside to massive perpetual monetary creation and favoritism towards the financial sector. Producers are punished for the profit of the non-productive financial industry. Putting aside moral implications, it's terrible economic practice. Though in the short run it can benefit farmers and producers if they catch the right wind of the speculative run-up, it can also devastate industries, and it has. The farming industry is now being pushed around like a child's toy by these forces in the very market they created for stability. Government subsidies keep large farmers profitable. Small farms can't make it. Though there are additional factors in farming to make it unprofitable, the loss of control over their futures industry to speculation is significant.

Most contracts are either rolled over or eliminated. A holder of a long contract will sell a short contract to close out his position. Because futures are traded on margin, traders can use higher leverage. Being an agreement to pay in the future, futures contracts only require a certain amount to be posted. In other words, a $100 contract may only need $10, for example, to secure it. If the futures price declines to $90, the contract owner must post the maintenance margin or the position will be automatically sold off at loss. This is one way that margin calls happen.

The other way is changing the margin requirements. Most commodities have a maintenance requirement lower than the purchase requirement, giving the buyer some wiggle room in the event of a decline. Maintenance requirements can be changed by the CFTC at will. If they deem a market too hot, they can raise the margin. This leads to the classic manipulation outcry. By raising margins quickly, repeatedly, and at odd hours, the CFTC can force a sell-off. Exactly this occurred when silver spiked to $49. The old, all-time high of $50 was fiercely defended by the regulators, who gut-punched it with 5 margin hikes in a few days at odd hours. Maybe they were just cooling the market off, but they do nothing of the sort when *stocks* are hot. The dotcom bubble never felt such regulatory tactics, nor did the housing market. Irrational exuberance is encouraged in most markets, but never in precious metals.

The typical minimum margin is 5-10%. In a more volatile market, the margin is higher. Because of this high leverage, the futures market is quite lucrative and quite dangerous. There is also a price change limit in futures. If a commodity moves by a certain percentage in either direction, all trading is shut down for the day. However, this rule is routinely ignored on massive gold/silver declines. No explanation is given.

Total gold production is about 2500 tons per year. Daily traded volume on these exchanges is 6700 tons per *day*. The trading volume of gold is almost 600 times the annual production. In fact, annual traded volume is 10 times all the gold that exists on Earth. Since only a small amount of physical gold stock is actually put on the market each year, it is the paper market that is inarguably controlling the price. No one contests this – they only contest if the market is deliberately manipulated. Of course, this amount of paper to physical creates a massive distortion, creating the ability to manipulate, and indeed manipulating, the market whether intended or not. It drastically cuts the price. If all that money were put into verifiably existent physical gold stocks, the price would be multiples higher as a simple mathematical calculation.

"Contango" is the normal situation for gold futures. In contango, the futures months cost more than the spot price, and each month out costs more than the closer ones. This reflects the cost of holding gold, for one thing, and the cost of future money versus present money, for another. It's not necessarily a speculation that the gold price will increase. There's a more immediate reason for not going into 'backwardation' – the reverse of contango.

Backwardation happens when the spot price is greater than the futures price. Arbitrage should clear this out immediately. If it's possible to sell gold in the spot market for $10 million, and simultaneously buy the same amount of physical for 6 months delivery at $9.7 million, then someone will do so, usually within seconds. The machines never sleep. The arbitrage (risk-free profit) will eliminate the backwardation. Backwardation can happen, but it tends to end quickly. Recently, however, it has been persisting for longer and longer periods, especially in silver. This may be because strong hands do not want to part with physical metal in return for a future promise. The metals are less and less available for large sales. Trust is falling quickly, withheld by smart investors. If backwardation persists and the spread widens, it is a serious danger signal that PMs are about to go parabolic. Big money knows that the supply is drained and is refusing to take free profits. They would rather make sure they have the metal.

Now for the real fix. The Cartel, the big bank consortium, uses the early morning grind most frequently. When the Comex opens at 8:20, there is a period of 100 minutes until the afternoon fix in London. In 2010, gold never rose over 2% between the morning and afternoon fix. Twice it rose only 1%. All other commodities have regular rises up to 6% or even 8% in this time range. Yet gold, in 2010, outperformed all other commodities save silver, due to demand outside this time period. It rose 24%. Still, almost every day, it ticks down starting at 8:20. Gold is hit almost daily at 10 a.m., the fix time. This is repeated at noon, when the Comex closes and electronic trading takes over. The game is to drive the metals lower when Western markets are open because the Cartel has less control over Asian markets. In a little known fact, gold is net down on the Comex markets for the entire bull market since 2001, despite rising from $250 to $1600. To explain – the average price at closing bell is less than the average price at opening bell: every day (on average), gold loses money during Comex hours and gains money (because it's a nearly continuous bull market) when the exchange is closed on international exchanges. It's so counterintuitive as to be impossible, short of intense manipulation.

Dmitri Speck offered striking evidence of gold intervention. Figure 31 shows the average intraday price of gold from 1993-2009. The drop at the p.m. fix is clear. It cannot be an anomaly – it's averaged over 17 years. The big banks have the power to set the p.m. fix. They have set it lower than the actual market price of gold. This is bald proof of market manipulation.

**Figure 31**

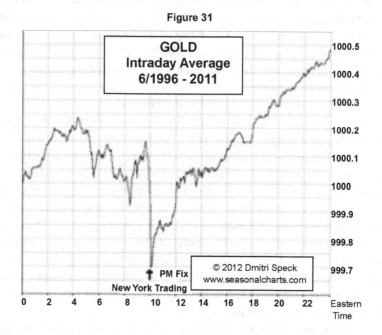

Market liquidity is highest for the four hours when London and New York are both open. A more or less daily attack occurs immediately on the opening of the New York exchange. Major attacks are typically made at 3 a.m. Because the market is so thinly traded at this time, the late night raid only makes sense as a manipulation. A large dump of gold will take the largest possible loss for the trader, so clearly making money is not the reason for the sale. Routine night sales drop the price as much as possible for the amount of paper gold sold.

A key indicator in the market is open interest (OI) – the number of contracts open at any time. OI divides into categories of large specs, small specs, and commercials (the Cartel). Commercial OI is what analysts watch because it indicates the direction of the market. Anomaly hunting is the game. Different theories exist – when the Cartel naked short position gets low, then price is set for a rise. Or the reverse. Theories seem to work for a time, then fail.

When the price drops and OI rises, however, naked short positions are increasing. This is because new positions are being opened. When the price drops and OI decreases, the longs are liquidating – closing positions. It's difficult to offer a simple explanation, so this rule of thumb will help someone looking at the weekly data sets.

The main suppressors are the commercial banks with big, big money, enough to push markets around. Technically, they need an opposite side to the trade – though suppression can be done by taking both sides of a declining trade to scare away smaller bids. The opposite trades are normally taken by small and large speculators. Short-term betting against the commercials is generally suicide. They exert an overwhelming market force that's tough to fight. However, they need to manage their short positions – paper gold sold without any physical gold to back it or a paper long contract to offset it. It's called naked shorting and it's illegal, but the banks are doing it anyway. No one seems to object, at least no one capable of doing anything about it.

The 3 largest commercials have had short positions as high as 65% of all shorts. Whether they have the gold to back it is not the issue. This level of concentrated position is market manipulation by definition. The commercial banks are pushing the price around with easy, clear proof and the regulators are covering it up.

Another technique, mainly for profit, is called a 'wash trade.' The large fund posts a simultaneous buy and sell order at a specific price outside the current price – say $98 transaction on $100 price. This tends to move the market price down without costing the poster anything – taking both sides of the trade gives a 'wash.' By buying options in the direction beforehand, the trader can take profits on the market movement he engineers. It's illegal and it happens millions of times a day in all markets with high-frequency trading.

In March 2010, Jeffrey Christian (a commercial bank precious metals expert) testified that banks leverage gold 100 to 1. This means that for every ounce of gold they hold, they trade 100 ounces of paper gold. Christian adamantly denied any intervention in the metals market, calling the past, open manipulation of the London Gold Pool "good manipulation." Soon after, he tells what's really happening – "intervention … it's much more effective if people don't know what you're doing." He expressly tells us that if the manipulation were occurring, it would be deliberately hidden.

Apologists for the system claim it is a contango arbitrage. Because futures typically sell for more than spot, buying physical and selling futures nets a profit. This ignores the cost of delivery, vaulting, assaying and security, however – which is the source of the price difference. Simply put – it costs money to hold quantities of gold, so its future value is greater because it factors in these costs over the time span. Contango arbitrage is a fig-leaf to cover the manipulation. The banks are actually selling 100 times the paper versus physical they own. When open interest (number of positions) grows enough, the banks 'harvest' the weak-hand longs by triggering automatic sell orders with a price dip. More on this in the next section.

Paper gold inflation has been called synthetic supply. In a testament to human creativity, the methods for creating synthetic supply are more than one might guess. Selling short futures is the most straightforward method. It's a brute force approach, requiring lots of capital, and is very high risk. According to analyst Victor the Cleaner, "you cannot manipulate a physically settled commodity contract from the short side for any period of time longer than the contract you are trading." This is technically true, but the implication he derives from it is not.

He claims that gold futures (and the gold market in general) is not and cannot be manipulated. He scoffs at those who suggest otherwise. But the claim asserts a full faith in the overt idea of the futures market and ignores its operating reality. The futures market ostensibly is a claim on delivery of gold at a specific date, but this *almost never happens*. Ninety-nine percent of gold and silver futures contracts are rolled over. The person holding the long side sells it before it matures. While the technical length of futures contracts is up to a year, the de facto length can be decades because no one forces the closure of open positions by calling for delivery. Gold supply is inflated in the futures market by many orders of magnitude. The rules for delivery are Byzantine, making calls for delivery far less worthwhile than speculation. The method is to play one game while calling it another.

In a sense, the Cleaner is correct. A commodities market cannot be manipulated against the prevailing trend for a vastly longer term than the contracts. A forceful and creative rolling can create a downdraft for some years on a one-year basis. All a big trader need do is steadily increase the short contracts around expiry. It's ridiculous to say that the term of contract is an absolute limit when the number of contracts can be steadily increased as a rollover method. The increase does not even need to be geometric – which would lead to a parabolic number of contracts. It only needs to be enough to overwhelm the longs. It is difficult to manage the steadily growing amount of contracts to be sure. But the approach is so simple and so obviously feasible that it's difficult to believe this analyst is giving an honest opinion.

The Hong Kong Mercantile Exchange was supposed to be a game changer. It was going to allow free trade of fully backed silver and gold futures, even featuring mini-contracts. This would allow even middle class Chinese to buy gold and silver from the futures market. Since it was fully backed, it would draw real physical from the world market. But that would have put a lot of strain on Western banks, the LBMA and the Comex through the fractional leverage enhancer. Instead, the exchange turned into a head fake – only offering more of the same unbacked shell games. It was a flop. On May 20, 2013, it folded after less than 2 years amid arrests and forged documents. All accounts were settled in cash. This was taken as a sign of precious metal shortage after a massive public buying spree. The accounts should rightfully be settled in the commodity itself, as this was the source of the investment's allure. But then, the EN+ group founded the HKMEx. And the head of the EN+ group? Nathan Rothschild.

Effectively, the HKMEx was just another delaying tactic seeking to slow the rise of gold. Eventually the market will suck out the underlying commodity and reverse the trend violently if it is held underwater for too long. The banks are obviously not manipulating gold steadily downward – the price is rising. Rather, the manipulation seeks to slow the long-trend, making the rises more gradual.

It is also a psychological war against investors seeking to secure their wealth in gold. When the price gets hot, a severe slam-down occurs. When conditions are urgent for a rise, the price is crushed. Volatility scares away the enormous pool of smaller investors, and even larger, risk-averse ones. Retirement funds, pension accounts, and 401(k)s, cannot tolerate risk. Artificially creating an unpredictable gold market scares away the bulk of middle class wealth which would drain the physical overnight. If the middle class went all in, they would buy coins from the local coin store. Physical supply would dry up immediately. By contrast, speculators (who prefer volatility) are welcomed with open arms. The futures market gives a huge nest for an ocean of cash while making virtually no demand on physical metals. A gradual increase in futures market participants is the perfect cover for suppressing the gold price. They help buy the retiring and new shorts, giving the Cartel a steady cash flow and keeping capital away from physical metals. In brief, inflating the apparent supply without getting bullion calls is the nub of the entire scheme. It has led to a 'short bubble.' Its resolution is unclear – it could drive paper prices much higher, when managed money panics in a price rise and covers. Or, more likely, it could lead to a divergence between paper and physical – with paper prices collapsing and physical soaring.

**Smackdowns**

*The speculators are focused on the next trade and their positions; the commercials are focused on mastering the speculators.*
*– Ted Butler*

On February 29, 2012 JPMorgan dropped 12 months' worth of silver production on the futures market in 56 minutes. It's called a smackdown, dropping the primary price marker – the futures market. It's part of the manipulation, but not just intended to depress the price again and again as in a managed retreat. It's also meant to alter market psychology. It's depressing to be a precious metals investor and watch your investment get hammered repeatedly. It feels like you can't defeat the powers. This scares speculators away from going long on gold. The smackdown is more than just a big dump of paper gold on the market. It's a specially timed, and sometimes highly orchestrated, event.

On April 12, 2013 gold got one of the biggest smackdowns in the whole bull market. The move was 5 standard deviations, which should happen once in 4776 years. The gold fund GLD moved by 8 standard deviations – that should not happen before the end of the universe. It was not typical market forces – it was the big desks manipulating the market in a well-coordinated assault.

The signal to traders was a 3.4 million ounce dump at Comex opening – the largest single order placement in history. It was a sophisticated operation complete with warm-up salvos. First, a false news story about Cyprus selling gold dropped it to $1550. That was a scant $25 above the 2 year low – a critical benchmark. Selling started aggressively in the London market, dropping it to $1542. When the US markets opened the actual attack got going in spades. After the opening dump, another *10 million* ounces hit the tape – $15 billion in a few minutes. No profit seeking entity takes such a risk.

Eleven hundred tons of paper gold was dropped on the market that day. Relentless sell orders tanked the price to the red line of $1525. The market capitulated. Massive stop-loss orders, of which the manipulators were aware because they operate the exchanges, were triggered. The market cascaded below $1500. Meantime, in London, investors started buying physical gold on the spot market because the price was so appealing. This worked against the shorts by bolstering the price. Lo and behold – the LBMA system froze, preventing the buyers from purchasing spot gold. The price was not supported by normal market forces. Speculators jumping in at a low point were blocked from performing their normal function, so the price fall had no natural arrests. The force working against the shorts was removed by a 'market glitch' at the perfect moment.

A similar lock-up happened during the price decline of Dec. 29, 2011. Traders were forced to forego the physical market and short the futures as a hedge. The tactic of dropping the price quickly, forcing leveraged longs to liquidate, and sending the market into confusion has a name – 'banging the beehive.' The attackers push the price down to the triggers, then let the market play out with the momentum established.

Sell stops are the essential technique for price manipulation. The commercials use technical analysis to determine where the resistance is to price drops. It's a simple matter of seeing where the price bounces off a low repeatedly. Just below that, the speculators put in stop-loss order. These are automatic triggers to sell when the price is dropping. The commercials drop a large sell order on the market of 500 contracts, for example. The price drops below resistance, triggering stop-losses for 1000 contracts. The commercials can then buy back their 500 new naked shorts and cover a few others. They manage to lower the short position and make a few dollars in the process.

The Cartel have to be precise, however. Too big a sell and they tank the price to where they can't make it up. Their average sell price goes too low. Also, if they overwhelm the sell orders underneath, then there aren't enough liquidations to buy back. Commercial open interest increases, which they're trying to avoid now because the long-trend of PMs is clearly up. If the sell bomb is too small, then the specs simply add to their long positions because the price doesn't break through resistance. The stop-loss orders are not triggered. Then the commercials are simply adding to a losing position.

This also explains why super-large sell orders that intensely crash the price are manipulation for a purpose other than making money. Super-large sell orders are a losing proposition because even though the price drops well below the average sale of the selling bomb, there simply aren't enough sell orders on the spec side for the commercial to buy back its contracts. If they tried to, it would raise the price far above the previous levels, leading to enormous losses. When a single seller overwhelms the market with a day's selling in a few minutes, there is some motive outside of the metals market per se.

It's very tricky to short-trade against the underlying trend. To do so, you must be big enough to move markets and nimble enough to ride them very quickly. It's also possible (and much easier) to engage in if you have advance notice of 'events.' Probably the best public notice is a Bernanke speech. Gold is almost always hit before, during, and after. A nimble trader could buy short term options on GLD, then take profits a few minutes later.

Back to the December 2011 big smash. With the market still falling and with no ability to buy or sell physical, holders of spot gold began shorting futures into the panic. Because it was on a Friday, they could have been hit with a nasty margin call over the weekend, forcing huge losses. It was a defensive hedge for them, but it pushed the price down more. The continuing fall broke undercapitalized traders like straws. Their positions were shut without mercy, shoving many more contracts for sale into the futures market, adding to the selling pressure. The market closed at $1490. Margin calls went out to the desperate longs, adding to the pain. They took the best option – liquidate in the aftermarkets, before the weekend did more damage. This pushed the price down to $1476 – an $88 decline in total. Sixteen million ounces of paper gold traded that day – an epic swan dive for the metal. At 500 tons, it exceeded all central bank sales combined for an entire year. Peak selling of 155 tons in one hour occurred just before the London fix. Sales were much greater than any possible holder of physical gold. All told, $24 billion was dumped on the market in one day. Not even the largest megabanks have that kind of capital on hand for a single operation. Only one entity does – the Federal Reserve.

The attack continued the following Monday, driving gold down below $1400. This was the most intense smackdown of precious metals ever.

Regulators frequently stop trading in other markets when faced with far smaller declines – yet they failed to do so here. Why? They are supporting the scheme. The monetary powers want stability in equities and bonds, and volatility in precious metals. Trading is never halted for gold declines, no matter how egregious and obvious the regulatory violations.

In a pretty extreme knock-on consequence, JPMorgan's eligible gold all but disappeared 11 days later when 8 out of 12.5 tons moved off the ledger. The vault listing for eligible gold (not available for sale) declined by 65% in one day. Somebody with deep pockets and plenty of clout had hit the bank hard with a call for delivery.

The smackdown operation had urgent cause. The details are tough to ferret, but it looks like a major supply squeeze was hitting the market. ABN Amro, for example, a Dutch bullion bank, had to settle its holders in cash. A run on the LBMA was in progress. The metal was not there and the cost in cash was sky-high. The massive take-down was orchestrated to permit the cash settlement to take place at a much more workable level. More importantly, it forced a few large holders to disgorge bullion and feed the demand.

High frequency trading (HFT) was used to manipulate the market. These systems get a heavy workout every day. The algos – computer algorithms – get access to data early. Thirty milliseconds is not enough time for a human trader to do anything meaningful, but it's a full day for a computer. By seeing the 'order depth,' the computer knows how many orders and how big are lined up on the buy and sell side. The algos front-run the market, determining the lowest price a large seller will take to unload his shares. This is below the market price because the seller will drop the price some by the size of his order. The algo, with advance information, short sells ahead of the big seller, clearing the market down to his minimum price. The algo then turns and buys back the shares from the big seller at the lowest price. Because the orders could have been filled at a higher price without the front-running, this suppresses the true market price. And it happens all day long. While HFT routinely manipulates markets both up and down for profit, an algo seems to exist that is specifically intended to push the gold market down.

June 7, 2012 offers an excellent example of HFT manipulation. Gold frequently swoons $10 over ten to fifteen minutes, maybe twice a week. But on this day it dropped $22 in one second. The detailed breakdown, brilliantly spotted by Dmitri Speck of SafeHaven, shows a complex algorithm attack by a highly sophisticated program. It came late in the day, at 21:21. Most seconds had 2 trades per second, but the 20th second had 501 trades, going down. The price dropped by $8.30 without any intermediate trades, a situation which could not possibly happen without some "unnatural" occurrence. Buy orders

Figure 32

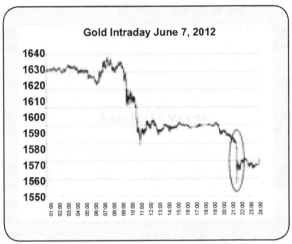

Figure 33

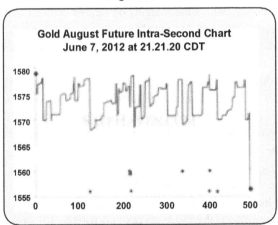

are *always* in place at intervals of 20 cents at most. Somehow, this seller was able to post a transaction below the bid, losing $8.30/ounce on subsequent trades. Each trade was tiny, only a single contract. It's a common HFT tactic, machine gunning tiny trades to drop the market. Only this time, the seller was able to sell to a much lower offer – possibly itself! The price bounced up, then dropped again by $7, five times during the single second. It settled $22 lower and stayed there for hours. The dots on Figure 33 are 'indicative prices' – prices set when trading is halted. Trading was halted, but later, so these prices *should not exist*. Someone understood the plumbing of the COMEX trading system and exploited it to drop the price of gold at lightspeed. It's a perfect example of manipulation and would be very easy to investigate. The source would not be hard to find. Yet regulators have done nothing, despite having it drawn clearly to their attention.

Market spoofing is basically a psy-op technique using HFT. The commercials (the ones who are suppressing the price) sell short some amount of futures contracts. They then 'spoof' the market by placing a series of declining buy and sell bids, then quickly retracting them before they are filled. This gives the appearance of a market sell-off. Speculative sellers rush in through automatic sell orders, trying to minimize losses. Buyers pull back, waiting for the bottom. After kicking the price down by a few percent, the commercials buy back most of the shorts.

Smackdowns are often politically timed. The London Trader, an anonymous insider, reported on several hundred tons of gold sold on June 7, 2012. The takedown went on for four hours and dropped the price $40. It coincided with a Bernanke speech. Gold went into heavy backwardation because there was no spot gold for sale. Backwardation indicates a lack of counter-party trust because it allows for risk-free profits. In backwardation, gold is more expensive for buying now than in the future. A trader can thus sell his gold holdings and buy gold futures, pocketing the difference. Even better, the arbitrageur gets to hold the money (minus the margin) on futures contract until the contract matures because contracts don't exchange funds until maturity. That's why it doesn't work in reverse. You can't sell futures and buy spot as an arbitrage.

Backwardations should very rarely happen. They should also disappear in seconds due to the riskless profits and algorithms constantly hunting the market for it. When backwardation lasts, it is because risk is perceived in holding gold futures. No one wants to part with real gold, only to have their futures contract redeemed in paper (or defaulted). They might make a bit of cash, but they would lose their gold. Backwardation in gold is a measure of distrust by big market players.

Bullion banks are trying to hide their large short positions. If aggressive hedges and speculators smell the blood in the water, they will attack, driving down the share prices and forcing fill orders on futures. Most bullion banks are very weak because they've been leasing gold from central banks for years and selling it into the open market. This creates good cash flow, but a nasty balance sheet because they owe the gold back to the central bank at today's far higher prices. Everyone in the market knows the game, but it's tough to spot the weakest entities to target.

## Allocated Gold, Pools, ETFs and Other Games

*Give a man a gun and he can rob a bank.*
*Give a man a bank and he can rob the world*
**– unknown**

In one of the most astounding sleeper stories of the whole Gold Wars, up to 60,000 metric tons of allocated gold has apparently been misappropriated. Allocated means that each owner has the specific serial numbers of their bars on the owner's account. The bars are required to be kept in secure vaulted storage. Many of these bars, however, are listed on multiple accounts. To put these holdings in perspective, all the world's central banks' gold reserves are only 35,000 metric tons. The multiply-accounted private gold is almost twice that. This is a mirror of the wave of national gold repatriations discussed later.

A number of class action lawsuits have been filed for missing gold in Switzerland. The physical gold was in allocated accounts, but was sold to other parties and replaced with gold certificates, pieces of nice looking paper. Other countries and banks have committed the same practice.

A sea of wealthy investors is waking up to the fraud and quietly demanding their gold. The host of Swiss lawsuits went unreported in the media. No one wants public exposure. It would make retrieval of the metals doubly difficult because a panic would ensue. When it breaks, this will be a gargantuan scandal, eclipsing LIBOR. Because allocated account holders have excellent legal recourse, the turmoil will be epic.

Egon von Greyerz, head of Matterhorn Capital, told of a customer who tried to move his allocated metal to Matterhorn, which has an impeccable reputation as a well-audited, fully allocated fund. The customer was told by his Swiss bank that the bars with his serial numbers were not there. They handed over different ones, but whose? The anecdote is telling – the fractional reserve paper gold scheme is starting to break down. To add insult to injury, the bank was charging the client storage on property it no longer stored. Greyerz has warned of the situation for years and openly suspects that the problem is systemic. Much of people's vaulted gold simply is not there any longer. Greyerz told of several new clients who had bought allocated gold before 2010, but received bars marked 2011. "At the point when confidence in paper gold is lost, and we know that Comex and other places don't have it, they will have to buy gold at whatever price. Investors should definitely not have their gold in the banking system."

Harvey Orgen testified before the CFTC in 2010. He had requested and been allowed into Scotia Bank's vault in 2008. The bank, which is a bullion bank, held only 60 one thousand ounce bars of silver as its working supply. Its gold holding was below 10,000 ounces. It's the biggest bank in Canada – and it sells gold directly to the public. But the mark-up is almost 30%, so no one buys from them.

There is a very strange connection to Scotia Bank. PBS revealed the existence of a huge gold and silver supply in the basement of World Trade Center 4 – 379,000 ounces of gold and 30 million ounces of silver. It was moved away quickly during the cleanup. *The New York Times* reported the metals belonged to Scotia Bank.

The Comex, according to the Times online, had $750 million of metals stored there for clients.The total dollar amount was $950 million. Mayor Guilliani announced on November 1 that $230 million of gold and silver had been recovered. Apparently, then, $720 million in gold went missing in the 9/11 cleanup.

When Venezuela wanted its gold, the demand was satisfied with old bars from London and Switzerland. It was not the original gold Chavez had deposited, so the institutions sending that gold are now short that amount in bullion. The allocated gold system is a teetering row of dominos.

The most secretive gold vault in London was found by Zerohedge to be located at 60 Victoria Embankment. JPMorgan had leased the building for some decades before buying it outright in 2010 after it was offered on a fire sale by bankrupted real estate billionaire, Simon Halabi. Halabi has since disappeared. However, JPM did not buy it first – that honor went to the infamous and secretive Carlyle Group, the investing house of George Bush I and Osama bin Laden's half-brother, Bakr. They shelled out $175 million for the heavily fortified property, then flipped it to the tenant, JPM, for twice that. One can only wonder why the bank didn't submit a bid, but paid out so much money in a transparent shell game, instead.

The plot thickened when some tons of gold were shipped to that address from various places, mostly with a Saudi investment fund name attached. The Saudis disavowed any claim to the gold and reneged on the payments – they had already received money forwarded by other commercial banks. Apparently no one claimed the gold and no one knows where it subsequently went. JPM makes no comment on the location of the vault. Allocated, physical gold actually has a cloak-'n-dagger reality that extends far back – one recalls the 100 tons of Nazi gold laundered in Swiss banks, of which only 4 tons were returned after the war. A lawsuit in 2000 awarded additional damages.

A more covert, less risky method for bankers to get their hands on a supply of gold is by using unallocated accounts. Inexperienced investors can be induced to buy unallocated gold – just a pool without any specific numbers assigned to investors – enabling the bank to lease the gold pool out to another party. The gold holder – HSBC, for example – collects twice, from the unallocated owner and from the party leasing the gold from the bank. The leasing party then sells it into the open market on the 'gold carry trade.' If the leased gold is retained in the vaults (as often happens), then the gold can be re-leased up to the reserve limits. This can happen many times over until a run on the gold becomes a risk. Notably, this mirrors the original fractional reserve gold based system stemming from the goldsmiths. It is how money first became inflated and is virtually identical to the Federal Reserve fractional system except that some real bullion must exist to cover a claim. And that requirement is the Achilles heel. This is how other nations are fighting against the Cartel.

The largest fund, SPDR Gold shares (GLD), is an exchange traded fund – unallocated gold. An investor can buy shares of unallocated gold indexed to 1/10th of an ounce per share. There is a lot of distrust of the GLD fund; many believe it does not have the gold it claims. The price of GLD is 3% less than the cost of physical. If the gold is there, then GLD is losing money hand over fist. The fund still has to source the gold at market cost. It cannot sell it for less than it pays for it – a basic rule of capitalism. Alternatively, the gold may be entirely made of paper. Certainly some gold is there, and probably much of the inventory. However, the inventory can be sold multiple times. GLD is 'unregulated.'

Gold ETFs first appeared in 2004 and have exploded in volume since that time. Currently, they account for 600 tons of gold demand per year out of global open market demand in 2012 of 5000 tons. (That does not account for unreported gold sales, which can be very substantial.) As the total investment purchases (as opposed to jewelry and other purposes) for gold globally is listed by the World Gold Council at 670 tons per year, that should mean almost all of the investment gold went to ETFs. However, many people, including deep pockets, buy gold. With production at 2500 tons per year, the ETFs cannot draw from existing stock – it's all used up in the total demand. The numbers do not add up for the ETFs to be drawing in physical gold. To demonstrate: large ETF investments do not move the price of gold, contrary to the laws of supply and demand – physical stock is not moving. From beginning to mid-2009, GLD added 340 tons of gold – 60% of global supply, yet the price only moved $1. From mid-2009 to the end, the fund dropped 10 tons while the price rocketed by 28% ($250). The supply/demand laws are suspended, strongly suggesting that very little physical gold is being moved – it's all paper. Let's break this down a bit more because it's a central plank of the price manipulation.

Formed as a trust, GLD is intended to track the gold price. The custodian is HSBC; the trustee is the Bank of New York. HSBC is demonstrably short massive amounts of gold futures. This is a classic conflict of interest – the custodian has a vested interest in a lower gold price because they must fulfill their gold futures contracts by buying them. A lower price benefits the bank. Holding the gold gives them the opportunity to sell the gold into the market, potentially. Only the prospectus would legally prevent that, but the prospectus is not a comforting document for investors. The fund "involves significant risk ... [the SEC has not] determined if this prospectus is truthful or complete ... the Trust's gold may be subject to loss, damage, theft, or restriction on access ... recovery may be limited, even in the event of fraud, to the market value of the gold at the time the fraud is discovered ... Trustee may have no right to ... examining the Trust's gold bars or any records maintained by the subcustodian, and no subcustodian will be obligated to cooperate in any review."

So: no holding of gold can be verified. Investors cannot get the gold they own. SPDR gold trust has no obligation to prove anything, even in the event of fraud. No one can legally force them to prove they even have the vaulted gold. Their prospectus deliberately screens any audit, assay or inventory of any gold held by a subcustodian. The investors are wide open to massive fraud, to having any gold sold right from under their noses. They will then be compensated with paper at the 'market value of gold.' But that value is based on spot value and the 'fix' price, not over the counter sales, which include a growing premium. The investors seeking to claim their physical gold must take the loss. And it can be settled when the fund wants – after a massive smackdown, for example.

The gold is held in an unallocated account, commingled with the Custodian's assets. "If the Custodian becomes insolvent," the prospectus reads, "its assets may not be adequate to satisfy a claim." The dangers of unallocated accounts are easily spotted – the gold does not have to be there. Most likely, the gold is owned by multiple parties, and is used as fractional reserve gold. The term 'gold deposit' used in the prospectus does not mean physical gold. Gold is physical metal. Gold deposit is a financial liability: it is paper.

There is no legitimate reason for a trustee as large as GLD to forego allocated accounts. Any party responsible to its investors and worthy of trust (such as Sprott's PHYS) holds gold that is allocated, inventoried, and audited down to the individual bar. Nobody with any sense who wanted the wealth protection of acquiring physical gold, and anticipated the need to obtain delivery would ever consider such a defenseless legal arrangement. Either the Bank of New York is incredibly naïve, or they have deliberately hung the dumb money out to dry. How likely is the former?

Auditors can ask politely if they have the gold, but can only audit the long side of the Custodial holdings. If HSBC, or a subcustodian, sells gold short in the futures market, they can use the GLD physical against this claim, and they are not even required to tell the auditors. In a recent rule change, futures contracts on the Comex can be settled with ETFs – of which GLD is far and away the most popular. Because the futures market is intended to facilitate price discovery, its function is totally subverted if the futures settlement is an ETF – a derivative of gold. The primary means to set the market price of gold does not involve any actual gold, even in final settlement. Using such means, the price is totally separate from the underlying commodity and thereby totally controlled by overwhelmingly massive and collusive players, the commercial banks.

This is a major reason for the recent huge upsurge in popularity with gold ETFs. Futures is a large market, so a steady stream of 'deliveries' is poured from GLD paper into traders accounts. Their lack of accountability and poor prospectus also explains why GLD trades at a discount to physical gold. It's usually about 3.5%, leaving a wide open hole for arbitrage which no one seems to take. An investor would need $10 million to stand for delivery, but they could buy 100,000 shares, sell an equivalent future at a premium, take delivery from GLD and deliver it to the futures buyer, risk free. Why does no one, and most particularly the big pockets, do it? Probably because they know they cannot get the metal from GLD.

Moreover, GLD can be shorted. If a brokerage holds GLD shares for an investor, it can short-sell those shares without the owner knowing – all part of the larger game. This punishes all long investors by artificially increasing the supply. As of this writing, 25 million shares are short – $3.8 billion. Any bank or broker can hold 1000 ETFs for a client and then sell short another 1000 to another client based on holding the first block.

Secretive movements of physical in and out of GLD are confirmed. On August 16 of 2011, GLD reallocated 790,000 ounces of physical gold, redeemed by JPMorgan, Merrill Lynch and Goldman Sachs. This was not public knowledge but was a leaked fax disclosed by Warren James. The commercial banks seem to be using the GLD bars to satisfy demand for physical for customers with vaulted storage.

The large banks have gold flow in other ways. They contract for forwards (unmined gold) from miners and later sell it to large investors, for example. GLD gives them a means of parking the flow between buy and sell. They exchange the gold for a basket of shares in order to free up capital. Later, they can redeem the basket (if the price of gold is up or flat), or buy shares in the market (if the price is down) to make a profit and recoup the gold.

19-Aug-11 0.40000 0.41600 0.42600 0.48800 0.51000
22-Aug-11 *0.48250 0.43000 0.35000 0.25000 0.08750*
23-Aug-11 0.40800 0.41600 0.42250 0.50000 0.52600

A second use is to replace reserves because the fractional selling of gold puts banks in a vulnerable position. They can be hit with a run on gold. This happened on August 22, 2011. The gold forward rate went into serious backwardation as seen on the LBMA chart. Somebody big needed a lot of gold fast.

When the numbers reversed, a big bank was looking in the spot market for a lot of gold quick. They were willing to give up the arbitrage to someone else. That's not a typical commercial bank M.O., so they must have been desperate for immediate gold. They bought near months and sold later months at discount. The above numbers are a screen shot – they were only on the LBMA website for a short time. The LBMA 'corrected' them and now the event has been shoved down the memory hole. But it's not trivial. It is an indication of things to come.

Indeed, the event repeated for Société General, three days in a row – August 9-11, 2011. They also coincided with huge GLD inventory drawdowns on those days of 1.5 million ounces. One of GLD's 'authorized participants' apparently drew the gold and swapped it to Societé General.

The conclusion is deliberately upended. If GLD reserves decline, the media claim that no one wants to buy gold anymore. In reality, the physical gold is being drained by the big banks to bolster their reserves. A lowering of GLD reserves indicates a growing open market demand for gold. That's because new inventory is not being parked at GLD for any length of time. It goes right out the door.

On April 5, 2011, the Sprott gold fund PHYS took in $340 million in a share offering. The next day, GLD declined by 234,022 ounces. At the price (then) of $1455, their holdings declined by $340 million dollars. Where the gold went is not clear, but the connection between the values is. GLD was drained to supply the gold to its ultimate destination through a chain of intermediaries.[1]

Victor the Cleaner called GLD the Central Bank of Bullion Banks. In an insightful analysis, he details the 'puke' indicator as predictive of gold price moves. A 0.5% decline in GLD stores consistently presages a rise in gold price 8 times faster until the gold is replenished. It's a big deal, partly because such a predictive ability is very potent. But more so, because it points a fat finger at major illegal activities. GLD is not supposed to be leasing and swapping gold. Its investors should technically own the gold.[2]

In a televised puff piece intending to 'prove' that all the GLD gold was in vault, reporter Bob Pisani went through a cloak-n-dagger theater performance. He was blindfolded and taken to an undisclosed location of a vault. There, he saw a good store of metal and even held up a 400 ounce bar. Amateur sleuths checked the serial number – ZJ6752. It didn't belong to GLD.

Almost a year later, Ned Naylor-Leyland of Cheviot Asset Mgmt found its owner. ETF Securities shared the vault with GLD. All the pictures of stacks of gold bars in the report were bars that belonged to someone else. The GLD prospectus allows for gold swaps. Translation – they can trade gold for not-gold (cash, gold certificates, etc.) and keep that not-gold on the books.[3] In other words, the commercial banks are shorting the shares of GLD. Meantime, they are using the stock for their own inventory, leasing it, swapping it, or exchanging gold 'certificates' for it. They then use this physical to satisfy demand delivery, most of which comes from the East.

But the well is running dry. The GLD fund routinely dips in holdings. First quarter of 2013 saw 125 metric tons go out the door. The media spun it as a decline in the gold market, but they neglected to mention the buyer of the physical gold. Since the purchases were so large, and the footprints are there, it was a major bank, or several, covering difficult short positions by raiding the GLD stores. Naturally, they short GLD shares right alongside this, to get a decent trickle of gold to move to insistent buyers without public notice. This keeps the price of gold low. GLD is often used as a proxy for gold because the price is readily available.

Here's the kicker. GLD (and SLV, the silver sister) are operated by two custodians who also are part owners of the LBMA clearing mechanism for physical bullion. That means they can use the GLD bars to 1) settle their own massive short positions when these are forced in physical, 2) back the GLD fund, and 3) settle out the spot market for the LBMA, the largest spot market in the world. They are exercising a massive leverage on the gold in vault.

Resistance to gold misappropriation is happening. People are learning about these issues and acting. The Texas Bullion Depository proposal is a bill that seeks to repatriate Texas gold from its allocated Federal Reserve account. The state holds 664,300 ounces at the Fed depository. By also allowing Texas pension funds to invest in physical gold for the first time, the depository could put heavy buying pressure on the gold market. It also sends a signal to the monetary powers.

Why would Texas want its bars back? Morgan Stanley provides an example. In 2007, Morgan Stanley pled guilty to fraud. It charged clients for purchase and storage of gold. The gold was never purchased nor stored. Though they denied the allegations, the firm settled without allowing regulators to examine the vaults. The payout of $4 million was a tiny signal of much greater events to come and demonstrated the above-the-law power of the banking cartel: the bank was charged with a crime, then paid a fine and was able to deny investigators access to the evidence! The firm initiated another scam with an 'allocated' metals account that does not demand true allocation. In 2011, suit was filed against UBS for similar activity, charging clients without actually buying or storing any silver.

It's getting harder to source quantities of the metal. Dutch bank ABN Amro issued a halt to customers' gold deliveries effective April 1, 2013. It's an interesting twist: if someone stores gold at the bank, do they still own the physical, or only its equivalent? Maybe not. If possession is 9/10 of the law, then the vault owner would seem to have a better claim, especially considering rehypothecation practices. Amro is settling in cash at market prices. If there is no shortage – as the powers say – why did they not simply source the gold directly?

## Central Bank Manipulations

*You are a den of vipers. I intend to rout you out*
*and by the Eternal God I will rout you out.*
—Andrew Jackson

Under current long-term conditions, the stock market is grievously overbought – price to earnings ratios are at lunatic levels. The bond market is almost entirely supported by the Federal Reserve. The housing market is in the toilet and slowly flushing down. All major currencies are losing public trust quickly. In a systemic event, gold would be the go-to asset, but even more – if gold becomes a 'hot' investment and rises dramatically, it would suck funds out of all these other wobbly sectors. If gold became the prime investment before the next black swan actually appears, that in itself could, and probably would, cause such an event. A raging bull market would stress out the major shorts and drain significant markets, possibly rupturing the system. That's one great fear of central bankers and a critical reason for its ongoing and desperate suppression of gold. Central bank suppression takes a number of forms, some even associated with warfare.

Confiscation is a favorite tactic. An Italian family going home had their gold taken by authorities crossing the border. Border guards don't need a reason – you do not have the same rights at a border. It was a full ton, valued at $50 million. (Bloomberg, in a basic fact-check error, erroneously claimed it was $6 million.[4]) But individuals are not the real prize. Libya lost 144 tons after the fall of Qaddafi. Libya's central bank held the gold, but after the overthrow, the country never received it back for rebuilding purposes. It's simply "gone." Iraq suffered a similar fate after Hussein's fall, but the amount taken was not disclosed.

However, not all gold confiscation comes on military heels. During the Greek shakedown, Greece almost lost all of its gold to the central bank. Public anger diverted the arrangement. In early 2012, the government was replaced by central bank technocrats, with Lucas Papademous installed as Prime Minister. The deal was 400 pages long and made Greece the first OECD country to "abdicate its rights of immunity over all its assets to its lenders." Especially angering for some independent members of the Parliament was the surrender of rights to Greek gold in the event of a Greek failure to pay.[5] But Greece is small beer. There's a larger potential gold grab should the southern EU nations serially default. Italy is the prize with a whopping 2451 tons of gold. Spain and Portugal also have 500 tons combined. Confiscation, after military action or by forced collateralization, is a primary means for getting access to large physical stores of gold.

The main game, however, is suppression of the price – and it's an old one. Fed Treasurer Arthur Burns wrote a memo to Gerald Ford in 1975 verifying an ongoing manipulation of gold. Governments and central banks, he claimed, should not be allowed to purchase gold at market rates ($170 at that time) but should pay the Treasury basis of $42/oz. Germany had a "secret agreement to not buy gold above the official price of $42.22." To let governments and central banks revalue holdings at market prices would "frustrate efforts to control world liquidity. Liquidity creation of such magnitude would endanger efforts to get inflation under reasonable control."[6] They feared the money creation from banks suddenly having much larger asset bases by their gold being worth a lot more. This would spark inflation.

Other CBs help. In 2007, gold shot from $680 to $1033. The Swiss National Bank dumped 22 tons to stiff-arm the price back underwater. A year later, the 2008 crisis hit – prime time for a gold rise. And again it banged over $1000. Central banks had to shovel out 220 tons this time, to skid it back below $900. Further back, the Swiss crashed the gold market on October 4, 1997. They announced a sell-off of half their gold holdings – 1400 tons. Gold dropped by 7% in minutes. One trader called the market "a war zone."

The central bank battle against gold is now 100 years old. In 1914, they temporarily suspended payment in specie (gold). After WWI, the gold exchange standard allowed only 400 ounce bars to be redeemed, cutting the common man out. In 1934, confiscation happened. But first, gold got the blame for the Great Depression. In 1944, the dollar took gold's place for trade settlement and silver left the coinage in the 1960s. The gold pool tried and failed to keep the price down. Then Nixon closed the gold window in 1971. Now the war has morphed into propaganda and marketplace suppression.

The Swiss gold sale came at a critical time for the market. The US market had a decadal fall the next day. The Hong Kong exchange was tanking rapidly. The Swiss banks even recommended a quiet policy to dishoard, but the same Swiss banking committee went quite public on another front. Attacking the gold price is a time-honored technique in crisis. It disrupts gold's role as a barometer to the economy. If things are falling, gold gets a market uplift. The CBs take extra measures to push it back down during crisis periods.[7] This is not to say that all gold price drops are due to deliberate suppression. There is certainly market activity and sells by large holders to get capitalized rapidly.

But why the war in the first place? Because people in government and top finance crave power. They long ago realized that power does not flow from the barrel of a gun – it rolls off the printing press. Those who control the currency, control everything. Exercising control through fear and the threat of violence is difficult. It incites revolt. It is obvious. It is aberrant to daily life. Currency is a normative part of most daily human life. People need it. It's much easier to control them by holding the tool they use to fulfill their needs – by controlling the currency. Gold, unlike fiat currency, cannot be controlled while still being issued in unlimited quantities. If people were to value gold over paper, it would lead to governments and central banks having far less power.

The CBs have documented their suppression of gold for all to see, should anyone care to look. A 1968 cable, weeks before the collapse of the London Gold Pool, from the US embassy in Paris to the State Department, describes the need for the CBs to remain masters of gold and describes a set of suppression schemes.[8] After the 1970s gold boom, Paul Volcker wrote, "Joint intervention in gold sales to prevent a steep rise in the price of gold, however, was not undertaken. That was a mistake."[9] "The price of gold is pretty well determined by us," Federal Reserve Governor Wayne Angell said in 1993. "We can hold the price of gold very easily." Angell's tactic was to use higher Treasury interest rates to make gold unprofitable, thus controlling the market – an impossible tactic now.[10] J. Virgil Mattingly, counsel to the Federal Reserve Board, stated that the Exchange Stabilization Fund had engaged in 'gold swaps' (a suppression technique covered later) and possessed the legal right to do so from a very broad mandate.[11] Dr. Zjilstra, former President of the Netherlands central bank, wrote in his memoirs, "Gold is artificially kept at a far too low price."[12]

Central bankers deny it whenever the subject comes up in formal situations, but the denials ring hollow. "The last duty of a central banker is to tell the public the truth," Federal Reserve Vice Chairman Alan Blinder said in a 1994 television interview. Gold Anti-Trust Action Committee (GATA) even won a lawsuit over a Freedom of Information Act request denied by the Fed. The court awarded GATA $2800 for legal costs and required the Fed to turn over some gold records. The Fed was allowed to withhold most records as 'proprietary information' – notably, an allowance only given to private parties, not the government. The released records revealed secret swap arrangements with foreign banks. The only reason for secret swap arrangements, as we will soon see, is price suppression. If it was for legitimate settlement of trade accounts, secrecy would be pointless.

The G-10 gold and foreign exchange committee is incredibly secretive. The Fed will not release members' names, keeps no meeting records, and the committee is not even listed as part of Fed activities.

Still, the CBs tell the right people and let information slip. The Bank for International Settlements even printed a brochure advertising intervention in the gold market as one of their services.[13] In its 2003 annual report, the Australian central bank said, "Foreign currency reserve assets and gold are held primarily to support intervention in the foreign exchange market."[14]

Many financial analysts working within the industry are fully aware of this – they just don't have a public forum to address it, and moreover, have negative incentive to disclose the knowledge. Nevertheless, Royal Bank of Canada caused an uproar with a leaked report in 2002. Top bank officials, it seems, believed in gold market suppression and felt it would eventually be ruptured. The document included a number of interesting points:

Increasing Evidence of Unsustainable Gold Price Manipulation

a. Aggressive gold lending, which from an economic perspective is indefensible, has filled the supply/demand gap.

b. NY Fed gold has been mobilized when the gold price is rising.

c. Timing of Exchange Stabilization Fund gains/losses corresponds to gold price movements.

d. Audited reports of U.S. gold reserves show unexplained variances.

e. Minutes of Fed meetings confirm officially denied gold swaps.

f. Rules on gold swaps revised but subsequently denied. However, individual central banks have repudiated the denial.

g. U.S. gold reserves have recently been re-designated twice, initially to "custodial gold" and latterly to "deep storage gold."[15]

In perhaps the most egregious and transparent example, between 1999 and 2002, Chancellor Gordon Brown lost Britain £4 billion, and most of its gold. More than half of English gold was sold at below $296/oz, sinking to as low as $256/oz. It was the worst financial move in precious metals history, coming at the absolute bottom of the gold market.. He announced it far in advance, which drove the price down heavily beforehand, thereby deliberately creating a lower price to sell off the gold. Selling the gold at auction shaved another 3% or so off the LBMA fixes. It also dropped the fix price for the later auctions. He deliberately drove the price down to help out the banks, irrespective of the damage that it would do to his country. A memorandum from the Bank of England specifically states that the lowest bidder (above a minimum price) will get the gold at the lowest possible bid. Why not the highest bidder?[16]

The commercial banks were involved in a gold/yen carry trade. They leased gold for a pittance, then sold it into the open market. They obtained yen (low-interest, steadily eroding value) with the proceeds as collateral to invest in higher yields. At the expiry of the loan, they unwound the yen position, bought the gold back in the market and returned it. It was a great money machine when gold dropped, but a big loser when the price spiked. At least one US mega-bank wound up in trouble – many tons in the hole and facing the long gun of insolvency. Along with it, Long Term Capital Management was allegedly short 300 tons. The interconnections among banks made it a disaster scenario for the global system. Brown threw Britain's gold down the loo, suppressing the price to let the banks cover their mistakes.

It's not a fringe theory either. Speculation became rampant after the event. Indeed, the matter was debated in Parliament and a group of CEOs from the largest gold mining firms wrote an open letter to the Prime Minister detailing the case of malfeasance by Brown.[17]

The British had been pressuring the IMF to sell $3 billion worth of gold to 'fund debt relief.' The IMF had no need to do so – the amount was small and fairly easy to pull together from international monetary printing presses. In fact, the sale would have harmed the nations needing relief as most of their economies were heavily gold-mining based. A drop in the price would have made debt repayments much more difficult. Even the suggestion of such a

Figure 34

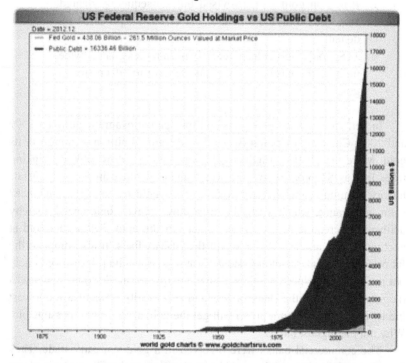

sale – a suppression strategy called 'jawboning' – was enough to drop the market well before any actual sales even took place. Several hundred tons at once was a lot for the market to absorb. That was then; now, the amounts are far higher.

Then came the Washington Agreement. Central banks agreed to limit gold sales to 400 (later raised to 500) tons total per year. The price went up almost 20% in a week. The shorts were getting crushed and pled their case to the central banks who responded. The Dow Jones reported "*Central Banks are selling gold in order to prevent a further sharp rise in prices from causing a major financial crisis* [my emphasis]."[8] In a subsequent lawsuit, the Governor of the Bank of England was quoted as saying, "At any price, at any cost, the central banks had to quell the gold price ... The US Fed was very active in getting the gold price down."[19] In 1999, the Central Banks were fighting tooth and nail to quell systemic risk associated with the gold market. Some of the bullion banks were helping because they had sold huge gold forwards, putting them upside down in a rising market. The situation is now many orders of magnitude greater. The CBs are getting desperate.

For decades now, gold has been a political prisoner of the monetary/debt system. The Washington Agreement publicly declared its intent to keep the gold price from falling too far and fast. However, it allowed a major twist in the lease arrangements. Bullion banks could settle their leased gold in cash. They did not have to buy gold in the open market, preventing a serious gold spike from lease unwinds and allowing much more leasing. Of course, it drained central bank gold. In fact, long-term Treasury and Fed official Edwin Truman said, "the modern counterpart of the [London] gold pool is the agreement among the central banks of some of these same countries to limit their market sales of gold."[20]

GATA has been saying for almost a decade that the gold market is manipulated. After years of ridicule, GATA Secretary Chris Powell has managed to appear more frequently in the mainstream media. CNBC ran a lengthy interview with him on June 21, 2012, where he made the startling claim that over "75% of the gold the world thinks it owns does not exist." It is merely paper claims against bullion banks.

GATA stores an impressive archive of manipulation evidence. In a lawsuit report, GATA analyst Michael Bolser used a deep statistical analysis to show market suppression of the gold price. The Comex had numerous order sizes three standard deviations from the norm where the LBMA had zero. Since the two markets trade in synch over 99% of the time, the anomalies reveal a set of manipulations. The report was pre-2000 and the Long Term Capital Management (LTCM) crisis took center stage. LTCM had a system-threatening event in 1998 when it was heavily leveraged on Russian bonds. They had used the gold carry trade (leasing gold and selling it to the market) to finance the operation. In order to keep market forces from driving the price higher, the Fed arranged for a massive off-market transaction to cover the LTCM short position. During the crisis, Italy lost a chunk of gold and British Prime Minister Tony Blair stepped up to the plate to serve the financial system by totally mismanaging Britain's assets. Some have called his actions treason. They definitely dropped the price of gold.

Central banks can easily suppress the price by a simple announcement of a major sale. Speculators sell holdings for a profit beforehand. Futures holders move from long to short positions, anticipating a price decline. Doing so, they push the market down ahead of any sale. The CB sale need not ever occur – merely an announcement has been shown to drop the price, though this technique is losing effectiveness.

Still, most western nations have sold the majority of their gold even as the price has gone up by 800%. Canada and Norway have sold everything.[21] The US appears to be the odd man out with a mere 1% in sales. But that is an accounting fraud with most of it 'leased' out and redeemed in cash or even forgiven.

The Fed has been caught lying many times. Most notably, they changed their ledger from 'Gold Stock, including Exchange Stabilization Fund' to 'Gold Stock' after intense questioning on the matter. Technically, the Fed owns no gold. The official claim was that the ESF owned no gold either, but the Fed 2001 ledger line item listed gold, which would not be possible if neither entity owned any. This is important because the ESF is tasked with stabilizing markets. If they own gold, the only reason is to manage the market – to manipulate it. The Fed indicated the ESF holding was 'slight,' at $41 million. However, this is not its market value. Remember that the Treasury official gold price is $42. That would make ESF holdings almost a million ounces. It's actually a lot of gold. The Fed went further – it scrubbed all reference to the ESF afterward.[22]

The ESF has no Congressional oversight, making it the perfect candidate to run a globalized suppression scheme. The opaque organization can secretly conduct gold swaps, because it has no obligation to report its 'investments.' The ESF's profits and losses are closely correlated with the rise and fall of the gold price. The Fed lists 9000 tons of gold on its books – most of it custodial gold for other nations. But they exempt themselves from audits, and have turned away German inspectors looking to examine German gold holdings. This gives the Fed a powerful ability to secretly funnel gold to the ESF through gold swaps. The ESF can then move the gold to bullion banks without overtly acting in the market. A steady supply of physical gold is necessary to maintain the price suppression. Without any physical gold, the market will detect the problem quickly and the suppression will break down. Other central banks are helping. The ESF and the Bundesbank swapped 700 tons of gold, for example, between 1995 and 2001. More on swaps in the Leasing section to clarify how this scheme works.

Most of the large banks have footprints in the scheme, as well. JPMorgan, HSBC, Goldman Sachs, Bank of America, and Citibank have different ways of 'participating.' Between them, JPMorgan and HSBC held 98% of all gold derivatives as of a 2008 peak. Other players have moved into the arena since then and the number has declined. When only one or two players hold such an overwhelming concentration of the market, it is manipulation – the fundamental understanding in market regulation. Regulations are designed to prevent just such a concentration of positions. Yet JPMorgan, with 78% of total gold derivatives, gets a pass from regulators. More on this later.

The short situation is extreme in these markets. Commercial net shorts hover around 3000 tons. These positions, being so large, distort the gold price, and much of gold investment goes to various paper shorts.

Paul Craig Roberts, the architect of Reagonomics as former Assistant Treasury Secretary under Reagan, and presently a fierce critic of government and CB policy, had this to say about the ongoing suppression:

When gold prices hit $1,917.50 an ounce on August 23, 2011, a gain of more than $500 an ounce in less than 8 months, capping a rise over a decade from $272 at the end of December 2000, the Federal Reserve panicked. With the US dollar losing value so rapidly compared to the world standard for money, the Federal Reserve's policy of printing $1,000 billion annually in order to support the impaired balance sheets of banks and to finance the federal deficit was placed in danger. The dollar's exchange rate in relation to other currencies becomes untenable when the dollar collapses in value in relation to gold and silver. As sharply rising bullion prices are a threat to the Fed's policy, the Fed has shorted the bullion market in order to suppress prices.[23]

The amount of fictitious gold is an important metric for understanding the scale of the suppression and the market reversal that will occur when it ends. The gold market has been called small but this is not so. Total daily trading in gold globally is a whopping $70 billion – ten times the amount the world spends on oil. Average daily trading volumes for the London markets exceed 20 million ounces – 600 metric tons. These are net trades; if a trader buys and sells on the same day, only his totals are counted. Gross trades are much higher – over 2000 tons. Annual mine production plus recycling is around 3600 tons. The spot market turns over more gold in 2 days than the physical market produces in a year. Every day, the London market turns over the entire LBMA stock of gold bars. Every 7 days, it turns over the entire global supply of gold bars. This is massively out of synch with all other commodity market ratios – except, of course, silver.

With only 15,000 tons of Good Delivery bars in existence, the LBMA cannot back the trades. Paul Mylchreest did a thoughtful analysis of the problem. The second most motile gold market is GLD, where 1/30 of shares turn over every day. Most markets, with audited physical holdings, turn over 1/100 or less. Gold is really a buy and hold investment, a store of wealth. If this lowest percentage – 1/30 – were applied to the London market, the LBMA would need 64,000 good delivery bars to back the trades. But only 15,000 such bars exist in the world, and far fewer are stored at the exchange. Every ounce of physical gold held in LBMA storage is consequently owned by at least 4 parties. That's because these markets are not allocated – tied to specific bars. Each contract is only an obligation to deliver, but all these obligations are, collectively, underwritten by the total amount of bars held at the LBMA for delivery.

This is actually a conservative estimate because GLD is much easier to trade – it moves like a stock in shares of 1/10 ounce. Probably, Mylchreest estimates, each LBMA ounce has 10-20 owners. This is, quite simply, fraud. Since the LBMA will not categorically state under oath that it is fully backed nor allow an audit, it is impossible to know the full extent of the fraud. However, as Adrian Douglass shows, likely around 50,000 tons of imaginary gold has been created in the London market alone – over 30% of all the gold ever mined.[24]

Gillian Tett defines financial repression as manipulating markets in a way that obliges investors to invest in government debt at negative real interest rates. Federal Reserve member Kevin M. Warsh resigned over 'financial repression.' He claimed the Fed was "suppressing market prices that they don't like" without stating which particular markets were being suppressed. How could the *Wall Street Journal* fail to ask that most compelling question in its interview? Here we have direct admission that the Fed is manipulating markets. No doubt the Bond market is a key target, but the logic of gold as sound money versus a failing fiat system, Tett writes, suggests a powerful motive to suppress gold as well.[25]

Is there legal proof? Blanchard and Co. sued Barrick Gold and bullion broker JPMorgan in 2003 for using Central Bank gold to suppress the price. Barrick protested that the Federal Reserve was also implicated in the charges, but could not legally be brought to trial because of sovereign immunity, and that therefore, as an agent of the Fed, Barrick should have immunity also. Barrick confessed to having used Central Bank gold to suppress the price in its plea to dismiss, and defended their actions by pointing out that a need to purchase the gold in the open market would subject them to "monumental financial losses" from higher prices.[26] Barrick settled out of court quickly.

Soon after, BIS chief William White talked about the five goals of central bank cooperation, one of which was to "influence asset prices (especially gold and foreign exchange)."[27] Citibank recently noted "resurgent central bank selling, which was clearly timed to cap the Gold price."[28] Nonetheless, the Federal Reserve refused to supply information about what it was doing when under a FOIA request, responding that it would include "information relating to swap arrangements with foreign banks on behalf of the Federal Reserve System and is not the type of information that is customarily disclosed to the public."[29] The Fed implicitly acknowledges gold swaps and explicitly claims the right, based on commercial interests, to withhold such information. But what are gold swaps? And why is such a benign sounding device linked to manipulation? The answer begins with 'gold leasing.'

## Leasing

*The Colonies would gladly have borne the little tax on tea
and other matters had it not been for the poverty
caused by the bad influence of the English bankers.*
— **Benjamin Franklin**

Supposedly, leasing is a way to make money off a 'dead asset' – one that doesn't bring dividends or interest. The Belgian Central Bank admitted to leasing over 40% of its gold as of 2010, for example. But the interest earned was a paltry 0.3%, clearly not worth the risk of default. It wasn't about profit. When gold hit $1900 in 2011, CBs quickly pushed lease rates further into the basement – negative territory. They essentially lost money to lease out their gold. Gold leasing rates first went negative in 2009 and have drifted lower since then. There are two situations here – one is called leasing and one is a swap. If the gold is leased, then the lessee makes interest payments on the gold it borrowed and still owes the principal. In this case, the lessor (who still owns the gold) does not lease at negative rates. In the swap case, the money for the gold is posted to the owner of the gold. Then the LIBOR (or London Interbank Lending Rate) is subtracted from the GOFO (or Gold Forward Rate). In other words, the dollars are loaned at LIBOR and the gold is counter-loaned at GOFO. (Don't worry about the details – it's needlessly opaque.) Each party gets what it wants – gold or dollars. If the prevailing rate on dollars is higher, then the lease rate appears negative. It's a sign of capital distress when banks loan their most solid asset out in exchange for equivalent cash and they pay for the privilege.

But inside of the operation is a scam – lease and sell. Bank A (usually a central bank) leases out gold to Bank B (a bullion bank, usually). Bank B then sells the gold in the open market and invests the proceeds. It's called a 'carry trade.' Here's how it operates for the yen. The yen has had a twenty-five year carry trade based on ultra-low interest rates. Borrow yen long-term at 1%, exchange for dollars and invest at 5%. The risk is a rise in value of the yen by the time the loan comes due. This risk is low because of the massive Japan CB money-printing which drives the value of the Yen down. However, if the trade is crowded – hundreds of billions invested – then the rush for the exits can drive the currency very high. Investors who borrowed, then sold yen need to unwind their investment to repay the yen, leading to a sudden shortage of yen as hundreds of trillions of yen are needed. This has happened a few times. Everyone needed to close their trades and there were not enough yen for all the buyers.

It works great if the item leased and sold is downward trending. Sell at 100, invest proceeds for the duration of the loan, and buy back later at 95 – a nice double profit. This was the gold M.O. during the late '90s and bullion banks did very well with it. Now the same practice has a different intent – to manipulate the supply of gold in order to depress the price.

But after such a transaction, the gold now has two owners – the open market buyer and Bank A, which continues to list the gold on its books as an asset, having only leased it to Bank B. This is one of many ways to multiply the apparent existence of gold. Much is made of the difference between physical and paper gold. Bank A owns paper, a mere promise to pay. If Bank B goes bust, then A is out of luck and out of bullion. Bank B may also be unable to acquire gold for return to A when the market dries up and be unable to settle in cash. An IMF paper called foul on the scheme:

> The guidance of paragraph 85 (iii) of the Guidelines, which is applied to gold swaps by paragraph 101, results in overstating reserve assets because both the funds received from the gold swap and the gold are included in reserve assets. While the gold is swapped, it cannot be the case that both the claims and the gold are simultaneously liquid and readily available to the monetary authority.[30]

The default scenario will happen again and again (it already is happening) in a number of different venues: futures market, ETFs, allocated and unallocated accounts, and gold leases. As trust drains out of the system, the desire to own actual bullion and in hand will mount. The numerous paper gold claims will be unfulfillable. The price of bullion will shoot up. The price of paper gold will separate from bullion at a lower price. Gold investments known to be trustworthy (Goldmoney, Eric Sprott's PHYS) will command towering premiums over suspect vehicles. Bullion banks will crash and be bailed-out as they try to source metal at far higher prices than they sold it for in years and months past. The futures market will become irrelevant and the physical market will set the price. Backwardation will become extreme as people are willing to pay far higher prices for gold now than for a future promise. At least that's one very plausible scenario.

Figure 35 shows the GOFO, or gold leasing rate. There is a notorious downward spike in 1999 concurrent with the Washington Agreement on Gold, when central banks agreed on how much gold they would sell in the open market. The WAG sent the prices of gold up by 20% in a few days. Somebody with a lot of gold (a central bank) didn't like that, so they leased gold out at a loss. Gold leases must be repaid in gold. They were willing to lend out 1000 ounces of gold and get back 996 in payment. Why would one party pay a second party to loan it an asset? If you rent a car from Hertz,

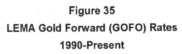

Figure 35
LEMA Gold Forward (GOFO) Rates
1990-Present

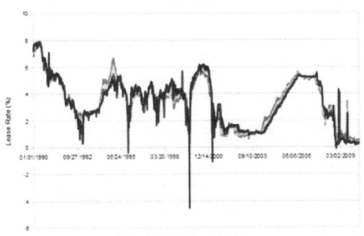

they don't pay you money to do it. The game was to arrest the price rise by flooding the market with gold.

When the lease comes due, the bullion bank would normally pay a miner and return physical gold to the Central Bank. However, the CB usually rolls the lease over. This allows for an early supply of gold to the market and a perpetual supply to be in the market while gold is still retained on the books for the Central Banks. The problem naturally arises when the price of gold rises more than the net profit – which it has for 10 years running. As the bullion banks cannot unwind the trade profitably, it should be expected to cease. Yet this unprofitable carry trade continues. How, and more importantly, why? The Central Banks appear to be covering bullion bank losses in cash to continue suppressing the price.

The scheme has been operating for some time. In 2004, Frank Veneroso crunched numbers and showed serious conflicts between official sources. The GFMS[31] cited gold leased out at 2200 tons for 1995. Veneroso used Bank of England data to show the amount leased was nearer 9000 tons. This is larger than the entire US gold holdings – leased out in a single year and 3 times the annual mine supply. And 1995 was the early days of such arrangements. They only ramped up afterward.[32]

The vast participation in this market was explained by Lehman Brothers in 2000. "Gold can consistently be borrowed much cheaper than money … a lease rate of 1.8% while a one-year bond is yielding about 6.6.%. Borrowing gold, selling it, and investing the proceeds at the risk-free rate is an attractive trade … the risk/return profile of the gold market favors the short side."[33] No doubt much of this gold was never moved as it was only in paper form. The quantities are simply too high for a true physical supply transfer to have taken place. However, a great deal, and perhaps all, of CB gold has been moved out of the vaults.

When the price rose quickly in the early 2000s, the bullion banks didn't want to undertake the risk of lending it out without a high payout. The gold lease rate jumped to a huge 10% – an increase of 1000% . But the lease rate (the amount earned by the bullion bank) equals the LIBOR minus the GOFO (the rate charged by the central bank to lease the gold.) The bullion banks earn the LIBOR because they reinvest by loaning the cash from the sale of gold into that market. When the price spiked, they added in the risk factor of a rising gold price, raising the lease rate dramatically. This caused the amount of available gold being sold in the market to plummet, shrinking supply in the face of a price increase. This would cycle into a further rise in price. The CBs feared a purchaser mania for gold. They flooded the lease market by taking a loss to cap the price rise. The bullion banks could simply borrow 100,000 ounces, sit on it, then pay back 96,000 ounces in a few months.[34] Free gold. Of course, it worked.

Gold swaps are a weird permutation on the 'lease' theme. In a swap, one Central Bank exchanges its gold for another's without the metal changing location. Each essentially moves gold on their ledger from owned to custodial; each one retains ownership of their gold, which is now officially held in storage at the other bank, while also enjoying custody of the other's gold. Next, the Western banks lease out the newly reassigned gold. Why bother with the swap? The Federal Reserve cannot legally lease out US gold reserves – the Fed doesn't own them. But there is no law against it leasing out other nations' gold reserves, so the swap allows the Fed and the corresponding central bank to lease out the very gold that was previously not legally available to them, simply by reciprocally changing its ownership. Or: the other nation may receive some trade benefit or currency payment for its part and may not know of the scheme to lease out its foreign-held gold.

In September 2001, the US Mint changed 1700 tons of gold from 'Gold Bullion Reserve' to 'Custodial Gold Bullion.' They quit owning the gold, but still stored it. It's a lot of gold – over 20% of US Reserves – to simply cease owning. No one mentioned it beyond the simple account statement, uncovered by an independent analyst.[35]

Another swap scheme was mentioned in a Bundesbank document. In this instance, two central banks can swap gold in the open. Each bank places a large sell order – through its bullion banks – at a specific price and a buy order at the same price, well below the market price. They buy each other's gold, sending a declining price signal to the market. In this transaction, physical gold sometimes flows to the other bank. However, the assets are then listed as 'collateralized loan' – to keep it on the books, increasing the illusion of supply. The sender does not subtract the gold from its balance sheet, nor does the recipient add it. For accounting purposes, there was no transaction. Similarly, this 'round trip' trade features two commercial banks posting large buy and sell orders on the open market at lower prices. This pushes the market down. This type of trade is unconfirmed in precious metals, but JPMorgan admitted to the practice in the oil market.

Analyst Alisdair MacLeod revealed a deep accounting deception – a gold swap scam – in the Bank of England's custodial gold (gold held for others). In 2006, the BoE held 2220 tons of gold for unidentified foreign nations. In 2012, that number jumped to 4691 tons – an increase of 2471 tons, over 100%. Next MacLeod showed declared gold holdings for all central banks (backing out those who hold no gold in London). Unidentified banks held 21,552 tons in 2006 and 21,088 tons in 2012, a decline of 464 tons. To clarify – BoE custodial gold jumped by 2471 tons at the same time that global CB gold reserves declined by 464 tons. The discrepancy is startling. Either a number of foreign central banks secretly shipped a further almost 12% of their gold to London, or London's new ledger entry is *not physical gold*. This type of ledger gold was probably created prior to 2006, leading to the conclusion that the BoE holds far less gold than it lists. Subtracting the gold entries that are clearly unbacked leaves a maximum of 3320 out of 5790 tons on the ledger – 57% – and potentially far less. The BoE is demonstrably running a *fractional reserve custodial gold system.*[36]

Mexico seems to have fallen prey to the BoE gold fraud. A citizens group legally petitioned the central bank for information on Mexico's 125 ton gold reserves, mostly purchased in 2011. After waffling, Banxico (Mexico's central bank) reported that the gold was held in London. However, the oldest central bank in the world was less than forthcoming about the status of Mexico's gold. They provided contract stipulations and payment information, but left out location, bar serial numbers, or any audit information – real evidence that the gold Mexico purchased actually exists. Normally, the BoE provides allocated accounts, but it appears the BoE felt that Mexico didn't even warrant this basic information. Banxico did not even know how many bars they owned. They seem to have bought a pile of unbacked gold certificates. Under citizen pressure, they are beginning to ask for a better accounting and may ask for physical delivery soon.[37]

The next suppression technique, creating an artificial supply, is called forwards. The means to manipulate the price are convoluted, almost incomprehensible at times. One of these, according to analyst FOA (Friend of Another), is the Central Bank 'ownership invoices' from large gold producers – forwards.[38] This is essentially one of the first means to manage flow and create artificial supply. Bullion banks bought the invoices from the CBs and sold them into the open market, as if they were backed by vaulted gold. In fact, Barrick (the largest miner on Earth) was selling its unmined reserves to the CB! The gold being sold was still in the ground. FOA calls it a back door means to nationalize the gold supply; the major gold miners have essentially hedged their production to the CBs for an indefinite period.

The Treasury lists Deep Storage gold for 94% of its holdings. Most people think this refers to the same unmined ore deposits, not some subterranean vault. Most US gold, it seems, has been sold and repurchased as ore in ground.[39] It also means the 8000 tons of US gold has been steadily sold into the market under cover of swaps, to suppress the price of gold long-term. The IMF even recommended specifically that central banks not distinguish between vaulted gold and gold receivables – gold that is owed to the bank. Most banks followed suit, combining them into a single line item on the asset sheet. This makes it impossible to know how much is actually leased versus held in vault. The strategy is clearly intentional. It is meant to mask the ongoing price suppression via leasing and to keep the gold market non-transparent. In this manner, public gold flows into the market invisible to the public.

The gold miners have to play this game to maintain enough cash flow to survive, but their hedge book crushes them when the price rises, especially if energy costs rise with it. That's because they've already sold the gold (hedging) at prices of years earlier, but have not paid to mine it yet. The suppression scheme dates back to the 80s. It's small compared to the current schemes, but still effective as it supplies the illusion of physical gold into the market. This allowed the OPECs to take delivery of physical from actual vaulted stores with the CBs replenishing those stores from the unmined reserves as they were mined. Simultaneously, it held the price of gold down in order to bury Western demand, since Westerners will not accumulate an asset that is not appreciating in price. The scheme was intentionally temporary – the strain to hold the price down indefinitely would not have been manageable. It was only meant to hold together the dollar hegemony, FOA claimed, long enough to get the Euro up and running. At that point, it was allowed to unwind slowly, but not fully, and the gold price began its continuing bull run.

Asia got in on the game finally, buying gold in the suppressed market. The CBs countered, preventing a price rise by openly supplying the gold. Of course, selling gold to long-term holders at suppressed prices only makes them want more. Eventually, the amount put out was unrecoverable through mining – the mines hit a production peak and could not supply enough. All these players, on both sides, wanted to move gold without the movement being visible.

Now, the strains have become too great, FOA believes. The system is about to break. No one with the power to do so wants to break it – they want to get what they can first and they don't want to be the global villain. But it needs so much maintenance that its end is inevitable. A new system has been erected in the past several years in order to accommodate global trade, FOA contends. It will be ready when the current one fails.

The current Gold Cartel evolved from 1990s when central banks began leasing gold in record volume. Though they did not disclose the amount, solid research shows it to be 12,000 metric tons minimum. This is multiples of annual gold production – 2500 metric tons. The gold went to strong hands – people who will not sell at the suppressed price. That's a big problem, because even if the money is printed to buy it back, the printing devaluation pushes up the nominal price without raising the real price. That's even before the intense price rise from buying it back. And in any event, these people will not part with their gold just because inflation is rising – quite the opposite. They see it as all the more incentive to hold onto the metal. The cartel banks were on the hook for all the physical gold borrowed and sold into the market.

Seeing the impossibility of getting the gold back – it would simply rupture the large banks – the Fed switched to ongoing suppression of the price. They allowed a 'managed' rise, holding it to 15% per year.[40]

Eric Sprott, billionaire gold investor and fund manager, examined this dynamic from the demand side. Market supply is roughly 2700 tons mined plus 1000 of scrap for 2012. Reports claim that demand and supply are extraordinarily synchronized, but they use the fudgy Net Private Investment (NPI) metric to match them up. Of course, NPI is just implied out of the difference between publicly asserted supply and verifiable demand. A true accounting would show a huge overmatch in annual demand to supply. China took in 785 tons – a single buyer grabbed 30% of the global supply. The Western central banks must be filling the hole – no one else has the resources. They want to prevent the pie in the face of a major gold default, but it has drained their reserves.[41]

Foreign powers are well aware of the gold price suppression and are making long-term plans against its unwind. Russian Central Bank Deputy Chairman Oleg Mozhaiskov spoke about the evidence of manipulation in 2004, implying a policy of gold accumulation for Russia.[42]

China, meanwhile, has bluntly expressed its opinion on state radio. "The U.S. and Europe have always suppressed the rising price of gold. They intend to weaken gold's function as an international reserve currency. They don't want to see other countries turning to gold reserves instead of the U.S. dollar or euro." A Beijing embassy cable released by Wikileaks suggests that the Chinese have a policy of steadily undermining Western currencies by accumulating gold.[43] A follow-up document accused the US of "doing everything possible to prevent China's foreign reserve from buying gold."[44]

Foreign CBs are buying gold in quantity. At a 600% increase from 2010, 2012 saw the highest gold buying on record since 1964, and that's just the admitted buying. Both Eastern and Western CBs downplay the amounts bought – for different reasons. The Asian side wants to accumulate as much gold as possible at fire sale prices. If they admitted to being major buyers, the price would spike. Western banks understate buying because they are parceling it out to Asia slowly to continue the game as long as possible.

Most of the gold is ultimately headed East. In less than 10 days, Andrew Maguire noted, 225 tons of actual physical metal rolled East. The gold almost certainly had other owners who will find out about their missing metal the hard way. The situation turned extreme in late March of 2013. On April 1st, the Fed put out an APB saying that institutional investors were about to dump their gold positions. Investment banks notified their clients and a wave of selling arrested the steadily growing buying pressure. By rolling together private and fund money against the market, the Fed temporarily crushed the bull market. The Fed actions were against its mandate prohibiting interference in markets. They were illegal. The actions were bold and smack of desperation. The signal to the alert person is clear: the US dollar and debt complex are in serious trouble.

### Regulatory Schemes, Cover-ups and Legalized Confiscation

> *When plunder becomes a way of life for a group of men*
> *living together in society, they create for themselves*
> *in the course of time, a legal system that authorizes it*
> *and a moral code that glorifies it.*
> *– Frederic Bastiat*

Carla Ruff had her safe deposit box listed as 'owner unknown.' The state of California broke into it and confiscated the contents, then auctioned them off, including a pearl necklace ($82,000 appraisal) for $1800. She had an account at the bank, her name was on the box, and her address was on multiple documents in the box. She wouldn't have been hard to find and her box had been meticulously paid for. Her critical papers were destroyed. This has happened to thousands of citizens who have active lawsuits. The California State Controller's unclaimed property division's attorney wrote a memo against programs to find the owners of such property as it would dry up needed income. Many states use the tactic and many citizens have found out too late. Delaware lists unclaimed property as its number 3 revenue source. Every state uses individual contractors to confiscate the property – a clear conflict of interest. This can be done for almost any type of account after 3 years of no activity, even if all payments are current.[45]

Many of these stories involve gold and silver. Apparently, the Patriot Act can be interpreted rather broadly, giving permission to ransack safe deposit boxes. In the 2003 Domestic Security Enhancement Act, Section 106 grants immunity for warrantless searches. Section 122 invokes the Patriot Act power of 'surveillance without a court order.'[46] Numerous anecdotal reports, difficult to confirm, exist of people who looked inside their boxes to find their gold and silver gone. This could become an increasing source of supply for the strapped bankers. "Banking and Financial Institutions are Critical Infrastructure," the DHS claims.[47] Indeed, the accounting regulations were changed in 2008, allowing banks to lie on their balance sheet as a national security measure. Since the massive banks are regarded as so critical to domestic security, one wonders where the line in supporting them is drawn. Private property has already been seized and distributed to the banks with PFG Best, MF Global, and Lehman Brothers, as well as the citizen bank accounts of Cyprus. If the banks are under threat of empty gold vaults, will the DHS step in to ensure a supply coming from safe deposit boxes? The logic is there and so is the precedent.

The regulations for holding gold by US citizens have become so Byzantine that Viamat (the world's premiere gold vaulting company) ended its relations with all US citizens. The US is perhaps their largest market, so this is a very big deal. The company is used to enormous regulatory stipulations. Something must have been completely out of whack for them to suddenly pitch this core business in the bin.

In Britain, police raided several safe deposit vaults. They seized the contents of all 6717 boxes, and forced the owners to verify their ownership before they were returned. Few had such proof and lost their belongings. Among them was a good measure of bullion. The owners will likely be compensated in cash rather than by the return of their bullion. A few of the box owners were involved in organized crime and that was put forward as the reason for the raid. However, this punished the innocent as well, merely for storing their valuables in the wrong place.

Private regulators are also actively manipulating the record and covering up complaints. Whistleblower Andrew Maguire, a very experienced precious metals trader, at one point witnessed traders toasting each other over a large and highly profitable takedown in silver that day. These manipulations cost ordinary people their savings and poor people (miners) their livelihood. Some even committed suicide over it. Maguire couldn't take it any more and paid a visit to the regulators. They listened – they had to. He showed them when the takedowns were about to happen. He described the process. Commissioner Bart Chilton paid attention. But after a four year investigation, there were no charges for malfeasance. Of course, the CFTC is underfunded. Why? It's a self-regulating industry. The CFTC is not a government entity. It gets its funds from the very companies it regulates.

Ted Butler has made a detailed case for such an investigation with mounds of evidence.

My allegations in silver are incredibly specific. I believe that JPMorgan, by virtue of a massive concentrated short position in COMEX silver futures, is manipulating the price of silver lower than it would be otherwise. If JPMorgan's concentrated short position did not exist, the price of silver would be substantially higher. It does not matter if the bank is hedging or engaged in market-making; the mere existence of such an unprecedented large and concentrated short position proves manipulation. That's a key feature of commodity law and is why the CFTC monitors concentration closely. The Commission looked into a 4% price decline in oil, yet ignored a 30% and a 35% decline in the price of silver.[48]

Just before the April 12, 2013 granddaddy smackdown, Comex stores were in waterfall decline. Silver dropped by 10% in a mere 48 hours. Gold stocks were being viciously drained by major players, including some sovereigns. One motive of the operation was to liberate physical gold from weaker hands, to get supply to the desperate exchange. It backfired. The gold stores were 'eligible,' meaning not for sale. The owners siphoned off 20% of stored gold in three months. JPMorgan took the biggest hit, with 90% of eligible gold leaving the vaults. Translation: clients do not trust the Comex custodians to store their gold any more.

The spot market is the price of gold to buy, today. The futures market more or less dictates the spot price, which is backwards. The physical should drive the paper price. Right now, if you buy on the spot market, you are an unsecured creditor with the LBMA – giving you a 'right' to take gold off. Few choose to do so. The tax is high, for one thing. Since the LBMA is 90% of the gold market, that equals a lot of paper churning and very little physical movement.

The Pan-Asian Gold Exchange (PAGE) was supposed to be the counter-assault on the suppression scheme. PAGE was set to sell 100% allocated gold and silver in smaller amounts – 10 oz of gold and 100 oz of silver. A lot of people would have dropped out of the LBMA and moved their money to PAGE. But it fizzled due to government regulations and internal sabotage.

Regulators have penalized banks owning gold for decades, requiring that they only carry 50% of its market value on their balance sheets. This is a massive disincentive to own gold. Of course, banks still do – it's the ultimate asset. But the consequences of a liquidity or solvency crunch are clear. A bank in real trouble will sell its half-valued gold for full dollars in the market. Even a healthy bank will not own a lot of gold. A rule change was proposed to the FDIC, the Fed, and the Treasury to end penalizing the banks for owning gold as a reserve asset. Gold would be valued at its market price for balance sheet purposes. The proposal failed.

Precious Metals Hunts

*That's why I'm richer than you.*
**– Jamie Dimon, CEO of JPMorgan**

In 1973, a team of cowboys participated in a shooting contest in Texas. The winners were awarded a protection contract. They soon found themselves loading boxes at New York's La Guardia airport and flying to Zurich. The cargo was forty million ounces of silver belonging to the billionaire Hunt brothers. H.L. Hunt, the father, was not trying to corner the market – he had a far more ambitious goal. He wanted to create his own currency. The last time anyone had managed to come close to owning the market was the Bank of England in 1717. The Hunts, it is said, created a bubble in silver. The claim is a half-truth, since gold rose at the same time.

Money, in my view, cannot be in a bubble. That's because the measure of a bubble is monetary; a ruler cannot measure itself. Of course, this comes down to whatever the world regards as money. The petrodollar standard shifted the world's idea from gold as money to the US dollar. For 40 years, this has been the basis of our understanding of what money is. In the absence of something else with gold's money-like characteristics, our conception is starting to swing back toward gold. It simply fulfills every characteristic. It's not magic – anything could fulfill those characteristics. It's simply that gold and silver do the best job. The gold price spike of the late '70s could be seen as a bubble because the world quit regarding gold as money at that time. The fiat forces won. Gold, which was sought after because of inflating currencies, shifted to being in a bubble only because the world no longer saw it as money.

When Paul Volcker raised US interest rates to a crushing 20% in response to out of control inflation, this extreme approach put the dollar back on sound footing. Currency was definitely not free and it was profitable to just hold cash. Bank CDs paid quite well. It didn't take long to get the economy back into sanity with a quick, sharp recession to flush out the malinvestment. It also accomplished the perception management of making the dollar appear to be real money by powerful and deliberate deflation.

There are other factors affecting the precipitous drop in the gold price. It was not the classic popping of a bubble, caused by big money choosing to leave because the market feels wildly overbought. The supply side dynamic was not so overbalanced. The demand side dynamic was artificially destroyed. The case of the Hunt brothers is a stunning example of the war on precious metals.

During their silver play, the Hunts got some deep pocket Saudis onboard. As the operation picked up steam towards 1978, the Comex and regulators got panicky. They held only 120 million ounces against the Hunt-Saudi team. With another large buyer making their own play, the exchanges looked likely to be in for a short squeeze, leaving them unable to make delivery on all their contracts. This would send the price to the moon, exactly what the Hunts wanted. The Commodities and Metals Exchange (CME) took action. They upped the margins on silver and limited ownership to 3 million ounces by any one party. Nine Comex board members, it later came out, held a 38 million ounce short position; they were deeply underwater. Their $1.88 billion position was in trouble. Bunker Hunt did not regard them as the neutral regulators they pretended to be, and rightly not. Silver soared to the mid $30s. The CFTC decided that Bunker's holdings were "too large relative to the size of the U.S. and world silver markets." A meeting was set for January 8, 1980 to stop the Hunts. The Comex, meanwhile, limited positions to 10 million ounces in futures contracts.

Hunt claimed he was being attacked without merit. "I am not a speculator. I am just an investor and holder in silver." Owning long outright is not typically thought of as manipulation. After all, it doesn't put anyone at risk who actually holds the asset. The only ones hurt are the naked shorts, people selling something they do not yet own. That type of risk is normally considered their problem; if they can risk it, they can lose it.

Silver fell for a day, then rose again. Under continued Hunt buying, it hit $50/ounce. The brothers had bought most of their silver for less than $10. They had made more money on balance sheet in six months than the senior Hunt had in his entire career. But getting out of the position entailed high taxes. They wanted to hold it and use the equity. Then the exchanges struck their death blow – a halt to buying. Silver holders could only liquidate. Essentially, they killed the free market in silver to protect their positions. The price fell from $44 to $34 in a day.

Throughout the price decline, Bunker Hunt kept making deals to buy. He rolled his futures, bought mines, and sought out more investor groups. As silver hit $21/ ounce, their holdings value had dropped by $2 billion. The margin calls on their 60 million ounces of futures were $10 million per day. On March 25, they got hit with a $135 million margin call and couldn't meet it. The losses were big, so big they put the brokerage house that the Hunts did business with in serious trouble. Bunker appeared in Paris, with an announcement about silver backed bonds based on 200 million ounces in holdings. It was too late. Silver tanked from $15.80 to $10.80. Other markets reeled, the Dow dropped steeply.[49] The private regulatory agencies won. The message was clear: precious metals investors would be fed to the sharks. The regulators were backing the short sellers. They were not impartial.

# Fort Knox, Fed Audits, Tungsten Fills, and Other Games with Gold Bars

*The two enemies of the people are criminals and government,*
*so let us tie the second down with the chains of the Constitution*
*so the second will not become the legalized version of the first .*
—Thomas Jefferson

Some gold war stories are enjoyable just for their spy novel quality. This headline is a work of art: "Trillion dollar lawsuit exposes secret Bilderberg Gold Treaty & funding of extraterrestrial projects." The article goes on to say,

A mysterious trillion dollar lawsuit filed on November 23, 2011 in the U.S. District Court for the Southern District of New York, claims that $145.5 billion worth of gold was secretly given to the U.S. government in the mid-1930s by the then Nationalist government of China for safekeeping. The lawsuit claims that 1934 U.S. Federal Reserve notes were issued to the Chinese government, and the gold transferred to the Federal Reserve Bank. It is claimed that a total sum of almost one trillion dollars representing both the principal and accumulated interest of the 1934 Federal Reserve notes was fraudulently taken from the plaintiff, Neil Keenan, an agent for the owners, a mysterious Asian entity called "The Dragon Family." What makes the lawsuit worth paying attention to is the link to the unresolved June 2009 case of two Japanese citizens caught on a train in Italy while traveling to Switzerland with 134.5 billion dollars in US Federal Reserve notes, bonds and other financial instruments.[50]

On a more down to Earth vein, the physical precious metals market has two mutually exclusive hypotheses – a glut of metal and a shortage. A glut will lead to ever-declining real prices in gold. A shortage will lead to a squeeze on the paper shorts, some of whose owners must fulfill their obligations with actual bullion, sending the price parabolically upward. Since money is always in demand and gold is increasingly the 'go-to' money in a world choking on paper currencies, the shortage theory seems more likely. Some big stories add fuel to this fire.

Barrick Gold is the whale in the mining tank. The firm is owned, originated, and led by bankers, unlike most firms, which are led by geologists. President Bush I was even on its board of directors. It has a huge forward hedge book. Barrick sold its gold while it was in the ground for less than $1000 per ounce.

They are deep underwater. In 2009, the mining giant issued secondary stock to erase its hedge book. The stock sold, but the book remained. Instead, Barrick invested the $3 billion in the Pascua Lama mine in Argentina. After tapping out the entire sum and more, numerous disputes mushroomed over mineral rights and other factors. Construction stopped cold, but sales of the 'deep storage metal' did not. The Comex is looking ahead to this lost mine for a lot of future supply that will never arrive. Barrick is tanking badly, with stock down over 50%.

But their back-story is far more intriguing. It includes a weird legend from WWII about Yamashita's gold. Supposedly, thousands of tons of gold seized from Southeast Asia were hidden by Japanese General Yamashita in the Philippines. The Americans later confiscated the gold, but agreed with the emperor to keep its existence secret. It was used to finance covert operations for decades. Barrick was created to launder the gold into the banking system. Barrick's awfully mispriced hedge book operated at spectacular losses for decades. As part of this operation, Barrick opened two refineries in Switzerland – a country with no appreciable gold mining. Barrick has no mines there, nor anywhere in Europe, which is also without gold. Why, then, was the mining giant refining gold there? Where had the gold – that then went into the major Cartel banks – come from? The FBI investigated, but their records of Barrick's gold-fixing actions were reported destroyed in the North Tower on 9/11.[51]

Whatever the truth of Yamashita and the origins of Barrick, a more critical story concerns US gold reserves. Ron Paul tried to get an audit on Fort Knox. The attempt was defeated in Congress. But there is no reason not to audit the gold unless, as some suspect, it isn't there. There has been no official audit of Fort Knox gold since 1953, in Eisenhower's day. Even that may have been a specious audit. In 1975, the General Accounting Office director wrote a letter saying that there was 'no good delivery gold' (99.5% or higher) left in Treasury vaults, i.e. Fort Knox.

After FDR made gold ownership illegal with executive order 6102, people were required to sell it to the Federal Reserve. With the resultant huge increase in the gold supply, additional storage was needed. In 1937, the Fort Knox bullion depository was built for $8.5 million (2009 dollars) and the gold was moved there. Featuring an 'atomic bomb proof' system with the largest vault doors ever made, Ft. Knox has stored the original Constitution, Declaration of Independence, the Hungarian crown jewels, European gold reserves, an original Magna Carta, as well as opium and morphine. Peak gold holdings were four times the current list. The officially removed gold was shipped to the Federal Reserve Bank of New York and to the London Gold Pool in the 1960s.

At the end of WWII, the US owned 22,000 tons of gold. Congress ordered an annual audit. In 1953, 9000 bars were assayed and found to be

.995 at 28.9 lbs. This was the last year the physical metal was audited. By 1971, the number of ounces had plummeted to 9000 tons – largely from the London Gold Pool. That's a critical point – it drained 13,000 tons to maintain the gold pool in the 1960s. Global population was a third its current level and money supply was 1/50. The reinstated suppression has gone on since 1999 – gold was mostly dormant before then. How much gold is left? The Treasury says 4600 tons are in Fort Knox. In 1971, rumors began that the gold was gone. In a photograph, when two Congressmen weighed a bar, it was only 22 lbs. The Secretary of the Treasury claimed the 30% error was caused by use of a household scale. But the photograph showed it was a postal scale, known to be quite accurate. And this was their best bar in the vault.

Ed Durrel spent $11 million dollars to get into Ft. Knox in 1974.[52] His team was only permitted to see vault 13, the smallest. They were not allowed to touch any gold and were only allowed to view it through peepholes. One reporter said it had a 'strange, orange tint.' According to analyst Bill Still, the color is normal with a high copper content. Treasury officials then admitted that almost all the gold in Fort Knox was inferior quality coin melt, not good delivery gold.

Victor Harkin oversaw the reserves until 1980. He said that an outgoing delivery of gold, never officially acknowledged, had required 30 trucks. It would account for removal of about 7000 tons of bullion. US gold had dwindled from 700 million oz. in 1949 to 260 million oz. Only 5% of that is presently claimed to be Treasury gold, according to the newspaper *The Globe*. The rest belongs to banks and investors. The Treasury claimed that all the sold gold was sent out strictly legally, but the official sale price was $42/ oz when the market price was four times that.[53]

Dr. Peter Beter worked with Bobby Kennedy closely. He brought charges, and soon appeared on radio shows nationwide, claiming the Rockefellers took gold to Mexico, then to Switzerland on a private jet. His work led to the 1974 Durrel inspection. No gold experts were allowed to inspect the gold, however. The story was taken quite seriously, appearing in Knight-Ridder, the *Los Angeles Times*, and the *London Times*. A Kentucky congressman, whose district included Fort Knox, confirmed that army vehicles were used to take gold out of Fort Knox by night.

On the other hand, analyst Jim Rickards claims the gold is still there and that the 'no audit' policy is for two good reasons. It covers the tracks of gold leased to JPMorgan and other banks. There would arise very sticky legal questions of ownership if the books were investigated. Much of the leased gold has been rehypothecated multiple times. Second, Rickards avers, gold is an unimportant legacy asset, not worth an audit. He compared it to auditing acorns in the national park. The second contention is nonsensical of course. Ft. Knox is guarded by 30,000 soldiers and 300 tanks – an

Afghanistan equivalent. The first is a good reason, if true. Not auditing hides the corruption.

In January 2013, Tom Cloud of National Numismatics issued a forceful claim on the score of Central Bank held gold: "Everybody in the industry knows the US doesn't have the gold and can't deliver. They've leased it all out."[54] Judge Napolitano on Fox News ran a feature story on the possibility of missing gold in Fort Knox. Head of the Mises Institute, Lew Rockwell, said that most of what the Fed says is a lie, so we should be skeptical of the claims that the gold is there. Only a full and impartial audit will reveal the truth.

Then on February 18, 2013, the *Los Angeles Times* ran an article on an audit of Federal Reserve gold that took place in the vaults 'five stories below' the street. The audit assayed 367 bars, or 1% of the gold, finding it purer than formerly thought. The team also found that security and internal controls were 'up to snuff.' They sealed off the vault, declaring an intent to do the audit annually. The implication in the article was that the 'conspiracy theorists' were proved wrong about the nation's gold. Everybody could rest easy. But the article is about Federal Reserve gold and never mentions Fort Knox. No doubt some gold is held by the Federal Reserve in New York. The Fed holds gold for other nations.[55]

The audit also ignored the fundamental question: is the gold encumbered? Just because it's being held by the Federal Reserve does not mean title has not been sold multiple times. An ownership audit was not conducted. The audit ignored the actual reason for conducting one, instead shifting the question around to make the holdings appear legitimate. The Fort Knox question is: how much gold is still there? The Federal Reserve vault question is: who owns the gold and how many parties have title to it? The debacle at MF Global and HSBC's legal battle with JPMorgan over gold ownership (covered elsewhere) proved how, in fact, gold is owned by more than one party. It's a matter of legal record now.

Another concern is that the audit was not 'independent' in any legitimate sense of the word. Treasury officials conducted it. Since the 1951 Treasury accord, the Fed and the Treasury are two wings of the same bird. At that time, Harry Truman squeezed out two Fed chairmen for claiming that excess bank reserves threatened hyperinflation, defying the Treasury in doing so. The next chairmen were more compliant and since then, all have accommodated Treasury policy. It may often be difficult to tell which is tail and which dog, but they are obviously one animal.[56] This may imply that now the Treasury controls the Fed, but it would be more accurate to say that government and the finance industry do not fight, but totally serve each others' needs. Some wonder if the Federal Reserve actually now owns US gold. The Fed claims to 'own no gold whatsoever.'[57] This may be true in actuality, but the Federal Reserve gold stock (US gold reserves) listed on balance sheet, May 30, 2012

– which reads "Gold stock 11,041"[58] – shows the Fed owns $11 billion of gold. At market prices, that's 214 tons. But since the Fed lists gold at $42.22 an ounce, that makes their gold stock 8133 tons. US gold is listed as $11 billion at official prices by the Federal Reserve.[59] It certainly looks like the Fed lays claim to US gold. Officially, however, they own gold certificates and the Treasury owns the gold.

> According to Goldseek, the Fed has an asset claim on $11 billion in cash. If the Treasury revalues gold, then they owe the Fed more. If the Treasury defaults, the Fed can lay claim to the gold. Jesse's Café Americain, a savvy gold analyst, thinks the agreement will not be enforced in any meaningful way in favor of the Fed. He raises the issue of whether the gold is, in fact, there and if other claims on the gold exist, but declines to speculate.[60]

An interesting side story comes out of all this. The last gold coin minted by the US (until recently) was the 1933 double eagle. It was never issued. The government destroyed them after the confiscation order. In 1944, one of them was reported to the Secret Service. A standing investigation has yielded 20 of them, with half destroyed. But King Farouk of Egypt bought one and applied for an export license. It was granted without knowledge of the Secret Service. Farouk would probably have returned the coin, but World War II got in the way. He was deposed in a 1952 coup d'etat and his possessions were auctioned off. The double eagle disappeared. In 1996, coin dealer Stephen Fenton was arrested and found with a double eagle. At first claiming it was purchased over the counter, he then claimed it was the famed Egyptian double-eagle. Fenton was not prosecuted, but a civil court reverted ownership to the US Treasury. The coin was stored in World Trade Center 7, then moved in July 2001, two months before the attacks. It landed in Ft. Knox until it was auctioned for $7.6 million, the highest amount by double of any coin purchased up to that time. Fenton received half the money. The question is: if the coin could be auctioned to an individual, how could the government claim the right to seize it from an individual? In 2004, 10 more coins were discovered and seized.

Other countries are lying about gold, too. The Royal Canadian Mint (RCM) was one of the most prestigious mints in the world. It lost its golden luster in 2009 with a series of increasingly thin fictions issued after the mint lost $15 million of gold bullion. The first claim was due to loss from the melting room floor. The Royal Canadian Mounted Police investigated and found bad accounting and problematic inventory controls. A number of the gold bars were actually tungsten. Gold bars can be counterfeited by using tungsten – which has a similar density – and plating it with gold. In an ISO 9001 certified institute, incompetence is highly unlikely. When combined with the evidence of tungsten laced bars elsewhere, that excuse vanishes. The mint apparently stores bars for customers without an assay – a very poor procedure. When the problem was discovered, the RCM looked like a fumble-fingered operation. The Mint lacked enough gold for the Maple Leaf coin program and, analyst Rob Kirby speculates, they melted down client gold and swapped it with bad delivery bars filled with tungsten. The RCM never mentioned the very public scandal in its annual report.[61]

China, meantime, reverses the US situation. They hold far more gold than officially declared. They only publish gold holdings every few years and the true amount is a state secret. In 2005, they revised their official gold holdings sharply upward. Many analysts have noted huge inflows to China and withholding of all China's production for government coffers. Yet the official gold holdings have not changed for years. They probably have 5000 tons minimum and possibly far more. They are preparing for a massive change – one we'll cover towards the end of this book.

Meanwhile, fake gold is circulating in fact and rumor. Australian Bullion Dealers provided photographic evidence of a salted bar – with 40% of the gold drilled out and replaced with tungsten. It passed xrf scans and ferro-magnetic tests, but was 2 grams underweight. The suspicious dealer cut it in half and found the bored-out gold.

Deutsche Bank, the Slog reported, fulfilled a large order with tungsten filled bars. This is a much higher order of deception than the bad 10 ounce bars in New York retail establishments. The source (Austria) is a sovereign entity with expert analysts fooled by one of the world's largest banks. The evidence put forward is still deniable, but the source is reputable. And after the LIBOR scandal, the willingness to believe in the occurrence of such malfeasances is much higher.[62]

Some malfeasance reports were even bigger. Gold Refiner Goldmelt Heraeus in Hanau, Germany found a 500 gram bar filled with tungsten in 2011. The story caused a stir and other events came to light.[63] In October 2009, the Chinese government received a shipment of gold. In a normal assay, they drilled out bars and found they were filled with tungsten. The serial numbers traced back to Fort Knox. Over 5000 400 oz. bars were found to be counterfeit. The question, of course, is how much of the Treasury gold is tungsten laced? Some of it has been shown to be so. Chinese officials caught and questioned some of the perpetrators. They traced the crime back to the Clinton administration under Robert Rubin's time at the Treasury helm. The reported swap was for up to 640,000 bars replaced by counterfeits in Fort Knox. Another 700,000 bars were allegedly sold into the market.[64] If these numbers are valid, then 10% of the world's gold is not gold at all.

## The End Result

*Capitalism destroys itself.*
**—Karl Marx**

Citizens and governments all over the planet are turning to precious metals as refuge against the storm. Central banks are now buying gold out of necessity to bolster their economies. Only in North America are the people still dumb to the virtues of genuine money. The trust in the currency has fallen some, but not precipitously. It will in time. Meanwhile, the people of Turkey own 5000 tons of gold and the government owns half that amount. Trade with Iran in gold is brisk, with each country giving the other what it wants, gold or oil. Gold is moving from strength to strength, gaining influence and power as it restructures the world economy in its simpler, more trustworthy image.

The gold bull is not exhausted, it is coming into its prime. Most bull markets are measured in dollars, but this one is entirely different. The gold bull will be measured in its shining comparison against oceans of mal-investment, against its destruction of fiat currencies, and its ultimate return to the world stage, understood as money. I am not a prophet arguing for the wonders of the free market or its capacity to solve all human problems. The 'free market' can be a terrible and destructive force, polluting poor nations, wrecking vulnerable economies and consigning the unlucky to a lifetime of miserable poverty. But those facts indicate how exceedingly powerful it is. The free market, which means the global mass network of trade and consumption, is growing rapidly distrustful of a marketplace stuffed with endless paper promises, crushing debt, nuclear inflation of toilet paper currencies, gross favoritism towards the elites, and a culture of corruption that will surely destroy the bounty of human integrity and liberty.

The Treasury Bond complex will collapse, eventually. When it does, all the gold restrictions are off. All the money fleeing sovereign US bonds will go to real assets – real estate, energy, and especially gold. The Cartel will be out of bullets (gold bars) to cap the price. All the gold is flowing to the East. In a rare testament, the price of wholesale gold is higher, with longer wait times, than retail gold. Central banks, buying by the ton, pay up to $30/ounce more and wait for months. And they can't source massive orders above a hundred tons.

The West will be obliged to enact a force majeure – a settlement on all gold liabilities in cash instead of metal. They simply cannot come up with that much missing gold (or silver). The consequences are uncertain, but it will be bullish for gold, long-term. Probably, there will be a Mother of all smackdowns before any force majeure to give the final settlement a lower price point.

Three great forces are at play in the metals (and all markets): foremost, there is debt – the flushing mortgage, housing, local, corporate, and finally, sovereign debt markets, with the massive derivative tail wagging the whole dog. The other two are central bank inflation, and accelerating manipulation. But a deep restructuring is taking place. The Comex is being wrested away from the manipulators by Eastern players and is now being used to destroy them. The shorting mechanism – the main tool of price suppression – has been used to attack the banks on their deepest level, solvency. The gold is leaving and a bank without real money is poor indeed. This will become more apparent as worldwide distrust of paper assets ramps up and bank balance sheets decline in value. Many will go up in smoke.

The decline is in full swing with one bank front and center. JPMorgan sold 99.3% of all the delivered gold on the Comex for Feb-Apr of 2013. It was nearly 2 million ounces. This is a massive physical drain. It's also a key manipulation factor.[65]

An economy and a monetary system are built on trust. When trust in the largest institutions fails, people turn to government. When trust in government fails, people move to end reliance on the system. But trade is a necessary component of civilization and trust is mandatory for trade. The necessary trust will largely be placed in gold and silver. They will become the media of trade – probably through representative monies, or backed currencies, rather than specie. When precious metals replace the role of fiat currencies, the revaluation of the latter will be staggering.

Global assets are worth several hundred trillion dollars. Much of that is derivatives contracts and the like. When gold is placed on the other side of the balance beam, it will slam down hard enough to send these instruments into space, where they can be forgotten. Then metals will take the money side of the real asset equation. They will be revalued to balance against real estate, food, energy, transport, labor, consumer objects and all other human needs. Having destroyed the illusion, they will then right the world's balance sheet.

Gold rides up on a wave of bad sentiment about the monetary system. There are a fistful of heavy problems, mostly from international currency wars and debt saturation. Thousands of tons of allocated metal have been leased out and otherwise pilfered – this accounting is quietly happening as a result of investors trying to claim or audit their holdings. Gold is sold in a fractional system; much more is sold in futures, swapped bullion bank metal, and dodgy ETF instruments than exists in the physical market. Gold mining production is in steady decline. Sovereign bond systems are failing in serial fashion. The T-Bond scheme has pushed real interest rates negative for over four years, enabling banks to borrow well below inflation. Negative interest rates are always positive for gold. People's trust in currency is declining. Lastly, more and more nations are rebelling against US dollar tyranny. This includes a novel trading structure coming from the Chinese-led coalition which will shove aside the dollar and use a gold component.[66]

Gold demand is inelastic, reversing the normal supply/demand logics. Typically, when the price rises, demand rises; when it falls, demand falls. The reason is simple; gold is not an investment, it is money itself. A rising price shows the loss of value in paper currencies and the value of sound, limited-in-supply money. When that weakness of fiat, paper currency is exposed, the true value of gold shines forth.

At some point, the paper price and the physical price of precious metals will separate. Currently, the separation is called a 'premium.' In 2008, when suppression and shorting dropped the price of silver from $16 to $8 spot price, physical silver could not be bought for less than $12 in the shops. That is a 50% premium over the listed market price.

Figure 36
The Separation of Physical Demand and Paper Demand in Gold

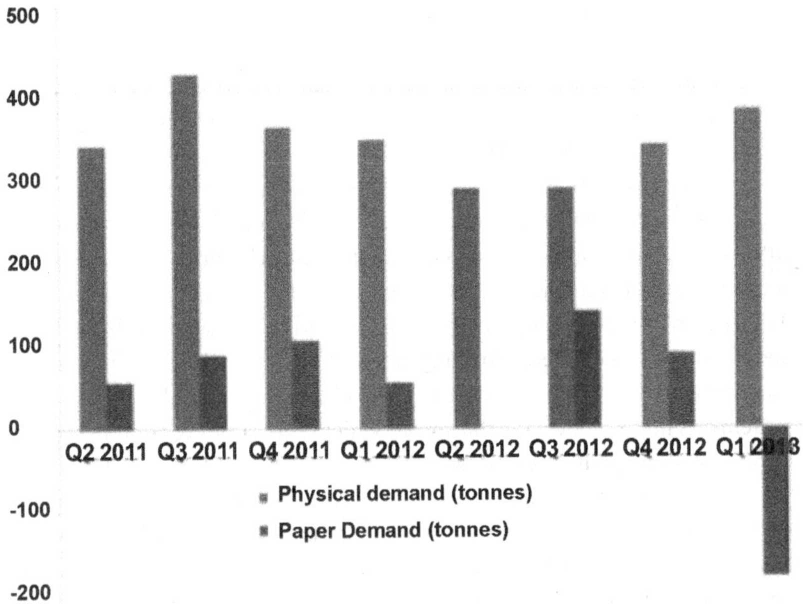

The two markets reconverged in percentage, but less so in absolute terms. Physical silver always sells for $2 to $3 more than spot price. Part of this is the seller's margin, to be sure, but even an independent seller can sell for the same mark-up. And the market buys it because people know that the paper price of silver is not the physical price, especially for small buyers.

After the 2013 major smackdown, retailers were buying above spot – a sign of major shortages. One of the strongest reasons is called stock to flow (STF). Flow is the material currently available for sale. Stock is global supplies. Much global gold is held in long-term storage by wealthy families and institutions. There it sits for tens of years, sometimes centuries. Insofar as it is not available for sale, it cannot affect the price of gold. Only flow affects the price, but it revalues the entire stock. If all stock became available – an STF ratio of 1 – the price would hit the basement in short order. If all flow disappeared – a ratio of infinity – the price would approach infinity, but only for actual physical metal. When the flow dries up, the price between paper and physical will separate. No one will be selling physical any more. It will all be in the 'strong hands' of owners who do not need immediate cash. They know the price will only go higher as paper currencies fail. They will not sell now when the future offers a far higher return, in fact to preserve wealth. This will only increase the price and demand. It reverses the usual logic of an increase in price bringing more supply to market. As demand chases non-existent flow, with hyper-monetary creation on top, the price will go Zimbabwean. In Zimbabwe, an ounce of gold cannot be bought in the local currency. It costs more than a quintillion dollars, due to the nightmarish hyperinflation.

The futures market will eventually dry up. It is primarily a short-term, speculative play. The longs cannot win because each time they try, the shorts overwhelm with illegal unbacked sales. Fools keep trying, but at some point, there will be fewer fools in that game. At that point, there is no prey to short upon. The market will move increasingly to physical. Superior exchanges, with fully audited, allocated metal, will prevail. The price will tear apart between Eastern and Western exchanges, a process already well under way. Arbitrage will increase, but Western players will be unable to deliver; the metal simply is not there. Arbitrageurs will increasingly face the risk of force majeure – a default on delivery. Mostly, they will get handsome cash settlements made quietly. As the spread widens, this arbitrage will become a torrent. At some point, the dam will break.

According to the Chairman of Leeb Capital Management, the banks do not have the allocated gold they are supposed to have. The banks hold customer gold on deposit, but then they lease the gold to be sold by a third party in the open market. This suppresses the price. The situation will cause havoc when people who thought they owned gold realize what's going on. A mass bank run on the gold will create a massive price upheaval as banks try to buy back to cover their ghost metals. There will be an attempt to use fiat money to paper over the problem, but many investors will not want it. The government may impose price controls, but the global problem won't stop there. It will only create international imbalances between the domestic controllers and the other nations. Gold will flee to greener pastures and become increasingly scarce in the manipulated countries. It will end in "total chaos."[67]

Some analysts believe their short position in gold will eventually overtake the commercial banks and that they will have to short cover and in doing so, they will drive up the price. But this is unlikely for two reasons: algos and force majeure. The banks are using algorithms (AI software) to push the price down. They can use a number of methods, but by controlling the exchanges, they are able, through the algos, to see 'market depth' beyond what other traders can see. Further, they can coordinate efforts and spoof to give a false market depth on the sell side. In other words, Bank A throws out a massive market price sell order, scaring away the big buyers who don't want to buy before a decline. Bank B 'catches' the sell order in front of any real, stable buyers who won't back down. Bank B simply returns the order off-market to Bank A with no money changing hands (or reverses the process later), but the market price has been dropped.

The Cartel is also suppressing the stock of mining companies. Along with lower bullion prices, this will work against them in a fierce but back-door way. As said before, the Achilles heel is the drain on the physical supply. Small and mid-size miners are going under at record rates. The majors are unable to meet profitable levels of production. A number of mines are being nationalized. This will have an enormous downside for global mining supply. Far less physical will be coming to market because the commercials have destroyed the mining industry.

Because the circle of paper gold expansion is largely closed inside the central bank/bullion bank consortium, breaking the manipulation will not happen by holders of physical – at least not directly. The CBs can continue the shell game for a very long time. The holders of physical cannot force the paper supply to shrink. They can only take the physical out of the loop and thus increase the risk of those inside when they increase the ratio. When the risk is too high, trust will begin to go. The propaganda will wear thin. Citizens of many nations will clamor for their CBs to repatriate their gold and stop selling it. Foreign CBs will turn against the West and seek the return of their gold from London and the Fed. That process is beginning and rapidly accelerating. Those with gold held by the Fed and the BoE don't want to rock the boat too much, though. If they expose the deception, they risk bringing on a force majeure – a default on getting their gold home. If they wait, they can get at least part of it from new mining supply over a period of years.

Probably the most fundamental mechanism for suppressing the price of gold is yoking it to the credit system of fiat money. This creates a forced discount of the price of gold because credit can be infinitely created. Analysts Another, FOA (friend of Another) and FOFOA (friend of a friend of Another) call this the freegold concept – what would the price of gold be if it was not denominated in credit terms? No one has any idea – the credit connection has been ongoing for over a hundred years. These analysts predict the end of the cycle eventually, when gold cannot be priced in credit terms because faith in the credit/debt fractional system will unravel. People will not value physical gold in those terms afterwards. This happens in hyperinflations, of course – no one trades gold for burning paper.

## Endnotes

1    "Did Eric Sprott Buy and Redeem GLD?" Kid Dynamite, April 7, 2011.
2    http://victorthecleaner.wordpress.com/2012/06/01/gld-the-central-bank-of-the-bullion-banks
3    "Ned Naylor-Leyland confirms actual owner of Bob Pisani's GLD gold bar", Silver-doctors.com, Jun 12, 2012.
4    Betty Liu, "One Ton of Gold Worth $7.5M Seized from Small Car", Bloomberg TV. April 4, 2013.
5    Rachel Donadio, "Growing Air of Concern in Greece Over New Bailout", *The New York Times*, 2/21/2012
6    Arthur Burns, Memo to the President, June 3, 1975. Declassified.
7    James Turk, "The War on Gold", Nov. 10, 1997.
8    Tyler Durden, "Declassified State Dept Data Highlights Global High-Level Arrangement To 'Remain Masters Of Gold' By 'The Reshuffle Club'", September 25, 2009.
9    gata.org/files/VolckerMemoirs.doc from Paul Volcker's memoirs.
10   Federal Reserve FOMC transcripts, July 7, 1993.
11   Federal Reserve FOMC transcripts January 31st, 1995.
12   Jaco Schipper, "Dutch central banker's memoirs confirm gold price suppression", Gata.org/node/11304, April 29, 2012.
13   Commodities Corner, CNBC. June 21, 2012.
14   Reserve Bank of Australia, 2003 annual report.
15   RBC GLOBAL INVESTMENT MANAGEMENT INC. Report on Gold, John Embry. Posted on freerepublic.com, June 24, 2002.
16   bankofengland.co.uk/markets/forex.goldinfmem.pdf from TacitOrdoSeclorum Gold Manipulation 5b, youtube.
17   Newmont Mining Corporation press release, OPEN LETTER TO PRIME MINISTER TONY BLAIR. July 7, 1999.
18   Dow Jones, Central Banks…, October 11, 1999.
19   *Howe vs. Bank for International Settlements*, from Embry and Hepburn.
20   Edwin M. Truman, Reflections on Reserve Management and International Monetary Cooperation, World Bank/BIS Joint Fourth Public Investors' Conference, December 3, 2012. From gata.org/files/Truman-WorldBank-BIS-12-03-2012.pdf.
21   Wikipedia.org/gold_reserve
22   James Turk, Freemarket Gold and Money Report, Letter No. 294, November 5, 2001 from Embry and Hepburn, pp. 48-9.
23   Former US Treasury Official – Fed Desperate to Stop Collapse. Paul Craig Roberts interview. King World News, 4/24/2013.
24   Adrian Douglas "How much imaginary gold has been sold?", GATA.org/node/7908 , October 16, 2009
25   Chris Powell, "FT's Gillian Tett provides the rationale for gold price suppression",. 24hgold.com, May 11, 2012.
26   Barrick Gold motion to dismiss Blanchard and Co.'s anti-trust lawsuit. February 28, 2003.
27   William White, Past and Future of Central Bank Cooperation, 4th Annual BIS conference, June 27, 2005.
28   John Hill & Graham Wark, "Gold:Riding the "Re-Flationary Rescue", Citigroup Global Markets Equity Research, September 21, 2007.

29    Federal Reserve's Response to the Freedom of Information Act request filed by GATA.

30    IMF Issues Paper #11. Hidetoshi Takeda. April, 2006. Cited in Kirby, Forensic Examination.

31    Gold Fields Mineral Services is a company that issues gold mining and market reports.

32    Frank Veneroso, "Facts, Evidence and Logical Inference A Presentation On Gold Supply/Demand, Gold Derivatives and Gold Loans", May 2001. Referenced in *Not Free, Not Fair: Long-term manipulation of the Gold Price*. John Embry and Andrew Hepburn, Sprott Asset Management, August, 2004.

33    David J. Hully and Peter D. Ward (Lehman Brothers), Reverse Alchemy: The Commoditization of Gold Accelerates. January 18, 2000.

34    Forensic Examination of the Gold Carry Trade. Rob Kirby, May 14, 2009.

35    *Howe vs. Bank for International Settlements, et al.* Plaintiff's Affidavit, Paragraph 29 filed April 12, 2001.

36    A detailed look at Bank of England gold, Alisdair MacLeod. Goldmoney.com, March 03, 2013.

37    MEXICO'S FEDERAL AUDIT DEMANDS PHYSICAL INSPECTION OF SOVEREIGN GOLD HOLDINGS, Guillermo Barba, Inteligencia Financiera Global. Feb. 26, 2013.

38    "Checkmate", FOFOA, March 5, 2013.

39    Dale Henderson, Stephen Salant, John Irons, and Sebastian Thomas, (1997), "Can Official Gold Be Put to Better Use?: Qualitative and Quantitative Effects of Alternative Policies. From Embry and Hepburn, supra.

40    James Turk, "A short history of the gold cartel", Gold Anti-Trust Action Committee, Mon, May 4, 2009.

41    Do Western Central Banks have any gold Left??, Eric Sprott and David Baker, 3/19/12.

42    "Perspectives on Gold: Central Bank Viewpoint". Oleg Mozhaiskov, Deputy Chairman, Bank of Russia. LBMA conference, June 3-4, 2004, from GATA.org website, node 4235.

43    "FLASH: China knows about gold price suppression, and U.S. knows China knows", gata.org/node/10380, Sept. 3, 2011.

44    "More Beijing embassy cables show China sees gold as central in currency war", Gata. org/node/10416, Sept. 5, 2011.

45    "Not-So-Safe-Deposit Boxes: States Seize Citizens' Property to Balance Their Budgets", Good Morning America. ABC. May 12, 2008.

46    Amber Harrison, "Debunking the DHS Memo About Safety Deposit Boxes: They Don't Need No Stinkin' Memo", American Live Wire, April 1, 2013.

47    Homeland Security: Banking and Financial Infrastructure Continuity, DHS Congressional Report, September 5, 2003.

48    Theodore Butler, "Transparency", Silverseek.com, September 24, 2012.

49    Harry Hurt III, "Silverfinger", *Playboy*, 9/1980.

50    Apple. news.exopoliticinstitute.org. March 12, 2012.

51    EP Heidner. *Collateral Damage: US Covert Operations and the Terrorist Attacks on September 11, 2001*, 2008, p. 11.

52    James Turk, "Edward Durrell and Fort Knox : We have a right to know", FGMR letter #256. December 13, 1999.

53    Bob Berino, *The Globe*, Dec. 15, 1981.

54    "Everybody in the Industry Knows the US Doesn't Have the Gold", John Rubino on January 31, 2013.

55    Andrew Tangel, "Gold at N.Y. Fed is intact, some purer than thought, audit finds", *Los AngelesTimes*, Feb. 18, 2013.

56    Tyler Durden, "Who Is Lying: The Federal Reserve Or... The Federal Reserve? And Why Stalin 'Lost'", ZeroHedge, April 21, 2012.

57    May 2012 hearing of House Finance Committee.

58    http://www.federalreserve.gov/releases/h41/Current/

59    Key to the GoldVault, US Federal Reserve. 2007.

60    "How Much Gold does the US have in its reserve?", Jesse's Café Americain, Oct. 13,

2009.

61      "Royal Canadian Mint's Tungsten Twostep?" Silver Doctors. November 28, 2012.
62      "Deutsche Bank Fulfilled Recent Gold Repatriation Request With Tungsten Salted Gold", Silver Doctors. November 27, 2012
63      "Fort Knox and the gold dipped tungsten bars", ProSiebeneSat1 Television, Germany. July, 2011. on youtube.
64      Rob Kirby, "GLD ETF warning: Tungsten Filled Fake Gold Bars", Market Oracle, UK. November 12, 2009.
65      Tyler Durden, "JPMorgan accounts for 99.3% of Comex gold sales in the last 3 months", Zerohedge, April 26, 2013.
66      Jim Willie, "June 2012 Hat Trick Letter – Gold and Currency report", goldenjackass. com
67      "All Hell is going to Break Loose on the Upside in Gold", King World News interview w/ Stephen Leeb, July 11, 2012.

# 9

# SILVER
# A SPECIAL CASE

*The major monetary metal in history is silver, not gold.*
—**Milton Friedman**

Billionaire Hugo Salinas Price wants to initiate a silver currency, in coin form, in Mexico. He suggests using it to save Greece. This method would move the flow of value back to savers and away from the elite. People who held silver would see their savings increase in value rather than decrease. Whenever the currency is debased, the government could raise the price of the silver drachma. Price's proposal is detailed. The government would convert a small percentage of their 110 tons of gold to silver and mint a 3 gram drachma. The Greek government has not responded.

Old silver coins have disappeared because of their face value markings tied to currency. The metal in a $1 silver coin is now worth more than $20. But coins marked in weight could be revalued on a floating basis and continue to circulate. The silver would be entered in parallel to a paper drachma. If economic policies were improved, then the paper would hold its own and even rise against the coin. The citizenry could choose sound money.

Salinas Price likes silver as money (or investment) for many reasons. First, less above-ground silver exists than above-ground gold. This counterintuitive, even shocking, fact is well known in precious metals circles, but not to the public. This fact alone makes it presently the single best long-term investment in history.

Silver was originally called the Moon's metal, and gold the Sun's. The ratio of 13 moon cycles per year led to a belief that the ratio of global deposits of silver to gold was 13:1. Not far off – it's 16:1. Mining and use of the metal began in earnest millennia ago in the Mediterranean nations, then moved to Spain about 200 BCE. Mining continued to produce about 1.5 million ounces per year until European explorers descended upon the Americas. Almost 3 billion ounces were pulled out of Bolivia and Mexico by the 1800s. By 1950, global stockpiles were nearing 10 billion ounces. Then everything changed.

Silver is the most reflective, most conductive, corrosion resistant, and second most malleable metal. It is second to oil as the most broadly used commodity. Despite the 16:1 supply ratio to gold, the price ratio is around 55 to 1. It's been as high as 100 to 1 recently. This is unbalanced, but that's only the footprint of the real problem. Most of the gold ever mined is sitting in vaults. Most of the silver has been absorbed into the economy for industrial uses, and is gone for good. Silver is the most useful industrial metal ever found. Obviously, far greater quantities of iron and copper are used, but silver enjoys more varied applications due to its properties. More important, these applications use only trace amounts of silver, so there is no question of recuperation by tapping large concentrations. The amount used by industry – electronics, solar power, mirrors, health care (antibacterial), lasers, even clothing – exceeds annual mine production. This situation has drawn down silver stocks, year after year, by hundreds of millions of ounces. Of the 45 billion ounces of silver mined throughout history, at most a few billion are still around as such.

About 750 million ounces per year comes from mine supply versus 80 million of gold, a 9 to 1 ratio. Add in recycling of 250 million, and we have 1 billion ounces in circulation each year. It's about an 8 to1 ratio in total coming to market. But this isn't the full story.

Only 30% of silver supply comes from direct mining; most comes as a by-product of base metal mining. In both cases, ore grades are deteriorating heavily. Average ore grades (silver/ton of earth mined) have declined 92% since 1935. Silver mining is hugely energy intensive. Shaft mines, holes in the earth, are disappearing as uneconomical. Only shaft mines for gold, which run to several miles deep, still operate. Most mines are open-pit – massive operations requiring machines so large that their tires are the size of a house. This will cause mining costs to continue upward. Likely, the production limits have been hit. Peak silver has probably arrived. The US geological survey has even predicted that the supply of silver via mining will almost disappear by 2020. This picture is massively magnified by the decline of cheap energy. Open-pit mines will soon become uneconomical without vastly higher prices. In fact, the largest silver miners posted net losses for 2012 with an average silver cost of $30. The supply price must be a minimum of $30 or miners go broke.[1]

Because silver has more industrial applications than all other metals combined, it is price inelastic – demand will not decrease with increase in price. For industry, silver is a tiny cost – maybe $10 for an Apple computer. Gold is not used very much in industry. Consequently, gold stocks have steadily increased due to mining – there is an estimated 5 billion ounces of above ground gold.

As silver becomes scarce, these industries will hedge, buying up physical supplies. This will push the price up. Industry uses up almost all mine production. As silver shortages hit, industry will panic buy. Apple cannot manufacture without silver. A genuine shortage threatens the empire of the largest company[2] on Earth. They will front-run the problem and buy a large store of the metal. Many other companies will do likewise. This buying binge will push the price of physical to unprecedented heights. A rising price will fire up demand, rather than the opposite.

The timeline for shortages is soon – a few years, tops. In 1980, there was at least 2 ounces per person. Now, there is about 1/6 ounce per person. We are still well below the nominal high of $50/oz and the CPI inflation adjusted high of $147. If one uses economist Walter Jon Williams' alternative inflation measure, the adjustment becomes $444/ounce. All other commodities except oil are posting record highs. There is about $1000 of gold and $5 of silver per person on Earth. Silver is enormously inexpensive relative to other precious metals – the signature of the long-term value investor.

To sum up: silver is a very energy intensive product. Energy is set to become increasingly expensive and mining is certain to use more and more per ounce of product. Industry will consume ever-increasing amounts of silver for a mushrooming array of end-products. Investment demand is rising dramatically in response to fears over the currency and economic systems. Most of existing stock is used up. Massive short positions in silver are floated in the financial arena. Central banks have no silver vaulted or on the books. Mining supply is beginning a steady decline, while demand has risen steadily for 15 years. As an investment, silver fundamentals are as good as any investment in history. Since 2007, investment demand for silver coins alone has risen 6-fold from 22 million to 128 million ounces. So why is the price so low?

**Manipulation**

*Crash JPMorgan. Buy silver.*
—**Max Keiser**

The word "dollar" comes from a Czech valley famed for silver mines. It was used to denote a silver coin before 1600. Historically, silver was priced a lot higher than it currently is. For centuries, it was above $500/ounce in 2012 dollar equivalent. That fell steadily, especially after some large mine discoveries. The price spike in 1980 was the anomaly, but the collapse after took it well below the mean. New forces have come into play and the market dynamic is set to change radically. Total investment in PMs is 1%. The norm used to be 25%. That major trend is reversing, starting in Asia. Silver is the new 'best' investment.

Billionaire Eric Sprott calls silver the investment of the decade. His large, properly audited, fully allocated funds offer redeemable silver or gold.

(He also has many other funds). He notes that his silver and gold funds sell in equal dollar amounts. With a 50 to 1 price handle, that means people are buying 50 times as much silver as gold. The US Mint has the same figures, showing Sprott's experience is not aberrant. He thinks the price potential is explosive, but that Western powers are capping price. That manipulation, he claims, will end.

For investment purposes, silver enters the market at 3 times the volume of gold. The total silver flow per year is a billion ounces, 750 new mined and 250 million recycled. Gold is 80 million new and 130 million recycled. But industry claims 650 million ounces of silver and 10 million ounces of gold, leaving a 3:1 ratio left for investment.

Data shows a normal distribution of silver purchase in 2008, 3:1 versus gold.[3] After the 1980 crisis, something big changes. Investors increase silver:gold buying to 45:1. The US Mint (the source of this data) is selling 10% of global physical investment silver. Dollar sales of silver are about equal to gold, but since the price disparity is 50:1, almost 50 times the amount of silver is being purchased as gold. This is a cursory analysis and leaves out the very important central bank allocations: all gold, no silver.

Total global gold value is around $9 trillion, but total silver value is only $150 billion. It is an unsettled question as to how long the market can withstand this lopsided investment – money flows into both metals at parity, but the ratio of available metals is massively skewed. Something seems amiss in the silver market.

Of course, gold has many excellent investment features. Most it shares with silver, but it beats silver by holding a more concentrated value and a more stable price. Still, silver seems to be superior in many other respects to gold, or any other investments. There are a number of reasons why.

- Massive industrial demand. Silver has 10,000 uses; it is the indispensable metal.
- Inelastic demand. Silver alone maintains high demand independent of price because of its industrial usage. Quantities for individual items are tiny, representing an insignificant part of the price. Yet silver is mandatory for the products.
- Most of the silver mined is now gone due to industry.
- Like gold, physical silver in hand eliminates counter-party risk. No one can default on silver, except society as a whole, and only by rejecting it as valuable.
- It's still well below its top price, much less its inflation adjusted peak of $178. With more traditionally determined inflation rates, the adjusted high is near $500.
- The citizen fight against the banking cartel cannot be won with gold,

but it can with silver. The supply can be drained enough to expose the deception. $1 billion would empty the Comex – 2 hours of US government spending would purchase the entire Comex silver stock. Governments and private wealth funds own no stockpiles of silver, but lots of gold.

- The ratio of silver to gold is mined at 10 to 1, but the price is 50 to 1. This imbalance will eventually correct because of the above stresses on the market.
- Too much printing. The CBs are printing money to oblivion, making it worth less and less, and eventually worthless.
- Physical assets are the place to store value, especially precious metals. They are rare and hold concentrated value.
- Steadily rising investment demand. Foreign nations are no longer playing the paper game and want real metal. Poorer people cannot afford gold and will choose silver.
- Conversion to real money. There is only slight demand for sound money. As people understand the structural weakness of fiat money, they will (and are beginning to) use physical silver coins as exchange media.
- It costs more and more energy to produce. It will not become less expensive to produce, short of a major energy revolution.
- Silver has always been money; it possesses the best useful aspects of money. Only recently has it been demonetized.

The 'eagle barometer' measures the amount of gold and silver coins bought, and thereby, public fears about inflation and the currency. This is in a parabolic trend. While the Silver Eagle was setting record sales in January 2013, it was also setting record premiums. The coins sold for $38.45 (more for small purchases), a $7 to $8 premium over the spot price. Even so, sales were capped at a meager 40 coins per purchaser, hardly enough to engage legitimate dealers. The true price of physical silver was far higher than the $30-$31 spot price during that time.

In January 2013, silver eagle sales jumped by 500% from the December rate, one month earlier. Total sales were 7 million ounces, even with a sales shutdown of over 10 days. The Mint could not source the silver, it claimed. At the same time, however, the SLV ETF added 572 tons of silver to its ledger, 18 million ounces. It makes no sense that SLV could find this much silver without disturbing the price, while the US Mint could not find a third of the amount. Except, of course, that the Mint needs physical silver. It can't play paper games.

The US Mint had to suspend silver eagle sales from mid-December to Jan. 7, 2013. It does this periodically when it cannot source enough silver to meet demand. Solid analysts use this as a metric to determine overall tightness of supply. If there was plenty of silver available, as most mainstream commentators claim, why does the US Mint need to halt orders? When they came back online, the orders piled in at 3,937,000 coins, the largest order day ever for the coin. The new order crushed the previous opening day record (2011) by 25%. Demand is clearly increasing.

Bill Haynes of CMI gold and silver testified to enormous buying. He sold more in a few days in late 2012 than in most full weeks prior to that. The customers had a unified view that 'the West is in real trouble here.' The buyers are very successful, wealthy people, with orders over $6 million. They are looking to preserve accumulated wealth.[4]

China increased its production of silver one ounce pandas from 600,000 per year to 6 million from 2010 to 2011. They anticipated (and got) hugely increased demand from legalizing silver ownership by citizens.

Another coin to gage demand is the Canadian silver Maple Leaf. They are blowing the doors off with a 50% yearly gain for 8 years. 2003 saw 684,750 units. By 2007, 3.5 million coins had sold. That went up 100% the following year to 7.9 million. In 2010 sales jumped to 17.7 million and 2011 recorded 23 million maples sold. The takeaway is that demand is exploding. Silver is the hottest physical commodity in the world.

**Figure 37**
**Canada's Silver Maple Coin Sales (in millions)**

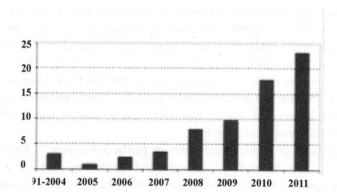

The trend is not welcomed by the financial powers. Bernard von NotHaus introduced a one ounce silver bullion coin intended to compete with fiat currency in trade. He and his associates want a return to constitutional money. The 'liberty dollar' was specifically said to not be legal tender, nor intended to simulate Federal currency. He made a million of these coins as an alternative to fiat currencies, taking a 100% risk (of prosecution and seizure) with absolutely no potential for reward. Since his coins indeed had the proper amount of bullion, he committed no theft or misrepresentation. Even though he could not possibly have profited from selling authentic silver bullion as counterfeited coins – the entire value of the silver was actually contained in the coins – and had no means of additional profit by pretending the coins were legal tender, Von NotHaus was convicted for counterfeiting because of this activity.

Several conclusions are possible: the powers that be do not want a silver currency because it would be mistaken for legal tender. They believe the man was legitimately counterfeiting. The other possible conclusion – the currency makers are afraid of any capacity of the public to switch to an alternative currency if people lose faith in dollars, so any alternative, especially a sound money one, must be stamped out. Another potential fear, with silver in particular, is a massive shortage in physical silver. This is a very real fear. There is precious little silver in the open markets and in government storage. Governments and the very wealthy do not buy and hold silver in quantity; they use gold. Whatever the correct reason for government action, the creation of an alternative *sound* currency is taken seriously, to the point of ludicrousness. Von NotHaus was actually labeled a terrorist by a US district attorney.

Government rejection of sound money has been slow and steady for decades. All silver was removed from US coinage in 1965. A '64 dime is worth 25 times as much. At this point, the US still had silver certificates. Even though gold was illegal, a citizen could turn in certificates in exchange for silver. LBJ ended that in 1968. One of the more interesting theories about the reason for Kennedy's assassination is that Kennedy had issued an executive directive for the Treasury, not the Fed, to issue currency backed by silver.[5] The bankers didn't like it and used the ultimate deterrent a few months later. The order was rescinded quickly by Johnson. Of course, we'll never know the real story.

There are as many 'smacks' to silver as to gold – probably more because it is a smaller, more easily controlled market and requires less ammo to take it down. When Ron Paul showed a silver coin to Ben Bernanke in March, 2012, a massive volume sell-off happened. Silver strikes seem to be frequently timed with official pronouncements. During Bernanke's short speech on June 7, 2012, silver volume spiked by 2500%. and its price dropped 78 cents during the time frame. An after-hours sell-off followed. A similar action happened in gold. By now the pattern is so predictable that it has a name: the Bernanke smack-down. When silver hit $49 in 2011, it was a warning shot and the banks acted. Soon after, the price dropped hard. The first fall is the key: $6 in two minutes. The full takedown took a couple of days and totaled $15 – 30%. This was a stunning decline, greater than any commodity decline ever. And there was no apparent political or financial cause. In any other commodity, manipulation would have been investigated and easily found. In this case, the regulators used their ongoing investigation (now resolved with no charges levied) as an excuse to make no comment. They did not even mention the events. Since overseeing these markets is their entire raison d'être, they can only be complicit in this criminal activity.

The price gets crushed, then steadily rebuilds. It's a recurring pattern. Between 10:35 and 10:50 on September 21, 2012, the market absorbed 62.5 million ounces. The 15 minute dump was double US annual silver production. It managed to keep the price below $35, a critical level. The selling was in the form of naked shorts – no one owns that much physical silver to sell.[6] The strikes have several purposes. First, to shake out the futures market longs and drop the price. Second, to liberate physical silver in the spot market. Third, to break the bull market in physical silver buying by discouraging the participants. Fourth, to release the stresses on the exchanges.

The stresses are revealed in the forward rate – a measure of trust in the futures market. The supply stresses are not welcome news, so the exchanges take pains to hide the information. When the silver forward rate went haywire, the LBMA simply stopped reporting it. The measure shows whether backwardation or contango is happening. When backwardation happens in silver, it's because investors don't trust the futures market to actually deliver silver, so they won't sell their physical silver for a guaranteed profit.

The following chart anomaly is crystal clear – silver lease declined to

**Figure 38**

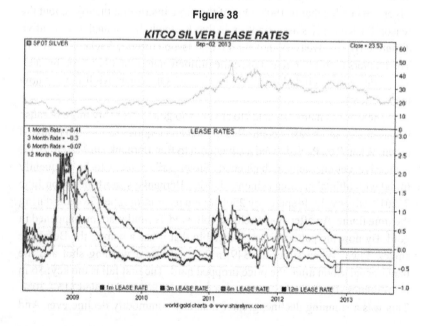

unprecedented lows and went completely flat. Lease rates have always had a ragged pattern, like most stocks and commodities. A pattern like this is clearly held in place by powerful players – it is manipulated. But to what purpose? The best answer is to assist a multi-month campaign to drop the price of silver. The game is to take it out of the desired asset realm. The Cartel wants the public, and in fact everyone, to stop buying and even to sell all their silver. It is made to look like an extremely unstable and high-risk asset through endless mechanisms.

The lease rate suppression allows a marginal profit to speculators who lease silver from various bullion banks, then sell it into the open market. The intent is to buy it back later at a lower price. The game is a very tricky finesse, of course. It cannot really maintain the down price if all other aspects are equal. The idea is to push the price down and make many speculators panic, selling their holdings.

The Cartel has used the technique with tremendous success for decades, in fact. But the utility is ending, its effect having a shorter half-life with each iteration. It also requires more ammunition per cycle. The law of diminishing returns is turning the tide on the commercial banks. Some bullion banks will be upside down and default in the event of a major metal shortage. The customer will be left holding the bag. In the case of the commercials who are bullion banks – HSBC, for example – they will most likely settle with the clients in force majeure as a cash settlement. They won't have the bullion, but have access to an infinite well of Fed notes.

Another anomaly in the chart is the sweet spot for the 3-month rate when it dipped to -0.6, well below the 1-month. It's difficult to understand this one, but it stands out as a big indicator that there is something wrong. Unmanipulated markets don't behave like that. Probably a big player pushed out a large share of 3-month contracts because (in their analysis) the 1-month lease would have turned around too quickly to discourage the market.

The Commodities and Futures Trading Commission (CFTC), which oversees the futures exchange, sets position limits, and the maximum number of contracts a participant can hold, is currently in great dispute. Many analysts claim they have fallen to regulatory capture (when the industry players get their people on the regulatory positions of power). The CFTC is largely staffed by Goldman Sachs-trained investment brokers. And here's why.

A unique situation developed in July 2012 in the silver market. Commercial open positions dropped to 17,000 net short. (Net short is commercial short positions minus long positions). JPMorgan is well-established to be about that amount net short. But the large specs also added short positions bringing them to 5000 net short. This means that the other commercials went net long 5000 contracts. For the first time, *elements of the Cartel were holding opposite sides of the trade.* They were not in unison. Furthermore, the other commercials went net long for a very good reason – they anticipated a rise.[7] They had been hammered in the big smackdown of April 2013.

Part of the Cartel, it seems, pushed the price down for a year. The main reason was to extricate themselves from their naked short positions. If the price rises, a naked short loses money. If they sold at $25, for example, then they would have to buy back at $35. In March, 2011 the commercials were 55,000 net short. At 5000 ounces per contract, that's a loss of $275 million per $1 rise or almost $3 billion for $10 rise. It's not hard to see how the April 2011 blow-off in silver to $49 put the commercials in deep red. So how did they collapse the price? The regulators did it for them by changing the margin requirements.

When silver hit $49, margins were raised 5 times in a few days. The first raise forced speculators to post margin or to sell. Most sold as high as possible, leading to a massive sell-off. This was multiplied by late-night mini-raids and continued margin hikes. The pressure caused a selling panic. The commercials stood by until they found their 'cover point' where they bought back all their shorts with lower losses.

They extricated from their short positions between April and July, 2012. They were net short 56,000 contracts in silver in April, which declined to 12,000 contracts by June 29. It was an 85% decline in net position over 3 months – a breathtaking reversal. The banks, analyst Turd Ferguson showed, were holding the price down to get out of their dangerous positions.[8]

The Comex helped them. The Commodities and Metals Exchange is a for-profit exchange which holds physical metal in vaulted storage for market participants and delivers it. For many years, no one took delivery from the Comex. They rolled the contracts over. However, in what is a recent phenomenon, since 2008 delivery is being demanded. The slogans 'blow up the Comex,' and 'drain the Comex' are now part of the metals proponents' vernacular.

There is a deliberate obfuscation in precious metals terminology. The Comex lists 'registered' and 'eligible' metal in its vaults. Again, eligible means it is not available for trading, but meets the technical requirements of purity and so forth. Registered means that someone has put the metal up for sale on the futures exchange.

Most of the metals movement in the Comex is in silver. Gold rarely moves, but millions of ounces of physical silver are relocated constantly around banking vaults and to SLV. This reflects stress in the physical market, taking from the major account to satisfy demand. Moreover, settlements are listed with weights to the third decimal place. Most of them end with .000 – impossible! It never happens, indicating that huge quantities of Comex silver are just paper.

It's fairly difficult to get delivery from the Comex. The paperwork is monstrous and the obstacles are growing worse since Comex wants to 'store' the metal for owners. Comex is the little brother of the London Metal

Exchange, part of the London Bullion Market Association (LBMA). There is ongoing collusion between the organizations.

The LBMA is not an exchange but rather, per its name, a marketing association of 11 banks. As it does with gold, the LBMA sets the spot price of silver daily, the 'fix.' Ten of the 11 banks are under investigation for massive fraud in the LIBOR scandal. In 2011, the LBMA traded 144 billion ounces of silver. This is about 4 times all the silver ever mined. It is around a hundred times all the silver currently in global stocks. Ninety-five percent of these trades occurred at the four smackdown times discussed in the gold section.

More evidence of silver price suppression comes from the LBMA itself. The LBMA is in trouble, staring at a default event. The usual LBMA inflow is about 30,000 kg. Between June and July of 2012, that increased to 169,000 kgs, a five-fold leap. They needed silver badly and got it. The system is being bolstered by major insider support. Of course, it comes from this side of the ocean.[9]

The US's silver bullion exported to the UK went from 19 metric tons to 291 in a year, a 1500% increase. The anomaly is unprecedented. The LBMA is experiencing huge shortages in delivery on silver and the US system is backing its British friends to keep the cracks papered over. How long it can last is the big question.

Bart Chilton is Commissioner of the Commodities and Futures Trading Commission (CFTC), the private regulatory agency for these markets. On October 26, 2010, he said "I believe there have been repeated attempts to influence prices in silver markets. There have been fraudulent efforts to persuade and deviously control that price. Based on what I have been told and reviewed in publicly available documents, I believe violations to the Commodity Exchange Act have taken place in the silver market and any such violation of the law in this regard should be prosecuted."[10] He later backed off the statement, disavowing manipulation in guarded bureaucratic speak.

The CFTC has received more complaints about silver market manipulation than all other markets combined. Position limits are the elephant in the room. A position limit is a maximum amount of holdings for a particular commodity. Position limits are a way to stop manipulation and they are enforced in every commodity – except gold and silver. In 2008, the CFTC found no problems in the silver market. However, they only based their investigation to the end of 2007, when the problems began. They deliberately omitted the failure of Bear Sterns even though they knew the short situation had caused it.

An August 2008 bank participation report showed that two banks held shorts at 20% of annual global silver supply. The naked positions were 30% of Comex stock and, at one point, these two banks held 99% of all silver short positions in the futures market. These are the largest percentage positions ever established in any commodity. Concentrated positions are the absolute hallmark of market manipulation. Manipulation is beyond question. Moreover, the holder of the largest position was found by a Congressman to be JPMorgan.

Max Keiser came up with an online campaign to 'crash JPMorgan, buy silver.' Keiser is a quite outrageous economist who speaks his mind. Often he yells about banker excesses, but always with a humorous flavor. His theory is that JPMorgan has collateralized its stock to sell silver short. When the stock price goes below the price of silver, it creates a huge strain. Further, any physical silver removed from the market is that much less that the giant shorts can take to hold their leveraged position. If the short is 100 to 1, then removing 1 ounce from global supply increases the JPMorgan leverage and risk by making it that much harder for it to source physical silver.

In another counterstrike against the bank, Asian national wealth funds have bought massive amounts of the SLV fund, a silver-backed fund that can trade on the stock market. It's the corrupt twin of the GLD fund, with similar practices. The Asian buying was an act of war against JPMorgan. The huge silver shorts held by JPMorgan are the soft underbelly of the beast. By buying shares of SLV, the silver price was steadily pushed up, creating massive pressure on the JPMorgan position. They were looking for buying capitulation. Instead they got regulatory interference. The Asian side lost the battle and the buying pressure on SLV has since let up.

Silver has been called the Devil's metal. It may not be far from the truth. A huge silver short position has travelled from house to house like a plague. Drexel Burnham held it in the 1980s. They failed. AIG took it over afterward, then failed. Bear Sterns took it from AIG. They rolled over. Now JPMorgan has it. There is an underground campaign, sponsored by Max Keiser, to use it against the banking giant.

The idea is a bit complicated, but basically it's geared at forcing the bank to honor some of these short positions in metal. If everyone buys silver, JPMorgan will not be able to source sufficient quantities. If they continue shorting, the separation between physical and paper prices will form an arbitrage, with JPM on the wrong side of the trade. Because of their high leverage, each ounce of silver taken away exerts many times that amount of strain on their silver positions. This position is then magnified throughout the overall leverage of the bank's asset portfolio because the physical silver is one of their only real assets – the rest is debt-based and trending worthless.

When Bear Sterns was sold to JPMorgan, the giant bank also took on its liabilities. These included a monstrous short position in the precious metals futures market. In fact, the company had been getting hammered with margin calls on those positions from December of 2007. The damage was $2 billion. JPMorgan got the asset buffet for pennies on the dollar, leaving investors to hang. But they then had the problem of what to do with the futures position. Back room deals were made and the details are well hidden. JPMorgan does enjoy total immunity, it seems, for its actions in the markets. Many speculate this immunity was part of the take-over deal. The US government and Fed needed these positions managed. They needed, for many reasons, to keep the lid on the precious metals market. The bank had to swallow the poison pill in exchange for the gravy side of the Bear Sterns portfolio. The gold positions were workable; the market enjoys high liquidity on both supply and demand side. The silver positions are less so – there is not enough silver to satisfy the demand.

JPMorgan reportedly had to cease market activities in May of 2011 as silver rapidly shot to $49. The bank reentered the market a bit later and the price was crushed. Nonetheless, it was hit with a $6 to $9 billion loss, Bill Murphy of GATA revealed. Its silver position is heavily implicated in the losses and is virtually impossible to close out though they have tried to do so through a number of unsavory tactics. When Eastman Kodak filed bankruptcy and shuttered its doors in 2012, a former JPMorgan executive was named the receiver for its assets. These included a sizable portion of physical silver. The bank got too little, though – it is short a far greater amount of physical silver.

Analyst Ted Butler finally claimed, after long resistance to the notion, that the US government was involved in suppressing the price of silver. Butler brought the case of silver manipulation by JPMorgan and other large

**Figure 39**

TWO BANKS NET SHORT AS PERCENT OF COMMERCIAL NET
SHORT & SILVER PRICE

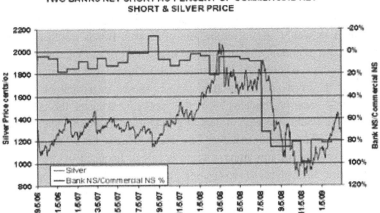

commercials to the CFTC. The enormous, concentrated short position was only possible as a manipulation tactic. The CFTC has ignored this position in its investigation even though the primary evidence in any manipulation investigation is a concentrated position. The silver position is the most concentrated in the history of the world, and evidence of it comes directly from CFTC data.

More than ignoring it, though, Butler thinks the CFTC is actively colluding in the suppression. Two 2011 occurrences support the idea. In the first week of May, silver plummeted 30% and in September, over three days, it dropped 35%. This is highly unusual activity for a globally traded commodity – possibly it has never happened. Any sharp decline of even 5% in a commodity receives a CFTC comment – all except this one. The price declines occurred with no real world reasons; the supply and demand curve for physical remained flat. JPMorgan got a sweetheart deal, Butler contends, when it took over the huge Bear Stearns silver short. The Treasury would prevent any investigation into manipulation. Butler closes with a message that the end is inevitable. The 'war on silver' can only end badly for the big shorts when the shortages of physical overwhelm their position. After all, silver has had some pretty serious runs with major opposition, but the previous holders of large silver shorts – AIG, Drexel, and Bear Stearns – are six feet under. And JPMorgan is looking pretty shaky.[11]

A follow-up investigation came because of Butler's allegations. After long years of interaction with the CFTC, Butler crossed the floor on May 28, 2012 and accused them of complicity in the ongoing situation. One clear signal of complicity – Butler and others who brought the charges have never been consulted to argue their case.[12] The four-year investigation only served to cover the continuing manipulation.

In fact, JPMorgan is the linchpin in most government market manipulations. If it fails, if its crimes are exposed, then the stresses on the other markets would instantly spiral out of control. Bonds would whipsaw, stocks would plummet, commodities would shoot up, and the dollar would become highly volatile. The Exchange Stabilization Fund will not let that happen if they can prevent it. JPMorgan is secure in its actions because of 'national security concerns,' which is probably actually the case. The government would lose a great deal of power and legitimacy. The political situation would become unstable. The consequences for JPMorgan of a massive backlash in any arena – legal, political, financial, or trustworthy image – are far greater than most people can imagine. Any investigation into its wrongdoing should be viewed as strictly a means to allow it to continue. That's why the investigation took longer than any in US history. The issue itself was not overly complicated.[13]

One of the cornerstones of the silver manipulation theory is the lawsuit[14] against JPMorgan which alleged and demonstrated that the bank deployed a devious methodology, engineering drops to force options traders to cover their positions, thereby enabling JPMorgan to buy them cheap. Saxo Bank was the front and Deutschebank was part of the operation. Saxo used its trading platform to 'telegraph' a pending drop in the price. The telegraph trade was a fake – it never made it to live trading – and it always happened between 5:45 and 6pm. The numbers were far off the spot price and showed a sharp price decline, followed by a rapid return. These fake trades always preceded a sharp drop in the Comex silver price.

This is a means to force options traders to sell futures. Not to make it overly complicated, but it works like this: these traders try to pull off a 'delta neutral' strategy – (meaning changes in their options value are balanced by changes in their 'hedge') for sales of futures contracts. Delta is the rate of change in options value versus the underlying asset, from 0 to 1. If silver rises $1, an option with a delta of 1 will also rise $1, with a delta of 0.5 will rise 50 cents, and with a delta of 0 will not move. The traders sold far out of the money puts – a bet the price will fall drastically – for a nearby date. JPMorgan was the buyer. Because the delta was 0, they did not hedge.

JPM's desk then sold silver futures to sharply drop the price. This caused the delta on the put options to rise, and the traders hedged by selling futures. By having many put options out there, a wave of futures selling was triggered, dropping the price and creating a feedback loop by raising the delta further.

The scheme occurred outside trading hours because then thin trading allows for much greater movements in price. JPM gained a double benefit – they were able to buy futures much lower than otherwise because the price drop was greater and no other buyers were in the market. This allowed them, by constant repeats, to cover much of their massive silver short position. They also made money by selling the options contracts, now worth far more.[15]

There were a number of other claims of price suppression in the lawsuit, including the outsize futures position. JPMorgan did not defend itself against the claim that its short position was in fact a concentrated one, capable of moving the market. In spite of this, Federal judge Robert P. Patterson dismissed the case, citing the plaintiffs had insufficient evidence of malintent.

At one time, if a bank could not redeem its notes for silver, they were prosecuted for fraud. Now, they can sell as much paper silver as they like without any backing and suffer no consequences. On May 23, 2012, 500 million ounces of silver hit the tape between 9 and 10am. While the price dropped $1, the important takeaway is the volume. In less than one hour, someone sold 2/3 of global silver supply. But the Leap-Day massacre, February 29, 2012, is perhaps the most famous smackdown, when 375 million ounces of paper silver (and 1 million of gold) dropped the price $2 in short order.

Wynter Benton is a pseudonymous writer/investor. The story is not verified, and Benton has gone quiet, but he claims to represent a host of terminated traders and wealthy investors who defected from JPMorgan in outrage. According to Benton, the MF Global collapse was due to an attack by JPMorgan to steal MF Global clients' silver – and indeed they got a load of silver in the settlement. This blocked the Benton team's goal of attacking the Morgan silver short position by getting delivery of a large silver order. Blythe Masters, a high-ranking Morgan exec and public mouthpiece, was a revenge target. Moreover, JPMorgan has a $36 death line tied to the silver price, meaning that if silver exceeds that price for any length of time, the bank will be hit hard on the balance sheet. Benton claimed silver would trade above $50 by December of 2012. Of course, it didn't happen. The overall story has some credibility, however, as Benton has forecast Cartel raids with solid accuracy.[16]

JPMorgan, Butler claims, is now the sole suppressor of silver, with government and private regulatory blessing. They have independently sold enough naked shorts to stop runs of silver in 2011 and 2012. But even with government largesse, blind regulators, and open-ended money printing, they cannot keep it up indefinitely. The mechanics of the market will prevent it. That's because futures are not the same as money. Futures are a contract to deliver the underlying commodity at a pre-specified date. Up till now, 99% of contracts are settled in cash and rolled – they are speculative bets, really. In a real shortage, some of those that need the actual commodity will buy it in the futures market. Nobody needs silver like big industry, since it is a critical element in millions of items from electronics to health care. When these companies buy silver in the futures market, their purchases cannot be settled for cash. Even a healthy 50% premium on the silver 'price' would be meaningless compared to the loss of profit on sales from their businesses.

Attorney General Eric Holder best expressed the reasons for fraudulent investigations and neglected prosecutions. Here he was discussing the banking system's money laundering crimes, but it would seem to apply across the board: "If you do bring a criminal charge, it will have a negative impact on the national economy, perhaps even the world economy."[17] Pundits are calling the phenomenon "too big to jail." According to the US attorney general, our banking system is now openly run by criminals who cannot be prosecuted. When the rule of law is not only violated, but openly abandoned as policy, democracy has failed.

## Endnotes

1    BREAK EVEN COST FOR SILVER RISES TOWARDS $30 AS COEUR, HECLA & SILVER STANDARD SHOW NET INCOME LOSSES, SRSrocco. Silver Doctors, November 9, 2012..

2    http://en.wikipedia.org/wiki/List_of_corporations_by_market_capitalization#2013
3    chart from US Mint. December, 2012.
4    "Public Buying "Monstrous" Amounts Of Physical Gold & Silver", King World News. Dec. 30, 2012.
5    John F. Kennedy, Executive Order 11110. June 4, 1963.
6    John Carney, "The Germans are coming for their Gold", CNBC. October 24, 2012.

7    TF Metals Report. June 23, 2012. Post 3940.

8    Turd Ferguson, "Squeeze Play", comment 184659. June 29, 2012.

9    SRSrocco table 5, June 2012, July 2012.

10   Eric Sprott, "Why are (Smart) Investors Buying 50 Times More Physical Silver than Gold?" December 22, 2012.

11   Ted Butler, "The War on Silver", 24hgold.com, July 24, 2012.

12   Ted Butler, "Illegalities", 24hgold.com, May 28, 2012.

13   Theodore Butler, "The CFTC Silver Investigation", Butler Research, August 10, 2012.

14   Commodity Exchange Inc Silver Futures and Options Trading Litigation, U.S. District Court, Southern District of New York, No. 11-md-02213.

15   "JPMorgan Allegedly Telegraphed Silver Price Smashes Using Massive FAKE TRADES on Saxo Bank Platform", Silver Doctors, September 18, 2011.

16   "Wynter Benton Returns, Predicts Silver Will Trade Above $50 by Dec 31, 2012", Silver Doctors, September 14, 2012.

17   Halah Touryali , "The Real Reason Wall Street Always Escapes Criminal Charges? The Justice Dept Fears The Aftermath", *Forbes Magazine*, March 6, 2013.

# 10

# RESISTANCE

*The money power preys on the nation in times of peace,*
*and conspires against it in times of adversity. It is more despotic*
*than monarchy, more insolent than autocracy, more selfish than*
*bureaucracy. It denounces, as public enemies, all who*
*question its methods or throw light upon its crimes*
*—Abraham Lincoln*

Resistance to financial repression is a time-honored practice. It has led to unfortunate consequences at times. In the crime of 1873, elite bankers demonetized silver. Where before the US was on a bimetallic standard, with silver the poor man's choice, they stipulated that all transactions above $5 could not be in silver. Large purchases, mortgages and so forth were henceforth to be transacted in gold only, making it far more valuable. This deflation made the holders of gold (the bankers themselves) far wealthier. But as a consequence, out of work, impoverished miners murdered the silver mine owners.

Even presidents are not immune. A few months before being assassinated, Abraham Lincoln was resisting taking loans from London despite banker insistence. It's well-established that European bankers wanted to back the South and Lincoln raised the slavery issue to force a moral crisis that threatened their reputations – they couldn't very well back the slavers.

Resistance has even been manifested in popular outcry and action. In France, 37 ministers of finance were tortured or hanged during the Middle Ages and Renaissance. Ordinary people have been at war with the bankers throughout history. The repercussions can be severe. Soon after Ghana requested the return of its gold from London, John Atta Mills, the Ghanaian president, died suddenly. Connections in some of these cases cannot be proved, but such seeming coincidences are worth considering. The Cartel plays dirty and always has.

Anyone thinking the word War is a metaphor or exaggeration, might consider the following stories. Kevin Krim, a CNBC VP, aired a story about a $43 trillion lawsuit against the banking cartel for racketeering. The story implicated high government officials, as well. Hours later, the story was removed. Krim found out that both his children were murdered allegedly by the nanny that same day. A career nanny, she had no aberrant history and had tended the children faithfully for two years.

In 1982, Chairman Roberto Calvi, was murdered in connection with Banco Ambrosiano. David Kellerman, the Freddie Mac CFO, also purportedly committed suicide in 2009. He was sitting on a mass of evidence, and was about to testify on some very large mortgage fraud. He never got the chance. Police did not investigate. Daniel Pirron, of Deloitte, caught a bullet, deemed by his own hand. He was heavily involved in an Iran scandal linked to Standard Chartered.[1] The list of such unusual deaths could fill a book.

When Greek debt hit 140%, the troika wanted to attach their gold under its debt obligations. A failure to pay would result in the Greeks losing their gold. The country was almost certain to default. Citizen outrage prevented the troika from attaching the gold. There seems to be a trend to protect national gold. The wave of repatriation was begun by Hugo Chavez. When he repatriated Venezuelan gold, the people turned out en masse to 'escort' it home, right beside the military. Outside the Western corridors, people view gold reserves very differently. They view it as the national wealth. They value it.

This view is landing in some Western nations, too. In 2000, Germany withdrew 940 tons of gold from foreign vaults. The question as to why they did so secretly is an open one. The Bundesbank had the legal right to reclaim its gold publicly. In a 1968 memo, the Bank of England surveyed 172 gold bars from the Fed, held in the Bundesbank account. The gold was inadequate – it was 'bad delivery.' The BoE agreed to the Fed demand that, since the matter impacted Germany and not England, it would keep it silent. The Bundesbank knows, of course, about the scam and probably knows of more than this verified incident. Since they own the gold, the last thing they want is to call its purity into question.[2]

German law requires a full audit of Germany's gold reserves every year. This audit stopped for several years beginning in the mid-2000s. No one noticed for a time, but then people began asking questions. Parliament got involved. The Bundesbank promised an answer soon. It took a few more years. The German court of auditors finally demanded a full audit of its gold reserves stored in London and New York. The demand was made upon the Bundesbank, the German central bank, which resisted the measure. But the stakes are high – at 3400 tons, Germany has the second highest official gold reserves of any nation. Distrust is rampant and growing among the German people. A political movement is afoot, similar to the audit the Fed movement in the US.

In September 2012, the New York Fed turned away German inspectors wanting to see their nation's gold reserves. The stated reason was that the facility lacked adequate space to conduct the audit. In November, the Bundesbank stated its full intention to leave the gold where it was and its full backing and trust of the Federal Reserve. Then in January 2013, it suddenly reversed course. The Bundesbank will begin repatriating its stock of gold over the next seven years. The retrieval duration is highly suspect. Why not seek the return of the gold all at once, if the Fed has it?

The requisition is for 50% of the total gold to be stored in Germany. Some 674 tons total will be brought from France and the US – if the agreed deal happens. It seems that Germany is the first major country to call the Fed's bluff. Much of the gold stored there has probably been leased out for purposes of gold price suppression. How much of the German gold can and will be returned is open to question, but the pressures will continue to grow in the direction of mutual distrust. The rush to get the gold home has begun, since Germany announced it publicly.

CNBC editor John Carney noted:

> In reality, it does not matter one bit whether the Federal Reserve Bank of New York actually has the German central bank's gold or whether the gold is pure. As long as the Fed says it is there, it is as good as there for all practical purposes to which it might be put. It can be sold, leased out, used as collateral, employed to extinguish liabilities and counted as bank capital just the same whether it exists or not ... For almost all imaginable operational purposes, the actual existence of the gold in Fort Knox or in the vault beneath the FRBNY's Liberty Street headquarters is irrelevant. The bookkeeping is what really matters here. So long as the Fed says Bundesbank owns X tons of gold, the Bundesbank can act as if it did own the gold—even if the gold had somehow been swallowed into a gold-eating galactic worm hole.

The disappeared gold possibility has entered the mainstream media, however, possibly to less manageable effect than Carney projected. Fastmoney featured one commentator's startling claim: when everyone claims their gold, there might not be enough after all the leasing and swapping done by the Fed.[3]

Meanwhile, Holland has followed the Venezuelan/German suit. The Dutch, suspecting malfeasance, want their gold to come home. Ninety percent of it is held elsewhere, mainly the US and Canada. Azerbaijan jumped aboard the train, repatriating one of its tiny 15 tons of gold from JPMorgan vaults. Ecuador has also gotten in line to bring its gold home. The small countries are not problematic individually, but they can aggregate to create a very troublesome situation for the bankers. They also create a signal: the floodgates are opening, trust is fleeing. Every man for himself is the next policy of central banks.

Even the conservative Swiss populace is raising the flag. In 2007-8, the Swiss National Bank dropped 250 tons – 20% of reserves – of gold on the market. The public is not happy about it. Luzi Stamm, a leader of the Swiss Conservatives, has spearheaded a steady movement with burgeoning popularity. He is a sound money advocate with a simple but powerful platform: the Swiss Central Bank must cease dishoarding gold, get national reserves up to 20% in gold, and repatriate all the gold it owns. There is, of course, no reason for the Swiss to hold gold out of country anyway. As a global banking center, their reputation is sterling. They can hold gold and move account ownership of gold just as well as London or New York. Stamm claims that gold is not meant to be a political whiffle ball or central bank speculative tool; it is the citizens' wealth. The group also is pushing for the Swiss Bank to offload its crippling Euro position – an event which will cause a category 5 hurricane in the currency markets. The Euro would implode, the Swiss Franc would soar and gold would shoot highest of all. As the fifth largest gold holder in the world, the tiny mountain country is a singular pivot point. Any referendum would take years to implement against stiff opposition.[4]

All this foot-shuffling and deck-chair rearranging solves nothing. It only pushes the problem down the pike. The only real solution to avert a systemic cardiac arrest is to liquidate the massive, insolvent banks. Let the ensuing debt default wipe out the failed enterprises and let the deadwood fall away. The too big to fails, by their very size, are destroying the global economy. The rest of the world, with a lot at stake, is watching. They are planning. And they are quietly preparing.

**Sino-Soviet Alliance**

*We are on the verge of a global transformation.*
*All we need is the right major crisis and*
*the nations will accept the New World Order*
*—David Rockefeller*

The China-Russia alliance is critical in world politics. It proceeds slowly but steadily. Centuries of mutual hostility are being breeched. In June 2012, Putin made a deal to increase trade from $83 billion to over $200 billion by 2020. China has production and Russia has resources. China needs water, gas, oil, and metal; Russia has them all. Russia needs a solid, large, dependable trading partner to vault it higher in the GDP sphere; China can provide. Both hate Washington for decades of hegemonic abuse.

Russia has openly stated that a currency war is taking place. It is no longer speaking in metaphor or bankerese. With Japan and Switzerland at ground zero of the currency wars – the franc is the go-to note for value retention and Japan is desperate to boost exports – they will scramble desperately to end the battle. Currency wars are not good for either leaders or citizens. Currency devaluations come hot and harder, angering the public which faces price inflation and rises in protest. These nations and others will increasingly discuss a gold standard as a stabilizing, war-ending antidote in the currency markets. They will turn away from the US to the east.

China is readying itself to comply with (according to Jim Willie's sources[5]) an emergent gold-tradable note. The note will circulate in a peer-to-peer system, not a centrally driven system. Trust will be high because anything will look attractive after the globalized, endemic corruption of Western banking. The Chinese yuan will link directly to the notes, making the yuan implicitly gold-backed and very attractive to value investors and merchants. In other words, this currency war will end with a paradigm shift.

It's important to note one thing: trade is the driver of banking, not the reverse. For decades, the system has been able to exploit a dollar leading policy, but as trade migrates to more and more non-dollar accounting, the banks will have no choice but to reposition or die. If the banks diversify away from US T-bonds, it will be their last defense of the dollar complex. Since they can only defend against that within a dollar-based global trade system, they will not be able to survive if they attempt to buttress the tide.

China stunned the investment world (except the US where it was not reported) by announcing it would pool its reserve assets with other central banks outside the dollar system. This new system would use the dollars and Treasury instruments, but outside the US locus of control, to establish a trading system that cuts out the destabilizing dollar printing as part of its operation. They may rebrand the dollars as Chinese-US dollars to separate and increase their value from other US dollars as their value would remain fixed, rather than diminishing by inflation as a result of increased supply.

China cannot go straight to providing the world with a reserve currency. Such a move would force them to remove their top-down economic controls. Capital has to flow in and out, be convertible, and be re-investable in the issuing economy. This problem puts them in a bind. Their political system is outmoded, unable to manage a leadership role in the modern economy.

Leaders in China are slowly making its currency a serious force, winning this aspect of the currency wars. London arranged for swap agreements with the yuan. England is the first of the G-7 nations to do so. Soon enough, the yuan could be fully convertible. China is resistant, because full convertibility in the open market sacrifices direct control of the currency. China is not putting the yuan on the Forex exchange. They do not want Western powers with their numerous financial techniques to push the yuan around. The US will not participate, so far, in the yuan swaps – perhaps out of pride, or ignorance, but it will likely prove disastrous for the New York financial wizards. They will be pushed out of the new system and gradually marginalized by a Chinese-led global trade coalition.

One interesting source reports a mechanism being put into place by Arab and Eastern billionaires, with government backing, to destroy the dollar in the next few years. Talk of deliberately destroying the dollar sounds far-fetched, but there may more credibility to the idea than it would seem. The plan is relatively slow-moving, and relies less on overt antagonism, than on erecting viable alternatives and steadily recruiting non-Western trade partners to join and increase trade outside of the dollar. There are many components, but the primary ones are an alternative oil sales system, a gold-backed trade platform, an international central bank outside of Western control, a framework for diminishing US influence, available natural resources, and a coalition of regional leader nations.

The primary nations are China and Russia, with Brazil, India, Venezuela, Iran and South Africa as regional political and economic leaders. China is the manufacturing, economic, financial, and industrial power. Russia is the resource giant. Germany is being courted as a key partner, but the outcome is not clear. Germany is politically divided on the issue, with the Western system proponents currently in power. The opposition forces are very strong, very prominent and gaining in credibility even as the current controllers are losing power and credibility steadily.

The ongoing currency war now includes a low-level trade war. Currency wars are simply the first and primary face of a trade war, anyway. Currency wars are an attempt to devalue the money to gain short-term trade advantage by lower priced exports. The mechanism is loudly announced printing campaigns. When a currency is devalued internationally, the domestic prices of products do not rise for a long time while it makes domestic products less expensive in global trade, helping business out and increasing jobs and income. Simultaneously, imported items become more expensive, so domestic items are more appealing for consumers, leading to increased economic activity. The effect is short-lived, at most two years. It's a testament to the myopic vision imposed by our political and economic system. The quick fix rules the day, but causes tremendous and growing downstream problems.

At any rate, China is surpassing the US in a steady pull. Its economy is growing, though fitfully. The manufacturing base is titanic. The capitalist ethos is urgent in all the citizens. Their work ethic is unbeatable. China's monetary reserves are enormous. The currency is very strong and much desired. It is increasingly being used for regional trade and moving into Forex (currency exchange) markets. Most important, it will probably soon have a gold component, signaling a worldwide return to hard currency. The battle will ramp up.

Most of the Chinese currency restrictions, both inward and outward, are self-imposed. This allows them to control the value of their currency – keeping it low, to aid in their export driven approach. This is one reason why their products are so cheap. But their policy is clearly changing. They have engaged in bilateral currency swaps, a clear first step to opening up the yuan for trade. Within a few years, it will publicly tradable, though they will try to maintain some centralized control over it. That will be difficult – you can't have it both ways. In the end, the forces wanting a more open currency will win. China must do this in order to become the new superpower, emerging from the US shadow as it recedes.

The coalition, led by China, could produce some more aggressive monetary attacks. The key approaches to currency wars are promoting a measured decline beneath public radar or unleashing an overnight steep devaluation, done before people can dump the currency. A real attack could use these approaches against the country. If China dumped enormous quantities of T-Bonds suddenly, the Treasury complex would suffer a cardiac arrest. Rates would shoot through the roof immediately. Buyers would flee the scene, leaving the Fed as sole purchaser to choke on the entire amount – all new Treasury issuance plus the Chinese dump. In fact, through Operation Twist, China (and other nations) converted all long-term Treasuries into short-term ones with one year or less maturity. Probably, a back-room demand was made with this sort of threat: either the Treasury complex gets hammered in the open market, or the Fed gives China an escape hatch. Now China has lots more dollars and T-Bills (which act like currency) than T-Bonds, which act like debt.

China could potentially spark a hyperinflation with all the US assets. By dumping dollars and T-Bills, China could cause the US currency itself to suffer a massive devaluation. If China announced it beforehand, then steadily hit the market with hundred billion dollar dumps with surprise timing, the Forex participants would panic out of dollars. The sell-off would collapse the dollar value.

China could also buy up huge assets while pretending to hold Treasuries. This seems to be happening. Many US and world real estate holdings, as well as massive commodity stockpiles seem to be accumulating in Chinese sovereign portfolios.

Another possibility mentioned above (proposed by Jim Willie) is that China will rebrand their held dollars as Chinese-US dollars – with some mark on them. As this cannot and will not be inflated, it would become a very strong currency. In this scenario, the US would actually become the first country in history to lose control of its currency to another country.

According to Hank Paulson, China caused the collapse of Fannie Mae.[6] By jettisoning mortgage bonds, they set off the mortgage crisis – which would have happened eventually. Foreseeing a drop in US imports – a decline in their export market – they created a number of trade agreements among Eastern nations to counter. Anticipating US currency challenges, they moved from long-term bonds to short-term bills. With a few helpful deals in European bonds and broader yuan distribution, the IMF moved in their direction. That would probably include a place for the yuan in the IMF's own currency, SDRs.[7] China is engaging in a multi-pronged approach to radically alter its US trade. China seeks to end the US dollar's reign as world reserve currency – and the US is paving that road for them.

Australia and China have announced convertibility of Aussie dollars into yuan.[8] This cuts the US dollar out of the trade loop. Checking in at $200 billion, the initial swap agreement is meaningful. Currency swaps allow for globalized exchange by placing yuan and foreign currencies in producers' hands for purchases. It moves the yuan closer to a global reserve currency status. In fact, since 2008, China has created currency swaps with over 20 countries.

On September 6, 2012, China announced it would buy oil in the yuan instead of the dollar from anyone who wished to sell it so. Russia complied the following day with an announcement of unlimited sales to China – all the oil it wanted, with no US dollar in the transactions. The step is momentous. Then they upped the ante.

Chinese Premier Wen Jiabao arranged currency swaps with Saudi Arabia for 35 billion yuan. The news is major, because it signals Saudi Arabia's potential willingness to trade for oil without using the Petrodollar. Once the oil giant moves outside the Petrodollar arrangement even slightly, the US dollar will lose massive value in short order. No one will need it anymore. Other oil nations will be able to dump the dollar trade. At that point, all the excess dollars and T-bills (short term notes that act like currency) will be unwanted. Nations will attempt to move them off without causing panic. It will be unpredictable, but US paper will lose a lot of value. If the Fed and Treasury lose control of the process, it could turn chaotic. The largest oil refinery in the world recently appeared in Saudi Arabia. By building and owning it, China is now the largest importer of Saudi oil. This gives them a political power not seen before, an ability to potentially push the dollar off the world stage.

China is locking up African resources, diverting them towards its homeland. Part of the operation is funding infrastructure projects, all of which serve Chinese interests. But the African sovereigns are happy. They lack the capital and engineering savvy to undertake the projects. However, the growing reality is that China is not accepting trade settlement with Africa in dollars any longer. The yuan will soon be the new trading currency. It is the pivot point, turning the global trade mechanism away from the standing system of dollar hegemony to a multilateral base with China as the de facto leader. A number of African nations are strengthening trade in their own currencies. Zambia's central bank actually prevented all US dollar transactions – a dangerous step. Africa boasts the motherlode of resources sans oil, so swerving the continent away from the dollar represents a very major change in the trade winds.

China has gained (possibly through coercion) several bank franchises operating in the US. Formerly, they could not buy US assets very readily, now through these banks, they will be able to. They can funnel the $2 trillion+ pile of dollars and bonds back into US-based assets. They can invest in gold and silver funds, buy companies whole, buy land and other resources. Moreover these banks, through fractional reserve, will give China the power to create US currency, and if they are backed by China's massive bond and dollar holdings, they can indeed create a lot. So far, the temperature is low, but in typical Chinese fashion, numerous weapons are aimed – overwhelming force makes victory more certain. American bankers are assisting by committing sepuku on their own enterprises.

More covert actions are probably underway. Chase Bank was shut down nationwide in March 2013 with customer accounts declining to zero. Balances were restored, but it showed the potential weakness of the system altogether. A denial of service internet attack brought the bank to its knees for hours before that. A number of cyber-threat experts have gone on record with a dire analysis – China and other countries have long since penetrated every major banking system in the US. If they want, they can cause havoc with a massive attack on the system. People would be left without available money. Anomalies have struck more and more individual banks. A systemic crisis/attack could be in the offing. It could also be held as a threat to bend the West to Chinese demands.

The West seems trapped in its steady decline of power and keeps making strategic errors. Jim Sinclair, a veteran investor and trader of the gold market whose calls are legendary and accurate up to ten years ahead (though he missed badly by calling a $1500 bottom on gold) thinks the Cyprus money grab is the biggest event in gold market history. The Euro-bank controllers scalped Cypriot citizens, seizing up to 70% from their bank accounts. They tried to take bank deposits from the Russian crime syndicate which leads through the KGB to Putin, a former KGB head, himself. The money was vastly more than was reported – in the hundreds of billions, possibly even tipping over a trillion. Russia does not use the Western covert banking centers like Switzerland or the Caymans. They use Cyprus as the financial gateway to the West and keep their deposits secret from the Cypriot Central Bank by agreement. It was an attempt to grab a significant part of the country's funds straight from their central bank. The Russians were not amused at the potential loss of such magnitude. They see the writing on the wall for any funds they have in the Western system: it is not safe. They have begun to switch from paper to gold and will enjoy Russian government support of the gold market.[9]

Cyprus has been invited to join the Eurasian Economic Community and leave the Eurozone. There, they would have access to Russian economic assistance to weather the crisis. They would also be involved in the growing global trade arena being developed by the Sino-Russian alliance. It's a tiny country, but a major precedent. Cyprus has been called, by insiders, the template for future crises. A number of countries have written policies to forcefully turn depositor funds into bank stock. The stock, of course, will be worthless because the scenario will only happen to an insolvent bank as a means to recapitalize it. Spanish savers got creamed with this scam.

The US preceded the Cyprus fiasco with its own club-footed harsh diplomacy. In an overt financial attack on Iran, leaders excluded the country from the SWIFT system, the mode of international bank payments. Numerous countries immediately began a set of loose arrangements to bypass the system and hence the dollar. They will now conduct trade with Iran in their own currencies. The US backed off the SWIFT embargo for most nations, but the damage was done. The back-pedal only exposed the mistake even further. And it was a big one, causing a massive blow to the Western banking cartel power.

Iranian imports jumped by a factor of 37 in one year. The SWIFT reprisals backfired on Western bankers, but had some effect. Iran seeks to ramp up its gold holdings in order to settle domestic turmoil and stabilize its embattled currency. Most of the trade is with Turkey, a gold exporter, in exchange for oil. Turkey agreed to cut back on its oil imports under US sanction requirements – but they lied. Instead, the country increased trade with Iran by 50%. Countries are no longer complying with US demands, even as they say they will. Their denial will become more brazen eventually, without even the lip-service. Time will tell if the US will be shunned and ignored, or actively fought against in the political theater.

Of course, the Iranian oil embargo puts stress on the trading countries. The decline in world oil supplies by taking Iran off-market pushes the price up. Meanwhile, Iran's oil is dropping in price because of fewer buyers. With most countries strapped for cash, they look to Iran for energy. The trade goes on without public notice.

The BRICS are creating an alternate trading system that includes a gold component and a sophisticated barter component. This system is taking shape and will grow stronger. It is different, far more decentralized. As foreign banks can increasingly use it, they will divest of US monetary instruments and take on these types of assets. The US will have to bid up resources in dollars in a competitive arena, without the requirement of all trade being conducted in US instruments. The dollar will decline rapidly – indeed the decline has already begun. As these instruments flow back to our shores, the tsunami supply of bonds and dollars will overwhelm the shrinking pie of resources – a recipe for massive inflation.

The ASEAN (Asian block) trade summit included the most ridiculous move ever by the United States. The administration tried to put forward a trading plan with Asian nations that would exclude China. The nations concerned roundly rejected this absurd demand to dismiss their principal and strongest trading partner. Instead, they created a comprehensive economic partnership with China and threw out the US. This is part of the inexorable, powerful, but subterranean movement to isolate the US and remove it from its primary position as global hegemon.

This reflects a power shift from the G-8 to the G-20. The G-8 is the union of the Western economic powers (plus Russia). The group consists of the seven wealthiest countries by assets, not GDP. The G-20 is far more inclusive and consists of countries that hold 80% of the world's wealth. Emerging nations have a voice, although only 15% of nations are members. At any rate, the G-20 is not dominated by the advanced nations.

More importantly, the BRICS consortium has created a structure outside of Western influence altogether, shutting the door on the US and Eurozone. They are creating a new world bank – excluding the US. The bank is intended to annul Western power, especially corporate control of third world resources and locking the nations out of any profitability from their own labor. The development fund attempts to get out from under the US dollar as primary trading mechanism. Ironically, the bank is funded by the massive US Treasury bond surplus. From that point, the $100 billion in paper will be steadily converted to gold. Most nations want out of the dollar yoke. They see the inevitable trap looming for the US, which will force it to inflate its currency or suffer massive debt default. They see the US staunchly resisting liquidation of the economic black holes – the major banks sucking in money at a galactic rate. They see the military enforcement of the petro-dollar standard globally. And they want out. They are banding together to end US hegemony. The OPEC nations may soon jump behind the ascendant power, following China and Russia into the new system. The coalition is anything but minor – it includes 65% of the global economy and 75% of global population. Participants have reportedly agreed to prices of $7500 minimum for gold and $150 for silver. Whether they can stick to that or not remains to be seen.

By losing control of the instrument for international trade settlement, the US will also sacrifice control over its own debt complex since foreign reserves of T-Bonds are used for making trade payments. As these US instruments serve as the primary asset for bank reserves, overturning that will usurp US hegemony over the international banking system.

That's a necessary and inevitable situation, since the current system is upside down. Trade normally leads finance, but since 1990 or so, finance has led global trade. This is primarily due to the abused and exhausted Treasury Bond mechanism. Such a system distorts prices and economies. That's ending, as the BRICS rise. T-Bonds will be dumped and disappear from the global stage. Nations will have no need to have Treasuries as reserves. Gold will again become the basis for trade and savings.[10]

When looking at the countries in opposition – the BRICS – one country stands out. Why is the economically anemic South Africa in this grouping? Because the country is historically the largest producer of gold by a huge margin. If gold became understood as money, and if gold came to back the world's currency, South Africa would immediately emerge as a world power. When the long-term campaign against apartheid is filtered through the lens of realpolitik, the goal becomes far clearer, and more ominous. Western powers frequently rebuked apartheid South Africa for human rights violations. But under the uncompromising microscope of genuine political analysis, such statements of motive always have a covert, self-interested agenda. Empires do not care about rights violations in themselves, it is always a proxy for a hidden agenda. In this case, the war against gold.

In 1965, the 'peaceful' Carnegie Endowment published a research paper on the possibility of invading South Africa. The signatory was the Carnegie president, Joseph E. Johnson. He was also honorary secretary for the Bilderberg group, suspected to be an attempt to create a world dominated by wealthy elites. The Leiss report suggested boycotting South African gold before committing to a military invasion. Such an operation would, the authors hoped, give them far greater control of the gold market. Most likely, the mines would have been given to Western corporations (as happened with Iraqi oil), then laundered and used to hold down the price.

They wrote: "A successful boycott on gold would, if followed, either require some extreme intensive policing operations or some method of shutting off the market or part of it." [11] They were willing to commit to a military enforcement of a gold boycott. Taking the somewhat cynical view that political actions are always motivated by self-interest, then the long-term campaign against Apartheid was a proxy for the war on gold. While tensions eased after apartheid, South Africa allying under the Sino-Soviet umbrella at the 2010 BRICS summit was a fait accompli, at least partly due to the long-term suppression of the nation's cornerstone economic asset.

For many people in the world, the need for resistance to tyranny is an everyday reality. Most of these people view the West, and mainly the United

States, as the primary source of tyranny, in contrast to Western propaganda about China and the Middle East being the main sources. These citizens are increasingly expressing resistance in a curious way: opting out of Western currencies, and necessarily, therefore, engaging in a quest for sound money. The more gold and silver they buy, the more embattled the failing currencies of the West, especially the dollar, become. And the weaker these currencies are, the less they are taken in trade, desired for savings, or demanded for other reasons by everyone else. The failure of these currencies is the failure of the key enforcer of the power of tyranny. Controlling the global monetary reserve and financial trade mechanisms permits the exercise of awesome power. When this power is multiplied by fractional reserve banking and unlimited fiat creation, the power is unrestrained. The sole check on such a power is rejection. Only if the world rejects the US dollar, the Euro, the British Pound and so forth will the Western powers fail. Unrestrained war will no longer be possible; it is too costly by far under a gold collar. Unrestrained government will no longer be possible; it is also too costly under gold. The fiat system has undone itself by abusing its power and destroying the world's faith in it. The story is as old as money.

Probably, the US dollar will be marginalized in trade, reduced to a regional currency. Western powers will still use it, but their power will shrink dramatically as the East rises. When the dollar is eclipsed as the favored instrument of world trade, T-Bonds will no longer be desirable for foreign national reserves. Existing US bonds will be dumped on the market, causing a vacuum in their value. Finally, the US will suddenly and openly devalue its currency.

**Gold Drain**

*As gold goes, so goes the power*
*—ancient proverb*

Central banks around the world have been buying gold since 2008. The total is 1200 tons, or an increase of 4%. Considering they were net sellers since 1980, dropping 4000 tons, the shift is very significant. Foreign central banks are opting back in to traditional money and out of the dollar. The shift does not account for Russia and China, which do not disclose their actual gold reserves. Those numbers, ferreted through market and other data, are stunning.

In 2012, China increased its gold imports by 780%. Then it went big, importing 1200 tons by March 2013. The Chinese government only makes an announcement of official gold holdings every four or five years. The numbers are not valid – China holds far more gold, likely multiples of the stated amounts. Official holdings are 1054 tons, but they imported 100 tons in one month, and just from their Hong Kong channel. China also takes all gold mined in China, now one of the top mining states in the world.

While a huge stack makes the best hedge against all the US debt and currency China holds, there may be more to the game. China is likely looking to unseat the US dollar as the reigning champ of world trade settlement. A yuan backed by gold would jettison the currency into the prime time. Currently, people want Chinese notes, but they aren't convertible on the open market. Chinese leaders don't want to relinquish control of their currency. It's intelligent, because the Forex markets are brutal and indifferent to the damage caused by speculation to legitimate trade. Third world economies burn up and people starve as a result of trades made by indifferent Forex sociopaths. China is easing into the situation, strengthening its currency and asset base for the move. It's trying to do so surreptitiously.

In a March 2013 press conference, Vice Governor Yi Gang of the People's Bank of China made a puzzling and contradictory statement. China had no plans to increase its gold reserves from 1054 tons, he said, since it's worried about adverse effects to the gold price. He then seemingly contradicted himself by pointing out China's goldmines produce 400 tons per year and the country imports 500 tons per year.[12] It was unclear how the 900 tons added to China's ledger did not increase reserves. A good share of the imported gold is going to the citizens as income levels increase. China recently made gold legal for ownership again and began promoting gold ownership aggressively in 2009. Buying gold is a Chinese tradition for storing wealth. This allows China to import gold without the political baggage of official government buying driving up the prices up. That allows the government to accumulate gold in a hidden manner – which it already admitted to doing in the past when gold reserves were revised upward suddenly by 600 tons. The next revision will be within a few years, will be several thousand tons, and will probably be used to back a trading currency.

The gold is being drained from the major Western banks (see Figure 40). The US Geological Survey published the following data, showing that gold flows out of the US are at record levels. The game is to keep the demand from powerful interests satisfied without raising the price. This is physical gold, so the endgame is coming. It's impossible to determine how much gold is left in bank vaults, because of the shell games. But it's a lot less than is stated.

A very strange change occurred in early 2013. The balance of trade deficit dropped when US industrial exports rose $1.2 billion from December to January. That would be a healthy increase, except that it was non-monetary gold. An antagonistic sovereign, likely China, is demanding gold in payment of US trade debts. The gold is sent from refineries to mask the reason for the transfer – it is classified as non-financial, ostensibly used for industrial

**Figure 40**

**U.S. Gold Import-Export Deficit Jan-Jul 2012**

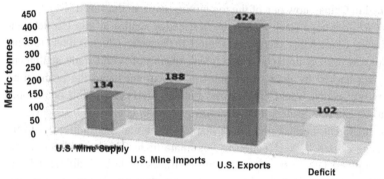

purposes. The truth is hidden, but the anomaly is strong enough to know that something is being hidden on the accounting sheets.[13] The strategy is primarily to beef up the yuan for the coming paradigm shift and end the dollar trade settlement. But there may be a second motive: revenge.

In 1999, China was granted most favored nation status. Along with this came an undisclosed agreement permitting Wall Street firms to lease Hong Kong gold and silver. The amounts are not transparent, but they are massive. Wall Street sold these assets into the open market to suppress the price, and when the time to return the metals came, they reneged.

There are other sources for inflow. China imported 315 tons of gold from Hong Kong alone in the first five months of 2012. That is more gold than the

**Figure 41**

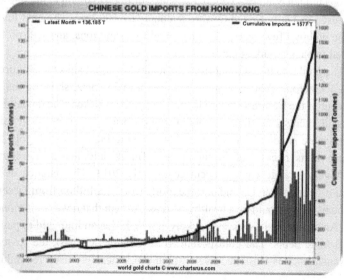

British empire owns. By September, China had imported more gold than the entire European Central Bank owned.

Iran and China are recasting tons of gold bars with new serial numbers. The apparent reason is to protect downstream interests. The original bars come from the LBMA, the Comex, and from Western bank vaults. Much of the gold is suspected to be allocated to previous owners. This situation has been proven on several occasions, so the countries are melting and recasting to avoid legal concerns in the future. [14] It's all part of the intrigue in the gold wars.

It's worthy to note that Russia is almost certainly playing the Chinese game. Russia has vast stores of gold, many times their official reports. The nation also imports far more than they officially state. As it is so similar to the China tactic, there is no need to detail it here.

Other trade war attacks are happening in the open market. The Shanghai Futures Exchange is putting out a crude oil contract at the end of 2013. This has the potential to change the game significantly, putting pressure on both Western price control of oil and the petrodollar standard. If oil contracts are routed through Shanghai, they will not need to be priced in dollars. This will set up an arbitrage against any manipulated prices in Western markets, where usually the oil price is artificially suppressed. Eastern traders will ruthlessly crush market manipulation by buying the risk-free Western-priced oil and reselling it higher in Shanghai. The system will face real ongoing pressure from the most critical commodity in the world – oil.

Traders have also been given a green light to oppose the Western bankers' trade in the gold market. Price arbitrage reached unprecedented proportions. In January 2013, the difference in silver was up an astounding 10% – $32.50 – on the Shanghai Gold Exchange and $29.61 on the Comex. Since arbitrage is risk free, 10% is an absolutely phenomenal profit. The Comex is not a spot price market, but it is not far off. That makes an arbitrage opportunity of $14,400 on a single silver contract. This is the thin end of the wedge for the price divergence between manipulated paper and physical.

The SGE has become the sound money ground zero warzone. The spread between Comex and Shanghai spot gold was $25/ounce December 3, 2012, a powerful opportunity for arbitrage and Comex attack from a globally situated player. A big player could scoop millions of ounces off the Comex, ship the physical East and with 40 million ounces, make a cool billion. The percentage spread on silver is much greater – almost 9% and growing. It would take a while and the price differential would have to hold to drain that much silver or gold, but it is clearly there because of US market manipulation. That level of arbitrage cannot hold in an open market. Few speculators are taking the trade, probably because of the risk of non-delivery.

This price differential puts China much more in the driver's seat. It also gives a second weapon of mass destruction against Western banks, especially JPMorgan. Morgan, of course, holds the largest short position in gold and silver. Most people think that China can only hit the US financially by dumping T-bonds (which also tanks its own portfolio). Untrue: now China can twist the screw of the metal prices. Since the big commercials do not have access to the silver to back it, silver is the great weak link. (They do not own enough gold, but can get access to other foreign and even 'borrow' client gold.) It may be a only a matter of time. Once China accumulates enough, or the West runs dry, they will be ready to send the price up. For now, they're happy to take metal in at the discount price.

Other countries are consorting with the West – India, surprisingly. But it's not working. When India tripled import duties on gold in 2012, the Indian people responded by buying 41% more than in the previous quarter. In spite of the government blockages and the record high prices in rupees, the public demand has become insatiable. Gold is an ancient Indian tradition, a preserve of wealth with a spiritual dimension. Indians hold over 18,000 tons in individual holdings – a staggering amount. India's Reserve Bank attempted to curb the flow of gold trading. Investors were buying directly from the banks, who were selling gold coins to hedge against high dollar movements. But the mass of incoming gold creates a current account deficit for India, so the powers tried, and failed, to halt it.

The big sleeper news is Turkey. The nation has a strong history as a world gold trader. Businesses in Turkey are importing gold from Europe, melting it and sending it off to Iran to facilitate trade around oil. Wealthy Iranians are operating as fronts for the Iran Central Bank. US sanctions against Iran's banking sector forced the country to move into gold to settle accounts. Sanctions have pushed Iran into a more defensive mode and the metal of kings is the best financial defense. Gold movements from Turkey to Iran were $13 million in 2011. In 2012, they jumped two hundred fold to $3 billion.[15] In April 2013 Iran imported 77,000 ounces – 12% of global gold production. The gold wars are in full swing.

## Monetary Reform Act and Local Currencies

*The real truth of the matter is, as you and I know, that a financial element in the large centers has owned the government of the U.S. since the days of Andrew Jackson.*
**—FDR**

The prime response to this, from aware citizens, is a desire to return to the gold standard. Ellen Brown and Bill Still disagree. The gold standard merely gave power to bankers who owned the gold. They would then use inflation and deflation of the money supply to get control of greater and greater wealth. Nothing would change. According to Still and Brown, gold and silver are not required to back money under the Constitution. They argue that "It's not what backs the money; it's who controls the quantity." Governments are no longer responsive to the electorate because they no longer control the money supply: the banks/central banks do.

The debt-based construct of money creation was designed to favor the banks, who profit from creating money out of nothing. The people are victimized by it through debt enslavement. The Federal Reserve Act was enacted though Congress had no right to sign away its money creation power. That power rightfully belongs to the government, according to the Constitution. The judiciary is bought and paid for by the fraudulent system, so there can be no redress there. The loss of that power by government has corrupted the system of checks and balances, leaving the monetary powers in control of everything. The nation, Still and Brown say, should issue fiat currency straight from the Treasury. The backing of money, they argue, is unimportant; who controls the issue is critical. With a straight-issued currency, the public would not have any national debt to contend with. Business, state and local governments, and individuals would flourish and wealth would increase. Currency is now a liability as it reflects a debt; it should be an asset.

The plan is simple: take away all monetary creation powers from the Federal Reserve and all banks. The Fed would no longer be needed. Banks would be required to maintain 100% reserves and simply become public utilities. The Treasury would pay off the national debt by direct issue. Because the national debt runs close to the monetary creation by the Fed and banks combined, paying off the debt and ending fractional reserve banking would net out, creating no inflation. The bubble and recessionary cycle would flatten out because massive creation and deflation would not be possible by a self-interested banking cartel. With the debt eliminated, there would be no need to pay $400 billion per year on interest. The personal income tax, which never existed until 1916, could be ended as unnecessary. Bankers would not be able to manipulate the money supply for personal gain, nor could they create money from nothing and charge people interest on that. The unbelievable wealth inequalities would be impossible without a finance-driven economy.[16]

Critics say this simply moves the problem from unelected bankers to elected politicians. Not so. While it is true that an unbacked currency could be abused by the government, any abuses would be clearly locatable; the Treasury would be to blame. Citizen outcry could force greater transparency whereas the Fed plays a double game of protecting its proprietary secrets. Moreover, critics ignore the obvious benefit – the system would not be predicated on debt to create money. Currency would exist a priori and debt would be a function of the currency supply, whereas now the currency supply is a function of the debt complex. Deflation could never be a threat because money would not be extinguished by extinguishing debt. Debt could not exceed currency, whereas now it must.

The State Bank of North Dakota (BND) has put some teeth into this proposal. The state created the bank in 1919 under populist pressure for low-cost loans, especially to farmers. Ever since, it has thrived. Since the 2008 crisis, the bank has listed record profits and no financial problems. The citizens, who own the bank, are delighted. The socialist implications do not concern the right-wing public; the bank works. Normally local taxes, over $1 trillion nation-wide, go into a bank account, usually on Wall Street. North Dakota deposits its taxes in the state bank where it does the citizenry some good. Part of the 'economic miracle' of the state is due to the oil boom, but most credit goes to the state bank. The bank makes below market loans to businesses if they create jobs. A national approach on this template would quickly create 10 million jobs, ending the employment crisis. As the North Dakota bank managers are public employees, there was never any incentive to gamble in the high-risk markets. The bank stayed solvent during the crisis and is stronger than ever. Moreover, North Dakota has one of the lowest unemployment rates. The deposit base pays the profits into state coffers rather than private bank coffers. This is not socialism, the citizenry feels – it is a defense against crony capitalism. The money is state funds, rightfully owned by the people. Any profits from its use should also belong to the people. Unlike when the national banks were bailed out – which socialized losses and privatized profits. The BND return to general coffers offsets tax liabilities, freeing up funds for consumers and small business people. The state of North Dakota also has *no debt* – unheard of in this day. No wonder the big banks dislike the BND.

Another interesting, if abstruse, discussion is the freegold concept. The concept has been taken to extremes from the poetic writings of Another, Friend of Another (his protégé), and the incomprehensibly verbose Friend of Friend of Another (FOFOA usually). The simple form is just as mentioned at the beginning of this book – currency and money are different functions. Gold will separate from paper and serve as a store of value only. Paper currencies will serve as media of exchange. The two will work together as a viable, emergent system. The system is not designed by anyone, but spontaneously comes into being under the duress the modern system places on the currency. People want a store of value, so they use physical gold. It's an ancient idea – the Romans basically practiced freegold.

Freegold has major consequences. Anyone saving paper currency would lose value steadily. Few people would hold savings accounts. Savers in gold would be free of the effects of CB monetary actions. Currency devaluation would backfire, draining the nation's gold as people convert out of paper. The third world would rise dramatically as labor and natural resources become power tools, supplanting paper currencies as tools of control. Limited supply of gold would slow down the debt-fueled fractional reserve monetary explosion because currency would only make sense for trade, not wealth creation/retention. Gold would hold that honor. In essence, people will exchange paper currencies for goods and services and store wealth in gold.[17]

While freegold is a natural evolution of the monetary system, others have designed or suggested active resistance to the system. Local Exchange Trading System (LETS) is one of a number of citizen currencies which operate on the basis of a set of principles: zero interest, of and for the community, transparency, freedom to participate or not, and pegged to the national currency. The last is contentious, as some members like the LETS idea because it potentially frees people from the ravages of inflation. The money is issued from a local board as a zero interest, permanent 'loan' to each member at a pre-set amount. LETS allows communities with little money to recapitalize internally. Plus, it's tax-free. There are estimated to be a few hundred such systems in operation, ranging from Nova Scotia to Africa.

The largest local currency is the Ithaca Hour in upstate New York, based on a labor hour, pegged at $10. The Hour mandate is fair trade, non-exploitation of nature, and collaborative economics rather than competitive. Hours are logged at a central accounting system where participants simply credit/debit their Hours themselves. The integrity of the system is maintained because both parties must agree to the exchange of payment.

The general citizenry feels stuck in the current central banking system, as if it felt no other choice is even conceivable, or if conceivable, is nonetheless unreliable. But this is illusion. At some point, people might realize that, by working together, the paper tiger of the banking hegemony can be destroyed.

**Local Resistance**

*Midnight is when the day begins.*
—Folk saying

Dissent within the elite ranks is not tolerated. On March 19, 2013, French authorities entered the apartment of IMF head, Christine Lagarde. The case was over a 2008 compensation payment wherein she was accused of embezzling state funds before she became IMF chief. She was cleared of charges.[18] It's shades of Dominique Strauss-Kahn, the IMF chair who was deposed for allegations of sexual assault, charges that were then dropped. There seemed to be some hidden agenda. Possibly, these were just political squabbles. When Kahn was arrested in New York, the conservative Sarkozy was French president, and Strauss-Kahn was likely to oust him. But Strauss-Kahn also had begun to stray from official, long-standing IMF policy. After the socialist Francoise Hollande won the Presidency, the newly appointed, more conservative Lagarde was investigated. LaGarde favored austerity, opposing the more socialist policies of Hollande. However, it's just as likely that both IMF chiefs were brought to heel for criticizing IMF policy. Whatever the actual reasons, a series of public 'vice' charges on leading financial figures generally indicates a deeper issue. Rarely are these people investigated for the reasons stated. Not that the charges are necessarily unfounded; they are often true. But if they were in favor with the right people, any malfeasance would be swept under and quickly forgotten. When this happens, the wrong line has been crossed – Lagarde, it appears, got a public warning, probably after a series of private ones.

At a lower level, Woody O'Brien quit being a federally regulated broker. He was pressured by regulators, who said a regulated broker could not give advice about buying physical gold and silver. Why not, he wondered, if it meets clients' financial needs? He tossed out his broker's license and gave his advice: buy physical gold and silver.[19] As a critical side-note for investors – brokers make little to no money on your transaction if you purchase PMs. And they receives no ongoing fees due to your owning it. So conversely, brokers may well be serving their own self-interest by advising you away from it, or advising limited purchases (10% of portfolio is occasionally recommended). They may advise you to invest in exchange-traded metals funds to 'get exposure' to the metals' price. This is not ownership of PMs. It is ownership in an unallocated fund which does not specify clear title to any physical gold. Settlement can be in cash and getting the actual metals out will not be possible for the normal investor. Seasoned analysts have expressed many concerns about ETFs. Your broker may also steer you toward mining companies. These have the serious problem of share dilution (lowering value) and ease of manipulation, but your broker gets a nice fee for your purchase of them. So any broker who does advise you to go buy some coins at your local shop is probably considering your best interest; he gains nothing by it. In fact, he loses the cream from the money you take out of his control.

Municipalities are joining the resistance – some big ones. The City of Buffalo comptroller, Mark Schroeder, withdrew $45 million from the banks after the Occupy Movement spoke with him about the predatory foreclosure practices. Because of the high leverage, each withdrawal is multiplied many times on the bank's fractional reserve, shadow banking balance sheet. Some people are stopping mortgage payments and demanding proof of title.

The City of Oakland lost $4 million per year on Interest Rate Swaps with Goldman Sachs, linked with the LIBOR manipulation. They terminated the contract with extreme prejudice. The penalty for termination was $15 million.

Oakland reneged, essentially daring the 'squid' to press for a public airing, knowing that it would reveal far more negative dirt about the bank than the city. Oakland set a precedent for many cities to follow. States and state agencies are joining in with lawsuits. Their borrowing costs were heavily damaged by the manipulation. Class action suits regarding the LIBOR are piling on. Home mortgages were doled out in fraudulent bases to the tune of $275 billion, as one aspect. There were 900,000 mortgages tied to LIBOR from 2005 to 2009.

Others are resisting Federal monetary authority. North Dakota may eliminate property taxes. It's an interesting argument, one that begins with a quote from a citizen – "When did we come to believe that government should get rich and we should get poor?"[20] The larger idea is one of true versus false ownership. If government can tax property, and punish people for not paying that tax, including confiscation of property or liens upon the sale, then a person *does not actually own it*. The argument is pretty strong – if you own something, it is yours to dispose of as you see fit. If the state can take it away for non-payment of taxes, then you are renting it. No other ownership item has ongoing taxes – sales tax is always a one-time situation.

Property taxes can be extremely difficult in hard economic times. If a person is unemployed or retired, they don't pay income taxes. They can cut their spending to lower sales tax burdens. Food is not taxed – it's a necessity. Only property taxes remain high, irrelevant to circumstances. Typically, they rise faster than CPI inflation. People can and have lost their homes.

North Dakota eliminated the personal property tax in 1966. This was a tax on all possessions owned. A campaign to keep the tax forecast economic catastrophe if it was repealed. The forecast was wrong. And while no US states have dismissed the property tax, both Great Britain and Iceland have. They repealed them due to popular outcry.

At some level, the issue is about local versus state control. It is an echo of the tenth amendment forces, which seek to limit the Federal encroachment of power. The tenth amendment states that all authority not specifically given to the Federal government is retained by the states. Several states have passed and others have considered laws of secession. New Hampshire, for example, has informed the government that it has the right to leave the United States and will do so if the federal government continues down the path of taking power away from the states. And to bring it back to the primary issue – Utah legalized use of precious metals as currency. Eight different states have proposed laws making gold and silver bullion legal tender. The Federal government is not happy.

Centralized power is cracking down with totalitarian authority. When Greece wanted a referendum on bailouts, the Prime Minister was replaced with a Goldman Sachs Vice-President. When Ireland rejected the EU constitution, they had to 'vote again.' Democracy is reduced to a deception; the choice desired by the elite must be endorsed. If the wrong choice is made, the process is redone until the desired choice occurs. It is a systemic restructuring, and an ugly one; according to Slavoj Zizek, it is 'a depoliticised technocracy in which bankers and other experts are allowed to demolish democracy.' Politics becomes theater with the end already written. There is now a 'tendency of contemporary capitalism to suspend democracy.'[21]

Still, people fight back, sometimes in odd ways. The Center for Armenian Remembrance sued the Federal Reserve on March 4, 2011. They claim the Fed purchased Armenian gold looted by the Ottoman Empire in 1915. The Ottoman Liquidation Commission put up a smokescreen of bank movements to hide the trail. It went from Deutschebank in Istanbul to Bleichroeder in Austria, then to the German Central Bank where it was listed as Ottoman Public Debt. After World War I, Germany turned over the gold as war reparations to France and Britain. Two members of British Parliament pled for the return of the gold to Armenia for its support of the allied powers. Instead, it was sold to the US government in exchange for Treasury Certificates. JPMorgan was the intermediary.[22] The Fed claims no knowledge of the gold.

There are many approaches to working against financial repression. On the petition website, We the People, GATA launched a petition to fully audit the Treasury's claimed 8100 tons of gold at Fort Knox. The provisions, crafted by GATA, were carefully laid out. They include full assay and weigh by outside inspectors.[23]

Others resist with their wealth. Investment funds with savvy managers are moving strongly into gold. Kyle Bass, David Einhorn, Pacific Group – all seasoned fund managers – have allocated 30% or more into precious metals. Their funds are doing very, very well, beating the other fund averages by 100% more returns. Michael Pento of Pento Portfolio Management predicted QE4 at the time QE3 was announced. He even got the timing right. He now says gold will hit $10,000 per ounce.[24]

The crème de resistance must go to Iceland, however. After the London banks blew up the economy, leaving it upside down and washing out the citizens' livelihood, the government sided with the people – after determined public action and long-shot political victories. Iceland repudiated all debt above 110% of asset value, effectively putting into place a debt moratium. They also threatened to jail bankers and defaulted on debt to the London establishment, then left the Euro. The country felt a sharp recession, then bounced back within two years. Some say the PIIGS – the indebted southern European nations – should 'go Iceland.'

To counter these large debt crushing trends some propose, even expect, a debt jubilee. In ancient times, debt jubilees wiped out all debts, allowing a system reset. These occurred every fifty years or so, so people could prepare ahead of time. Nowadays, the debt system is too complicated to do this outright. It would also heavily benefit debtors over savers. Another approach would be to uniformly distribute a preset sum of money to each citizen. They must use it to pay down debt. If they have no debt, they can have the money. Savers would not be punished and the debt holocaust could be essentially unwound. In today's ultra-complex system, such a solution would be near-impossible. The derivatives mess would create havoc and the banks would probably fail. Of course, they could then be replaced with public banking, to general benefit.

## Endnotes

1    Jim Willie, "Currency War Report", Hat Trick Letter, August 2012.
2    Tyler Durden, "GOLD AND FOREIGN EXCHANGE OFFICE FILE: FEDERAL RESERVE BANK OF NEW YORK (FRBNY) – MISCELLANEOUS, May 31, 1968. from Exclusive: Bank Of England To The Fed: "No Indication Should, Of Course, Be Given To The Bundesbank...", zerohedge. December 9, 2012.
3    Market Mystery. CNBC's Fast Money, January 17, 2013.
4    "Swiss right-wing forces referendum on banning SNB gold sales", Reuters, March 20, 2013.
5    Jim Willie, Hat Trick Letter, February-June, 2013.
6    "Paulson Says Russia Urged China to Dump Fannie, Freddie Bonds", Bloomberg. January 29, 2010.
7    The SDR is made of a 'basket' of other currencies.
8    China's currency is the Renminbi (people's money) and the primary unit of account is the yuan. The terms are used somewhat interchangeably outside of China to denote the currency.
9    Jim Sinclair, "Cyprus Disaster Is Much Bigger Than Being Reported", King World News, March 19, 2013.
10   Jim Willie, Hat Trick Letters, August, 2012 – April, 2013.
11   Amelie C. Leiss, Apartheid and the United Nations, Collective Measures, New York, Carnegie Endowment for International Peace, 1965.
12   Dorothy Hosich, "Massive increase in Chinese gold reserves unlikely – PBOC", Mineweb, March 15, 2013.
13   Jim Willie, "Gold and Silver report. "US Trade Gap...", Hat Trick Letter, February, 2013.
14   "Does China Plan a Gold-backed Renminbi?" Mountain Vision. Gold Silver World, August 19, 2012.
15   "Iranians in Turkey Collecting Gold for Central Bank, Zaman Says", Bloomberg, June 11, 2012.
16   themoneymasters.com/monetary-reform-act
17   Freegold, Wikipedia.
18   Angelique Chrisafas, "Christine Lagarde not charged in embezzlement investigation", Guardian.com. May 13, 2013.
19   www.abolishfiatslavery.com
20   Monica Davey, "North Dakota Voters consider eliminating property tax", The New York Times, June 12, 2012.
21   Zizek, Slavoj, "Save us from the Saviors: Europe and Greece", NYT Review of Books, June 7, 2012.
22   armenianweekly – 2011/03/18/lawsuit-against-u-s-federal-reserve-seeks-armenian-gold-looted-by-turkey/
23   Perform an assayed public audit of all the Treasury's claimed 8,100 tons of gold and net of swaps, loans & sales, Tom G. Hereford, petitions.whitehouse.gov January 9, 2013.
24   "Man That First Spotted QE4 Now Says Gold To Break $10,000", King World News, December 28, 2012.

# CONCLUSION

*None are more hopelessly enslaved than those*
*who believe they are free*
—Goethe

According to historian Carroll Quigley, who had free access to the records of elite groups, those elites meant to use financial weapons to dominate all nations' political systems and erect a global, hidden government. At the top was the Bank of International Settlements, owned by the private central banks. This 'feudal' system used the Treasury bond apparatus to essentially enslave each nation by debt.[1]

For this to continue, they must run down gold. As Alan Greenspan himself wrote many years before leading the Fed:

> In the absence of the gold standard, there is no way to protect savings from confiscation through inflation. There is no safe store of value. If there were, the government would have to make its holdings illegal, as was done in the case of gold.... The financial policy of the welfare state requires that there be no way for the owners of wealth to protect themselves.... [This] is the shabby secret of the welfare statist's tirades against gold. Deficit spending is simply a scheme for the 'hidden' confiscation of wealth. Gold stands in the way of this insidious process. It stands as a protector.[2]

In this light, there are many reasons to own gold.

1) The ongoing JPMorgan derivatives fiasco will require massive bailouts, negative for the US dollar.

2) China is making gold the de facto money and its citizens are using it for safe haven.

3) Major countries are allying to break dollar hegemony. An important aspect of the game is central bank gold buying by China, Russia and other nations in the East.

4) The Facebook IPO was a massive pump and dump scheme, the first in several years and perhaps the last in the West. It failed miserably.

Trust in such paper shell games is near death. Big investors are on to it. Soon the general public middle class will learn the lesson, too. Their savings and investments will flow into sound money.

5) The real estate bust left little in the way of hard assets to invest in that promise a rise in value. Gold may be the last man standing.

6) The dollar is under worldwide siege. Many resentful nations are dedicating their best efforts to ending US dollar hegemony. The US can stand against any country in the world, but not all of them.

7) High frequency trading has decimated the stock market. The public has been fleeced in flash crashes again and again, and is exiting. The algorithms have taken to eating one another. Stocks are unendurably volatile.

8) At least 140,000 people lost funds in the MF Global heist. No prosecutions were attempted; no charges were made. Trust in the trading system is vanishing. Gold, with no counterparty risk, will rise on the tide.

9) Southern Europe is facing runs on its biggest banks. The strain on the interconnected global banking system will be incredible.

10) Gold is more and more difficult to source in quantity. Physical metal in hand or well-audited is relatively scarce from the big player perspective.

11) Gold is returning to its role as a form of money.

12) Easy money policies like quantitative easing and zero interest rates create a flight to quality mentality.

13) Resentment of elite control is leading to alternative currencies among the world's poor. Silver will be the great beneficiary of this as people seek to trade in an affordable, sound currency.

### Figure 42
### Paper Gold and Physical Gold Divergence

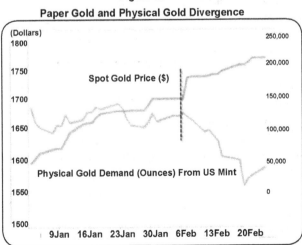

The premise that gold is in a bear market is based on a fallacy – that bear or bull is tied to falling or rising *price*. Wrong: it is tied to falling or rising *demand*. Paper gold is losing demand while physical gold is soaring. But paper holds the power of establishing the price, for now. It does not command the true value. Hence the moonshot in demand.

Eventually, the price of gold and silver may well go dark – no international price will exist. Global prices will be in wide differentiation, with the highest in the Middle East and Asia. The futures exchanges will separate radically from the physical price. Metals will not be available in quantity at any price. The process began in 2012, then took several sharp turns upward in early 2013.

The consequences are far greater than the mere value of gold, or even regarding it as money. It is War – as the book title says. If the public cannot summon an understanding of the debt-enslavement system, they cannot possibly act. If we do not terminate the power of this awesome bankster weapon – fiat currencies – we will consign our children to a lifetime of serfdom. This situation is in a clear, worsening trend. Liberties are vanishing. The financial industry has insinuated itself into the government and the mushrooming police apparatus as critical to national security. The banks own the assets we claim. We are unsecured creditors. The justice department officially pronounced 'no prosecutions' for banks as policy – it would threaten the global economy.[3] Regarding your assets, does this combination make you feel safe?

If global debt collapse decimates the global economy or the dominos of a falling financial sector or an energy crisis cause a serious GDP contraction, then the chances of turning those paper claims into the real assets they point to will be gone. Even worse, an irreversibly shrinking economy will shred the fractional reserve banking and monetary system which demands perpetual growth. Why? Because a growing economy allows for debt service, including interest. A shrinking economy destroys even the principal, never mind the profit. The warp-speed credit engine has expanded debt many, many times the real economy's capacity to service it, and the mismatch is fatal for the global economy. Declines in cheap energy multiply the effect by crushing the productive economy. We are witnessing the death of production under the burdens of resource depletion, financial engineering, off-shoring and naked profit motive.

A crisis of confidence will let loose a hurricane of fear. Mass owners of paper certificates will dive into the few lifeboats, exchanging an ocean of paper for a fistful of tangible commodities. Gold and silver will lead the herd, followed by energy, real estate, and other resources. Those holding such assets, with iron claims, will find themselves far wealthier. Hoarding of cash for essentials always happens in a financial crisis; before currency becomes worthless, it spikes in value. This would further restrict the ability to turn certificates into real holdings. A massive surge of cash would likely be issued by panicky central banks, leading to very uneven inflationary effects and possibly hyperinflation. In the massively complex web of today's global economy, just-in-time supply chains would be prone to major disruptions, leading to a cascading failure and contagion between more complex manufacturing and financial service centers. The manufacturing centers would be increasingly abandoned and scavenged. Our financial, paper-based asset complex is a Ponzi system, top to bottom. As such, it only awaits a crisis of trust to implode from realized deception and long-vanished integrity.[4]

The risk of high-level catastrophe is increasing. The powers that be have not addressed or even acknowledged any of the fundamental conditions that plague our world. Most may simply be too large and complex to solve. But a failure to even attempt mitigation is dereliction of duty. The game has been to push the separate and lower-level risks uphill and into the future. By minimizing immediate problems, the systemic threat is increased. The risks are now far more deeply connected and past the ability of even the most determined and coordinated international efforts to correct. Since the various sovereigns show little will or coordination, the crisis will end badly.

## Counterparty Obligation

*Debt is the money of slaves.*
*—Norm Franz*

Perhaps the most important and simple thing to understand about the interrelation of gold, currency and the economic system is *counterparty obligation*. It may be the most enticing aspect of gold ownership. Physical gold in hand has no counterparty obligation. No one has to honor a debt, or uphold a stock price, or provide any asset in exchange for the paper certificate claim on that asset. Virtually all forms of wealth have counterparty obligation. Stock can be diluted and companies can fail. Bonds can be defaulted or new bonds issued at higher rates, devaluing previous bonds. In a debt deflation, this is the great problem. The numbers are so massive that a domino of debt defaults could bring down the whole system. That was the reason AIG was nationalized – G-Sax and other major banks were in trouble from the derivatives held by AIG. LTCM, Lehman, Greece, MF Global, Bear-Sterns. The list is very long and the reason is always the same – a default by one of these companies would trigger a wave of defaults and systemic collapse. It's the main reason for the tens of trillions that has been injected into the system.

Some would argue that the currency is a form of debt. In one sense, it's true – the currency is created out of debt. In another sense, it's false – the currency, once created, separates from the debt itself. A person with lots of currency may not be in debt and therefore is really not at risk regarding counterparty obligation (but does face the risk of value loss due to inflation.). A savings or checking account, however, is a counterparty obligation; it entails the threat of a bank run. If enough people draw out their money, the bank's 10% reserve collapses. Having money in a bank account does not mean you have cash. You have a bank's obligation to give you what you put in. But banks can fail to meet that obligation. The FDIC is supposed to cover it, but they are massively overtaxed and likely could not cope in the event of massive bank failure.

Looking at all forms of modern investment, every one relies on some form of counterparty obligation – essentially, debt. Only paper currency (in hand) does not have this problem. It relies only on a general acceptance by society. It's similar to gold with a critical difference. Physical gold cannot be replicated ad infinitum. Paper gold, by contrast, is subject to counterparty obligation, as is physical in someone else's hands. If your gold is vaulted, the holder has the obligation to surrender the gold when you wish, but due to rehypothecation, where client assets are pledged for a bank's own investments, anything in a vault is at risk. And the risk is rising. It is almost a certainty, if you have some asset on a listed deposit with a bank, the bank has pledged that collateral for its investments, and the next bank may even have collateralized it again. In London, this is standard practice. If those investments are called in and the bank cannot pay, your assets can be seized by the counterparty. It's happened several times recently. Newer legislation honors the counterparty claims to your assets above your claims – this is what happened with MF Global.

In the event of a systemic global crisis, counterparty obligations will be defaulted on a very wide scale. Those that can be paid by printing (government obligations and so forth) will be repaid, but in a decreased value. In a sense, even physical currency has a counterparty obligation: the central bank must not over-issue or they will weaken, possibly destroy, the value. The counterparty obligation falls on the central bank and the government to maintain the value of the currency. As matters presently stand, this puts them in a terrible bind. They cannot maintain the integrity and value of the currency while holding the global economic system together. The debt mathematics is inescapable. More money, as debt, must be printed in a parabolic trend to service existing debt. This does not prevent the consequences; it only pushes them downstream and magnifies them. Currency holdings face the definite reality of perpetual erosion of value and possibly sudden, total loss. In the former instance, the counterparty obligation is not met, but the default is so gradual that people do not detect it. Holding currency long-term is an awful investment. Every seasoned investor knows this. Holding cash in a bank has become risky, too. Cyprus proves it.

This is why physical gold and silver, held in a secure, accessible manner, proofed against rehypothecation and back-door sales, are the go-to asset in economic crises. In such a situation, they will rise dramatically in price. The main critique against holding PMs in such a scenario is "you can't eat it." But there are many things that can't be eaten that still have value. The question is not whether you can eat something (or live in it), it's whether people will accept it in exchange for something else. It's certainly possible that all exchange based on currency will disappear, but it is extremely unlikely. It's simply too difficult to measure value without a referent medium in the form of a currency. A global barter system without a central basis of reference is impossible. In that scenario, either global trade ceases to occur because no one wants the failed paper, or people demand a commodity backed currency stable in value.

If the global economy chooses to survive by seeking such a currency – and it will – the backing will almost definitely be gold with a possible silver component. Gold will become dramatically more valuable because it will tend to replace almost all other existing currencies on the planet, at least for international exchange. This does not mean that physical gold must be exchanged. A gold standard with an independent audit and provable base, exchangeable for the currency, is all that is required. Because trust is the essential component of any centralized global exchange system, and because trust is more or less being gunned down by the corruption and deceit, whoever can manifest that trust on the global stage will be the next leader in the global economy. The nation that does this must have enough gold to do it. It will likely be done by a consortium of nations.

Global power is shifting, moving East. Financial structures are cracking and may not survive. The system of monetary creation is under threat, fighting for survival. It is growing old and enormous stresses make that survival look unlikely, even impossible. In that shadow, people and nations are seeking security for their savings and assets. Concerned about the strains of the current system, many now look to the ancient answer of gold as a fortress against the ongoing economic storms and corrupt depredations of the elites. The battle for the global economy is happening now. Conflicts will steadily increase over the following years. It will take time to run its course, but in this battle one thing seems more and more certain – the best ammunition is gold.

## Endnotes

1        Professor Carroll Quigley, *Tragedy and Hope*, 1966. p. 324.
2        Alan Greenspan, *Gold and Economic Freedom*, 1966.
3        Mark Gongloff, "Why DOJ Deemed Bank Execs Too Big To Jail", Huffington Post. March 6, 2013.
4        David Korowicz, Tradeoff, June 2012.

# GLOSSARY

AIG (American Insurance Group) – a company that speculated on the wrong side of derivatives and was backstopped by emergency government measures in 2008.

Allocated account – gold with bars listed by serial number to a specific owner.

Arbitrage – exploiting a price difference by simultaneously buying in one market and selling in another. It must be risk-free to qualify as genuine arbitrage.

Austrian School (Ludwig von Mises) – theory that believes in free market, competitive money, usually gold-backed.

Backwardation – Futures prices where nearer months are more expensive than later months.

Barrick Gold – World's largest gold miner.

Bernanke, Ben – Current Federal Reserve Chief.

BIS (Bank for International Settlements) – The Central Bank of Central Banks, dictating global banking policy from Basel, Switzerland.

BND (Bank of North Dakota) – A state bank owned by the public whose profits go to the state.

Bretton Woods – International monetary conference in 1944, creating a global system.

BRICS – The loose consortium of non-Western trading nations, led by Brazil, Russia, India, China and South Africa.

Brown, Ellen – Author of Web of Debt, advocate of government issued currency.

Bubble – massive increase in demand followed by a massive increase in supply overwhelming demand.

Bullionist Controversy – one of the first national debates (in England) over paper currency.

Bundesbank – German Central Bank.

Carroll Quigley – Economic historian given access to elite group records, author of Tragedy and Hope.

Carry Trade – borrowing low-interest, exchanging for a different currency/ instrument and investing at higher returns – a common tactic of large funds and banks.

Cartel, The – pejorative term for the coalition of large banks. A cartel in general is a consortium of industry leaders working together to maximize profits and control the market, essentially a monopoly.

Central Band – A nation's bank, charged with keeping unemployment and inflation low and regulating commercial banks.

CFTC (Commodities and Futures Trading Commission) – Regulatory body overseeing US commodities and futures exchanges.

Comex (Commodities Exchange Corporation) – US site for sales of gold, silver and all commodities.

Commodity – a physical asset.

Contango – Futures pricing where later months are more expensive than nearer months.

Contradiction of Capitalism – a phenomenon where increased efficiency in production decreases wages and money in circulation, lowering corporate revenues.

Counter-party – The party required to fulfill the opposite side of an obligation.

Counterparty Obligation – Obligation of the opposite side of any trade to fulfill.

CPI (Consumer Price Index) – government measure of price inflation.

Crime of 1873 – Law demonetizing silver, causing hardship for the poor and middle class.

Currency – Unit of financial account used in trade and investing.

Custodial Gold – Gold held by one Central Bank for another to settle trade accounts.

Deflation – a decrease in the money supply.

Derivatives – investments whose value is derived from an underlying asset.

Disinflation – lowering of inflation rate.

Dragon Family – a possibly mythical Asian consortium fiercely opposing the Western Cartel.

ECB – European Central Bank.

Eligible (gold/silver) – Comex held metals unavailable for sale.

ESF (Exchange Stabilization Fund) – A secretive agency, nominally part of the Federal Reserve, that manages aspects of the marketplace.

ETF, ETN (Exchange Traded Funds/Notes) – stock market vehicle for getting exposure to an underlying asset without taking possession of the asset itself.

Exter, John – Creator of Exter's Pyramid, a graphic of debt and monetary value.

Fat Finger – a trade accidentally higher because of entry error.

Federal Reserve – US Central Bank.

Fiat Currency – currency declared lawful by the state.

Fix – daily setting of the gold price by a group of bullion banks.

FOA (Friend of Another), FOFOA (Friend of a Friend of Another), Another – a series of pseudonymous, enigmatic bloggers on the gold market.

FOIA – Freedom of Information Act.

FOMC (Federal Open Market Committee) – a Federal Reserve committee which sets policy for Fed actions in the marketplace.

Force Majeure – 'Superior Force,' a term included in contracts to annul obligations after catastrophes and unavoidable harm to the counterparty.

FOREX – international market for exchanging currencies against one another.

Fractional Reserve Banking – Creation of money with only partial backing.

Freegold – gold absence of credit-based market distortions with price separated from paper.

FRN (Federal Reserve Note) – The currency issued by the Federal Reserve, the US dollar.

Fungible – asset where any unit is equivalent in value to another unit – e.g. a $1 bill.

Future – a contract to purchase a commodity in the future at a pre-set price.

G-20 – Group of 20 larger economies meeting to set policy and trade agreements.

G-8 – Group of 8 powerful economies meeting to set policy and trade agreements.

GAAP (Generally Accepted Accounting Principles) – The proper code of business accounting, suspended for major banks in 2008.

GAO (Government Accountability Office) – Internal government watchdog department.

GATA (Gold Anti-Trust Association) – A citizen watchdog organization documenting gold price suppression.

GDP (Gross Domestic Product) – The measure of a nation's total financial transactions.

Glass-Steagall – A 1930's era law separating commercial banking from investment banking, repealed in steps during the 1990's, attributed by many as a principal cause of the crisis.

GLD – an Exchange Traded Fund for investing in gold.

GOFO – Gold Forward Rate, the rate to lease gold from a bullion or central bank.

Gold Swap – exchange of ownership between Central Banks, usually without moving the gold.

Golden Jackass, Jim Willie – a colorful, contrarian analyst.

Good Delivery – a standard of purity for gold bars sold in exchanges.

GSax – Goldman Sachs, a politically powerful, old investment house.

Hedge – an investment to limit risk on a larger investment.

HFT (High Frequency Trading) – the now-dominant form of trading, involving supercomputers executing millions of trades daily in fractions of a second.

Hyperhopethecation – rehypothecation (collateralizing customer assets) multiple times for each asset.

Hyperinflation – a repudiation of the currency through massive increase in money velocity.

IMF (International Monetary Fund) – Organization ostensibly created to stabilize global trade and help failing nations economically through loans.

Inflation – an increase in the money supply.

Interest Rate Swaps – the largest nominal market in the world, designed to insure or hedge sovereign debt markets.

Jekyll Island – Birthplace of the Federal Reserve.

Keynesianism – reigning economic theory (currently under assault) that the economy can be managed through government deficit and surplus.

LBMA (London Bullion Metals Association) – World's largest metals trading exchange.

LETS (Local Exchange Trading System) – system of locally issued currency.

Leverage – Use of borrowed money for investing.

LIBOR – London InterBank Offer Rate – the key global interest rate for setting transactions.

Liquidity – available financial capital.

London Gold Pool – a union of 8 countries openly selling gold to hold the price fixed.

LTCM (Long Term Capital Management) – a hedge fund that threatened the global economy when it collapsed in 1999.

Margin – Use of borrowed funds to invest by posting collateral.

Margin Call – a demand to put more money into an investment or be forcefully liquidated.

MERS (Mortgage Electronic Registration System) – Database of mortgages. MERS was found illegal in court.

MF Global – Investment fund that broke the 'commingling of customer funds' wall, losing billions of dollars in client assets.

Minsky Instability Hypothesis – an economic theory that stable economies tend to degrade from financial engineering. See page XX

Monetarism (Friedmanism) – Economic theory that central banks can manage the economy through controlling the money supply.

Monetization – printing currency to pay off government debt.

Money – Unit of financial account used for storing wealth.

MOPE – Management of Perception.

MSM – Mainstream Media.

Nixon Shock – The date Richard Nixon severed the dollar's tie to gold in 1971.

Norman, Montagu – Eccentric head of England's Central Bank from 1920-44.

Obsolescence – breakage or gradual uselessness of products due to low-quality manufacturing or industry progress – can be deliberate or incidental from cost-cutting.

OI (Open Interest) – number of futures contracts outstanding in a market.

Operation Twist – A Fed operation to redeem long-term bonds for short-term bonds.

Paul, Ron – Former congressman and head of the House Finance Committee, strong critic of the Federal Reserve.

PBOC – People's Bank of China, the Central Bank.

Peak (oil/gold/etc.) – Theory that commodity production will or has maxed out, leading to a decrease in supply irrespective of demand.

Petrodollar Standard – An agreement to accept only US dollars for oil and recycle the dollars into US Treasuries.

PIIGS – Portugal, Ireland, Italy, Greece, Spain – the southern European nations in a debt crisis.

PM's – Precious Metals – gold and silver.

Ponzi – fraudulent investment scheme using new investors to pay profits to previous investors.

PPI (Producer Price Index) – Cost of raw materials for producers.

QE (Quantitative Easing) – Printing money.

RBE (Resource Based Economy) – Radical idea for restructuring the system to accommodate all human need without money or the need for property.

Registered (gold/silver) – Comex held metals available for sale on futures or spot exchanges.

Rehypothecation – using client assets as collateral for a bank's investments.

Rothschilds – most powerful, early banking dynasty.

SDR (Special Drawing Rights) – the synthetic currency of the IMF.

Second Bank of the United States – the second US Central Bank, from 1816-32.

Security – any tradeable asset, such as debt, stocks (equities), or derivatives.

Shadow Banking System – The system of unregulated investment banking.

Short sale – selling something the trader does not own, but must buy in the future to supply.

Silver Eagle – The one ounce bullion coin issued by the US Mint.

Solvency – asset value exceeding liabilities.

Spot Market – price of gold for immediate delivery.

Sprott, Eric – CEO of the Sprott Fund and lead investor in precious metals with a fully allocated and audited gold fund. Well-regarded for market commentary.

Stagflation – inflation with rising unemployment.

Still, Bill – Fed critic and advocate of government issued currency.

Stop-Loss order – automatic sell orders triggered at a pre-set price point.

SWIFT – system of international banking payments.

Ted Butler – key commentator on the silver market.

Tenthers – movement that argues against excessive Federal power, claiming the tenth amendment guarantees those rights to the states.

Treasuries – Debt issued by the US government. Bills are short term, bonds are long-term.

Triffin Dilemma – the need for a reserve currency to have simultaneous net outflow and inflow of currency.

Unallocated account – gold owned as part of a pool, without title to specific bars.

Velocity of Money – number of times the currency supply changes hands per unit of time.

Washington Agreement – 1999 agreement for Central Banks to limit gold sales to 400 tons.

Weimar – The German government of the early 1920's, which hyperinflated its currency.

Williams, Walter John – Analyst of government statistics, arguing they are deceptive.

Yuan (Renminbi) – Chinese currency, "the people's money."

Zerohedge – the premiere contrarian website, run by pseudonymous former trader Tyler Durden.

ZIRP – Zero Interest Rate Policy. The Central Banking policy of keeping interest rates below market reality to finance debt, support indebted banks, and prime economic activity.

# INDEX